History Unleashed

Also by Christopher Carosa...

50 Hidden Gems of Greater Western New York
A Handbook for Those Too Proud to Believe
"Wide Right" and "No Goal" Define Us

A Pizza The Action
Everything I Ever Learned About Business I Learned by
Working in a Pizza Stand at the Erie County Fair

Hamburger Dreams
How Classic Crime Solving Techniques Helped Crack the Case
of America's Greatest Culinary Mystery

Hey! What's My Number?
How to Improve the Odds You Will Retire in Comfort

From Cradle to Retirement: The Child IRA
How to Start a Newborn Baby on the Road to Comfortable
Retirement While Still in a Cozy Cradle

The Parent's Guide To Turning Your Teen Into a Millionaire
And How To Do It Before High School Graduation!

For Complete List go to:
https://chriscarosa.com/books/the-complete-list/

History Unleashed

Lafayette's Remarkable Tour

of the

Greater Western New York Region

by

Christopher Carosa

Pandamensional Solutions, Inc.

Mendon, New York

This book contains both original and previously published work. Some material contained herein represents the opinions of the individuals quoted and not necessarily the opinion of the author. In some cases, for metaphorical purposes, this work contains fiction. In such circumstances, names, characters, places and incidents are either the product of the author's imagination or are used fictitiously. Any resemblance to actual events or locales or persons, living or dead, is entirely coincidental.

Limit of Liability/Disclaimer of Warranty: While the publisher and the author have used their best efforts in preparing this book, they make no representations or warranties with respect to the accuracy or completeness of the contents of this book and specifically disclaim any implied warranties or merchantability or fitness for any particular purpose. No warranty may be created or extended by sales representatives or written sales materials. The advice and strategies contained herein may not be suitable for your situation. This book is sold with the understanding that the publisher and author are not engaged in rendering legal, accounting, investment or any other advice. If expert assistance is required, you should consult with the proper professional where appropriate. Neither the publisher nor author shall be liable for any loss of profit or any other commercial damages, including but not limited to special, incidental, consequential or other damages. If you actually read this, go to "X" in the Index right now.

COPYRIGHT © 2024 BY CHRISTOPHER CAROSA

Published by Pandamensional Solutions, Inc., Mendon, NY

Cover design by Catarina Lena Carosa
Cover image credits:

Marquis De Lafayette (1825), NPG.82.150-National Portrait Gallery, Ary Scheffer, Public domain via Wikimedia Commons
1825 Map from David Rumsey Map Collection, David Rumsey Map Center, Stanford Libraries.

ALL RIGHTS RESERVED
INCLUDING THE RIGHT OF REPRODUCTION
IN WHOLE OR IN PART IN ANY FORM

ISBN-10: 1-938465-18-0
ISBN-13: 978-1-938465-18-5

What Others Are Saying About Christopher Carosa's
History Unleashed:
Lafayette's Remarkable Tour of the Greater Western New York Region

"*History Unleashed: Lafayette's Remarkable Tour of the Greater Western New York Region* would make a wonderful film. Chris Carosa provides us with both detailed descriptions and broad overviews, helping the reader conjure up each scene as if they were actually present."
- ➢ Chuck Schwam, Executive Director, American Friends of Lafayette

"*History Unleashed: Lafayette's Remarkable Tour of the Greater Western New York* has proven to be an invaluable resource for me as I develop plans to help local communities commemorate, recreate and celebrate the bicentennial of Lafayette's visit in 2024-2025. Chris Carosa writes in great detail about Lafayette's adventures using information that is well researched and documented, as he makes learning about early American history, and the remarkable Lafayette, enjoyable. Reading *History Unleashed* will deepen your appreciation for our country, and Lafayette's contributions to our country and its unique history."
- ➢ Catherine Blind, Lafayette Bicentennial Committee Chair, Monroe and Ontario Counties and Registrar, Irondequoit Chapter of the National Society Daughters of the American Revolution

"In *History Unleashed: Lafayette's Remarkable Tour of the Greater Western New York Region*, Christopher Carosa revives a forgotten episode in western New York's storied past. Writing in an animated style, Carosa takes us along on Lafayette's journey from Westfield to Auburn, introducing us to people and places as they were in 1825. The excitement felt by regional residents in meeting this famous hero of the American Revolution is palpable."
- ➢ Robert Emerson, Executive Director of Old Fort Niagara

"The historian spends many hours seeking out knowledge of the past in all sorts of dusty books and now computer screens of all shades of brightness. While such an endeavor may not seem like a heroic effort, the historian is the unsung hero of society, for it is through their very effort that the historian reminds society what it is to be heroic. They do this through painstakingly researching and then telling the story of real heroes living heroic lives. That said, there are few who have lived a more heroic life than Marie-Joseph Paul Yves Roch Gilbert du Motier de La Fayette, better know as Marquis de Lafayette. Even today, this important man's life has things to teach us and ideals to strive for. In *History Unleashed: Lafayette's Remarkable Tour of the Greater Western New York Region*, Christopher Carosa has gone down this road to remind us who our Masonic Brother Marquis de Lafayette was, and how he touched Western New York nearly 50 years after the Declaration of Independence was signed, reminding us all who we are as nation and why his generation were heroes."

> ➢ Brother Lee Justo, Lafayette Project Coordinator, Grand Lodge of the Free and Accepted Masons of New York State and Master of Huguenot Lodge No. 46 (which has a direct connection to Lafayette)

"*History Unleashed: Lafayette's Remarkable Tour of the Greater Western New York Region* is not the first book regarding Lafayette's journey, but it certainly is unique in its approach! Chris Carosa's research is thorough and exemplary. This reference will undoubtedly prove to be seminal!"

> ➢ Michael A Miller, Historian - Auburn Lodge #124

"Chris has brought to light the joy and excitement of life in not only the young American nation but in our small towns and villages in 1825. To have seen the Marquis de LaFayette in person, a celebrated hero of the American Revolution who served under General George Washington, would have been an experience of a lifetime! Chris reminds us that we all should cherish and protect our town's history for generations to come. It is wonderful to know that LaFayette first entered NYS in Ripley!!!"

> ➢ Dr. John P. Hamels, Town Historian, Town of Ripley, New York

"*History Unleashed: Lafayette's Remarkable Tour of the Greater Western New York Region* is a masterpiece in research and presentation. Chris brings in not only the history but the relatability especially to specific local families involved in the American Revolution. Many of these same families were touched by Lafayette's presence with his return 1824-1825 and will again be present for the Bicentennial in 2024-2025. I did have relatives in Dunkirk and Fredonia when Lafayette visited in 1825, so I was thrilled with the mention of Olive Risley Seward. Thank-you for this timely publication."

> Gail Pugh Dash, Co-chair for the Lafayette Bicentennial Committee Chautauqua County, NY; Jamestown Chapter National Society Daughters of the American Revolution, Charter Member of the Celea Sampson Cole Daughters of 1812, Chautauqua County Genealogical Society

"In *History Unleashed: Lafayette's Remarkable Tour of the Greater Western New York Region*, Chris Carosa brings together a winning combination of comprehensive research, engaging storytelling, and fascinating details about General Lafayette and his fast-paced journey through New York State in June 1825. Chris skillfully helps the past come to life and makes it relatable for today's audience. It is exciting to connect with General Lafayette and the citizens of Greater Western New York through these pages as we commemorate the bicentennial of this unique chapter in American history."

> Patrice Birner, Honorary New York State Regent, National Society Daughters of the American Revolution

"*History Unleashed: Lafayette's Remarkable Tour of the Greater Western New York Region* his book traces the historical and geographical contours of Lafayette's grand tour over the roads and canals of Western New York in 1825. By examining both the precise route and the meticulous preparations made by the towns and cities responsible for welcoming the "Nation's Guest," Carosa offers an invaluable survey of the region's rich history, while skillfully sifting through documented accounts to separate fact from the legends and myths that have emerged over the past two centuries."

> Maxwell Walters, Curator of Collections, Darwin R. Barker Museum, Fredonia, NY

"Chris Carosa has masterfully described the story of Marquis de Layfette's farewell tour of Western New York. My middle schoolers are able to independently read this narrative and connect with fascinating local history that is seldom retold in textbooks. This work is also the foundation of a larger research project where students further explore the culture, community, and events of Western New York, shared in the book, developing essential reading, writing, and presentation skills. I highly recommend this book for all social studies teachers who would like to complement their curriculum."
- ➤ Jason Steinagle, Middle School Social Studies Teacher, Hamburg, NY

"Often history books can be dull, boring and long-winded: this is not the case with Christopher Carosa's *History Unleashed: General Lafayette's Remarkable Tour of greater Western New York*. The insightful narrative told in a conversation manner, is well documented, thorough, readable and very satisfying."
- ➤ Catherine L. Emerson, Niagara County Historian

"Chris Carosa has produced a fascinating and insightful history of the passage of a Revolutionary War hero through Western New York! Lafayette's 1825 journey shares an exciting moment in our history and lets the reader glimpse our budding American culture of 200 years ago. Kudos to the author for saving an almost forgotten tale and rescuing a hero from the shadows!"
- ➤ Leif R. HerrGessell and Author, Canandaigua, NY

For Dad:
…tell Lafayette I said, "Hello!"

TABLE OF CONTENTS

Foreword xi
Acknowledgements xiii
Prologue: It Was Twenty Decades Ago… 1

Act One: The Setting
Lafayette And America In The Era Of Good Feelings

1. What Took Congress So Long? 7
2. The Duty That Held Lafayette Back 111
3. A Message From An Old Friend 15
4. America in 1824 18
5. And The Lucky Winner Is… 21
6. America Welcomes The Nation's Guest..........................25
7. Why Lafayette?...29
8. Overview Of The 1824-1825 American Tour (Part I) 33
9. Overview Of The 1824-1825 American Tour (Part II) 37
10. Lafayette Prepares To Enter The Greater Western
    New York Region 42

Act Two: The Main Event
Lafayette's Tour Of Western New York

11. The State Of The Greater Western New York Region
    in 1825 49
12. The Making Of The Buffalo And Erie Road 54
13. Special Delivery To Westfield, A Fitting First..................59
14. Gaslighting The General..66
15. Fast Fredonia Frenzy...71
16. Dunkirk, The Last Frontier..78
17. To The Dunkirk Dinghy By The Dawn's Early Light 81
18. Rebuilt Buffalo 84
19. Regal Reception In Buffalo's Blossoming Queen City 88
20. Peter B. Porter's Home Sweet Home..............................94
21. Breakfast At Black Rock Then On To Tonawanda 98
22. Augustus Porter Could Have Danced All Night 101
23. The Natural Wonder Of Niagara Falls, Goat Island,
    And Lewiston..105

24. Riding The Ridge (Road) 109
25. Fort Niagara And The Man-Made Wonder Of
    Lockport 113
26. Remembering Silvius Hoard 117
27. Competing Memories Turn Lafayette's Rochester
    Visit From History To Mystery 122
28. Timothy Barnard, A Soldier's Story................................ 129
29. Dispelling Mendon Myths... 133
30. John Greig Lives The American Dream......................... 137
31. Canandaigua Anxiously Waits Before Jubilation And
    An Elegant Supper.. 140
32. How Commonality Saved Captain Williamson And
    Western New York.. 144
33. Pomp And Circumstance Before Lunch In Geneva......... 151
34. The Great Central Trail Becomes The State Road 156
35. Wowed Waterloo Overcomes Tragedy To Welcome
    Hero 161
36. Bigotry Cannot Defeat A Good And Honorable Man 164
37. Through Seneca Falls, East Cayuga, Then A Masonic
    Welcome And A Final Adieu In Auburn 169

Act Three: The Impact
Lafayette's Legacy

Epilogue: A Favor Returned, D-Day 50th Anniversary 181
Appendix I: Lafayette And Freemasonry 185
Appendix II: Lafayette On The Folly Of Tolerance 188
Appendix III: June 17, 1825, Bunker Hill Monument
    Cornerstone Ceremony 192

Bibliography 209
Endnotes 215
Index: 240
About the Author... 249

Foreword

It is probably true that every author has at least one ideal reader in mind as he or she writes. For Chris Carosa it was me. As I have been a "Lafayette-ist" for over fifteen years now, this book spoke to me in a way no other book has. It is not simply a biography or a description of events, but a detailed explanation of Lafayette's remarkable tour through one his favorite areas of our country.

This book certainly goes a long way in fulfilling our common goal of making sure that Americans understand that Lafayette was an important figure in our War for Independence, but also just how important his tour was 43 years later. Sharing Lafayette's legacy with the general public is a top priority of the American Friends of Lafayette. This extraordinary book clearly proves that Chris Carosa has the same goal.

History Unleashed: Lafayette's Remarkable Tour of the Greater Western New York Region does a perfect job of helping us understand Lafayette's importance in the early 19th century. Chris Carosa also helps us comprehend what early 19th century United States was like. He does a remarkable job of intertwining both stories. It's as if we are looking through Lafayette's eyes.

I am asked about Lafayette films quite often. My answer is that it would be impossible to cover his long, complicated, and fascinating life in a two-hour movie format. Maybe a ten-part miniseries could capture it all. However, History Unleashed: Lafayette's Remarkable Tour of the Greater Western New York Region would make a wonderful film. Chris Carosa provides us with both detailed descriptions and broad overviews, helping the reader conjure up each scene as if they were actually present.

Lafayette was an abolitionist, a proto-feminist and a friend of the Native Americans. Lafayette as a human rights champion was on full display in Western New York and Chris Carosa helps us appreciate this very important mind-set that Lafayette brought with him to

America. Of course, Lafayette was a daring young general, but he was much more, which is outlined perfectly in History Unleashed: Lafayette's Remarkable Tour of the Greater Western New York Region.

Chuck Schwam
Executive Director
American Friends of Lafayette
July 31, 2024

Acknowledgements

It may be my name on the cover, but the words behind that cover come from many people.

"History," goes the adage, "is written by the winners." Said another way, "History is a Rorschach test." It is what you think it is.

Cynics use this to question the relevancy of the past. Others see this definition as an opportunity to promote change.

In reality, history never was a strictly defined as those right/wrong grade school tests implied. Had we been first taught the history of history, we may have looked at it in a different light.

Cicero, the accomplished Roman orator who stands as the paragon of rhetoric—the art of speaking—labeled Herodotus "the father of history." Mind, while Cicero lasted long enough to witness the last days of the Roman Republic, Herodotus died four centuries earlier in the first years of the Peloponnesian War.

While Herodotus most famously entered the tales of the Greco-Persian into the annals of history, it was how he did it that probably most impressed Cicero. Herodotus interwove actual events with ancient myths and lore to tell a compelling story perfect for the mass market of his day.

Except not for everyone. His contemporary critics didn't think of him as "the father of history." They considered him "the father of lies." Chief among these detractors was Thucydides. A generation younger than Herodotus, Thucydides practiced what might be called "scientific history." For those who remember the TV series Dragnet, Thucydides was the Sgt. Joe "Just the Facts, Ma'am" Friday of history. He didn't appreciate the dramatic license of Herodotus.

To his credit, Herodotus claimed he merely reported what others told him. You can therefore make the case that he was more transparent than Thucydides in that he told it through the eyes of the witnesses.

Thucydides, on the other hand, would say he told it like it really was, based on immutable evidence.

Thus explains the inherent conflict of history. It contains elements of both science and the humanities. It is both fact based (either George Washington slept here or he didn't) and interpretive (what was George Washington thinking when he made his decision where to sleep). It's a constant tug-of-war. Some believe history becomes a choice between Herodotus or Thucydides. Others believe a happy medium exists, a place where factual integrity and good storytelling seamlessly blend together.

For my purposes, this two-hundred-year journey back into time required me to rely on eyewitnesses as reported in the newspapers of the time. For this, I owe a great deal of gratitude to the many digital libraries that have preserved these publications for all to see. As you'll see in the end notes, almost all the citations reference newspaper articles published at the time of the events covered. In some cases, I reference history books written later, but in nearly all cases my bias is to rely on books closest to the actual events, as subsequent interpretation of later volumes might blur the picture of reality.

Well, at least the reality of 1825. My goal in this project is to present Lafayette's tour through the Greater Western New York Region as if you were there. That means unadulterated use of language as those early Americans used it. Some of it might be fingernails-on-the-chalkboard grating, but that's the way they spoke back then. If you really want to know what it was like, you've got to breathe the air they breathed.

Along my journey, I discovered plenty of helping hands, far too many to call out by name. I can say that across the region, and indeed throughout New York State, I've met with members of the Daughters of the American Revolution (as well as a few Sons), members of the Masonic fraternity from the Grand Lodge of New York to the local Lodges in the communities I write about, and a plethora of historians from individual museums and municipal historical societies to the vast network of fellow members of the Association of Public Historians of New York State and the Government Appointed Historians of Western New York.

Many of these people read the chapters relevant to their areas of expertise and offered helpful feedback. Like I said, the content within the covers of this book represents the work of many hands.

Finally, as always, I must give a shout out to my wife Betsy. Once again, she proofed all but two of the chapters in this book. So, if you find an error, it means either I made a change after she proofed it, or it's one of those two chapters. Or this Acknowledgements section.

With that, I invite you to sit back, turn back the hands of time, and enjoy the ride.

Christopher Carosa
Mendon, New York
August 15, 2024

Prologue:
It Was Twenty Decades Ago...

Two hundred years ago, in January 1824, a struggling Congress asked President James Monroe to dispatch an invitation across the ocean to the only surviving general of the American Revolutionary War. The fifth President of the United States and the last Founding Father to fill that role, Monroe wanted to send a message—on both sides of the Pond.

It was a time of transition. It was a time of hope. It was a time to remember.

Domestically, America had just won its second war of independence from Great Britain. This one-time adversary had now fast become a firm ally. Concurrently, the old monarchies of Europe reappeared, threatening to undo the republican movement in the western hemisphere.

On the verge of his sixty-seventh birthday, Monroe accomplished much by the end of his second term despite a series of controversies and setbacks that marred his first four years as President. Initially elected to the nation's highest office in 1816, Monroe set his focus on wrapping up a treaty with Great Britain following the conclusion of the War of 1812.

Two treaties—the Rush-Bagot Treaty (signed in April 1817) and the Treaty of 1818—helped define the geography of the North American continent. It also established what would become the world's longest peaceful border between the United States and Canada.

Peace with Britain led to repercussions, both positive and negative. This new Anglo-American alliance led to increased trade. Britain upped its purchase of American cotton. This encouraged our new allies to avoid involvement in the Seminole Wars. Later, it would influence the decision of the southern states to form a confederacy that led to the Civil War.

Expanded trade didn't shield America from the Panic of 1819. Likewise, the budding division over slavery began in earnest with the Missouri Compromise in 1820. But that year would be noteworthy for an event that occurred for the second and last time.

Like George Washington, Monroe worried political parties would ruin our country. Elected under the banner of the Democratic-Republican Party in 1816, Monroe was determined to rid the nation of political parties upon taking the office. He toured the country seeking to unify Americans by giving them a sense of national purpose.

Monroe's visit to Boston impressed journalist Benjamin Russell. On July 12, 1817, he expressed his views in the Boston Federalist newspaper Columbian Centinel. In his article, Russell referred to that time in America as "The Era of Good Feelings."

The physical tour proved a success (and may have inspired the idea for another tour). By 1820, the Federalist Party was all but dead. For the first time since Washington's election, Monroe ran for reelection with no opposition.

While Americans view the War of 1812 as an extension of and the final act of the Revolutionary War, Europeans see it as a minor set piece in the broader Napoleonic Wars that extended from 1803 through 1815. In fact, conflict with its long-time European rivals likely eased Great Britain's peace with the United States.

At the same time, those rivals found themselves weakened. Spain could no longer bear the cost of an expansive empire. Monroe seized this opportunity and purchased Florida from the beleaguered European power through the Adams-Onis Treaty signed on February 22, 1819.

As Spain's influence in the New World waned, its former colonies broke free. Like the United States, each achieved its own independence from its former European overseer. Initially, Monroe maintained an official stance of neutrality. Still, his provocative "Aquirre Mission" sent a delegation to Buenos Aires to learn more about what was happening in South America.

By 1823, Spain had made motions to reclaim its old colonies. Seeing the potential for the return of Old World ways of thinking, Monroe, devoted a small portion (only three paragraphs) in his annual address to Congress on December 2, 1823, which framed what would become our nation's definitive Latin American foreign policy. You may remember learning about this in history class. It's called "The Monroe Doctrine."

Meanwhile, on the other side of the Atlantic, France found itself in chaos. This wasn't new. Since the French Revolution, this long-time ally of the American cause convulsed from one form of government to another. The ongoing spasm either killed or imprisoned political rivals. Among these included Marie-Joseph Paul Yves Roch Gilbert du Motier de La Fayette, also known as the Marquis de La Fayette.

We call him Lafayette. He was a hero in our war of independence. And he was its last surviving general.

Monroe's old friend, Lafayette was the man the President invited to become "Our Nation's Guest."

The 50th anniversary of the signing of the Declaration of Independence neared. Monroe thought asking Lafayette to conduct a "farewell tour" might instill a renewed sense of unifying patriotic spirit. It would act to pass the baton from America's Greatest Generation—that of the Founding Fathers and Revolutionary War Heroes—to their children and grandchildren so these descendants would not soon forget the memory of our nation's independence.

And Monroe knew first-hand how a tour could make this possible.

ACT ONE:

– THE SETTING –

LAFAYETTE AND AMERICA IN THE ERA OF GOOD FEELINGS

ACT ONE

CHAPTER ONE:
WHAT TOOK CONGRESS SO LONG?

James Monroe entered the final year of his second term feeling good. It was, after all, the "Era of Good Feelings." In eight years, the nation's fifth President had accomplished much. His country had many things to feel good about.

And there was more coming.

Monroe's decision to not seek reelection confirmed the tradition of the self-imposed limit of two terms as president. Before this, however, people had a legitimate thought that Monroe would run for an unprecedented third term. He had other thoughts. In a way, they were bigger thoughts.

But he had to wait for a slow-moving Congress to give the formal thumbs-up.

Independently, several citizens took it upon themselves to invite Lafayette to return to the nation where he first made his mark in history. While they weren't necessarily serving in any official capacity, they reflected a growing sense of patriotism. The nation within a couple of years of its 50th birthday, what better way to celebrate than hosting the Revolutionary War's "last surviving" general?

Joseph Wheaton was a member of Captain Olney's Rhode Island Light Infantry Company during the Revolutionary War. He wrote a nostalgic remembrance to his former commander General Lafayette in 1823.

In Lafayette's response, dated December 20, 1823, he says, "I wish, my dear sir, it was in my power to express to you personally my affectionate, faithful remembrance of my companions in arms, my particular sentiments for you, and to enjoy the sight of American liberty, prosperity, and virtue… duties to the cause of Freedom make it, if not a matter of hope, at least a point of honor, to keep my present post; but, so soon as I can do it with a safe conscience, I shall indulge my ardent wish to visit the happy shores of the U. States."[1]

Similarly, Dr. James Thatcher joined the revolutionary cause at the age of 21, serving as a surgeon's mate before making his way as a full surgeon for the Massachusetts 16th Regiment. Nearly five decades later, he authored the "highly interesting" *Journal of a Surgeon in the Revolutionary War*. On June 12, 1823 he sent a copy to General Lafayette.[2]

The General delivered his reply in a letter dated January 12, 1824. His communication concluded: "You invite me, dear Doctor, to the happy shores where so many unutterable emotions await me. Far I am from giving up the delightful hope. At this moment a sense of duty keeps me on the European side of the Atlantic."[3]

Note the dates of these two letters from Lafayette. Both predated congressional debate on formally inviting the Revolutionary War hero for a return visit.

In fact, and not without irony given the date of Lafayette's letter to Dr. Thatcher, it wasn't until Monday, January 12, 1824, that Col. George E. Mitchell, a representative from the State of Maryland moved in the House of Representatives to invite Lafayette to America and send a national ship to pick him up. Lafayette, for all the mutual respect he received from the United States, might have been surprised to learn the motion failed by a vote of 84 against and 74 in favor.[4]

Lewis Williams of North Carolina apparently spoke for the majority when he expressed concern that Lafayette might not accept such an invitation. Louisiana's William Leigh Brent, in answer to his North Carolina counterpart, said he possessed the proof Williams sought. "He had seen a letter addressed to Mr. Davezac, of New Orleans, wherein Marquis Lafayette stated that it was his intention to visit the United States once more before he died. One of his colleagues, also, (Mr. Livingston,) had received a letter to the same effect."[5]

To satisfy Williams, Charles Rich of Vermont amended the language of the motion. In addition, Lewis Condict of New Jersey felt the resolution would best be referred to a Select Committee. This motion passed without opposition.[6]

Mitchell reported the results of the committee work on Tuesday, January 20, 1824, and the next day, the House passed the following resolution:

"That the Marquis De Lafayette having expressed his intention to visit this country, the President be requested to communicate to him the assurances of grateful and affectionate attachment still cherished towards him by the government and people of the United States.

"And be it further resolved, That, as a mark of national respect, the President cause to be held in readiness a ship of the line, and invite the Marquis to take passage therein, whenever his disposition to visit this country be signified."[7]

The House then sent the resolution to the Senate, which promptly sent it to its own select committee. On Monday, January 26, Senator Robert Young Hayne of South Carolina returned from the committee the following amended resolution:

"The Marquis De La Fayette having expressed his intention to revisit this country –

"*Resolved, by the Senate and House of Representatives of the United States of America, in Congress assembled*, That the President be requested to communicate to him the assurances of grateful and affectionate attachment still cherished for him by the Government and People of the United States.

"*And be it further resolved*, That, whenever the President shall be informed of the time when the Marquis may be ready to embark, that a National Ship (with suitable accommodation) be employed to bring him to the United States."[8]

The House passed this amended resolution on Thursday, January 29, 1824[9] and President Monroe signed it into law on Wednesday, February 4, 1824.[10]

Monroe drafted the letter to Lafayette as instructed and dispatched it with his Minister to France, the honorable James Brown. Mr. Brown set sail from France aboard the *USS Cuane* from Alexandria. Should Lafayette promptly accept the invitation, the *New York Gazette* reported he would be picked up by none other than Old Ironsides herself, the *USS Constitution*.[11]

Lafayette's response was not prompt. It turns out his "sense of duty" was more serious than the Americans imagined.

Chapter Two:
Mankind's (Second) Greatest Invention

Take a look at his name: Marie-Joseph Paul Yves Roch Gilbert du Motier de La Fayette, Marquis de La Fayette. It exudes aristocracy. With Lafayette, that proved a mixed blessing.

On one hand, it meant he benefited from an elite schooling in proper behavior. On the other hand, it meant proper behavior shackled him. It would make him a hero to some. It would also earn him real shackles.

Born in south central France on September 6, 1757, he followed in the military tradition footsteps of both sides of his family. On his father's side, one of his ancestors served as a Marshal of France and accompanied Joan of Arc's army during the Siege of Orléans in 1429. His maternal great-grandfather commanded the Second Company of Musketeers (a.k.a., the "Black Musketeers") until his retirement in 1770.[1]

For the curious, the "Black Musketeers" had black horses while the First Company "Grey Musketeers" mounted gray horses. The Musketeers were a special forces unit that reported directly to the king. They received not only top military training but also learned how to behave as perfect gentlemen. If you're thinking James Bond or *Kingsman: The Secret Service*, you wouldn't be far off. The Musketeers represented the epitome of aristocracy.

To give you a sense of aristocracy, just follow the "Marquis" title. When Lafayette's uncle died in battle, the title passed to Lafayette's father. Likewise, when an English cannon ball cut his father in two during the Seven Years' War,[2] Lafayette became Marquis. Of course, he was only two years old, so his mother inherited the estate.

In 1768, Lafayette left his father's estate and moved to Paris with his mother and great-grandfather. The latter enrolled him in the elite academy that trained the Black Musketeers. Unfortunately, in 1770, both his mother and great-grandfather died. That same year, his uncle also died. Lafayette inherited an annual income of 125,000 French Livre.

This was equivalent to 9,000 British Pounds in 1770[3] or over two million pounds today.[4] That equals more than two-and-a-half million dollars.[5] Every Year.

Lafayette was rich before he was a teenager.

That's not all he was. Six months before his fourteenth birthday, Lafayette received his commission as *sous-lieutenant* in the Black Musketeers. It was the lowest level officer position; it allowed him to march in military reviews and parades and appear at the Court of Versailles before King Louis XV.[6]

Being young, he developed an idealism for liberty that would remain with him his entire life. It would pit him against family, against country, and against the traditional European way of life.

Before that though, Lafayette became a wunderkind within the French royal circles. Despite his marriage being arranged, he genuinely fell in love with his wife, the daughter of a prominent nobleman who requested Lafayette be commissioned a lieutenant in the Noailles Dragoons.[7] He was later promoted to major general in anticipation of going to help the American cause during the Revolutionary War.

The French aborted their official effort to send officers to America when the British discovered the intent. Lafayette, inspired by that youthful idealism, rejected this decision. Defying his father-in-law (and possibly his own military), he bought a sailing ship with his own money and made his way to America.

Though initially skeptical of young Lafayette's experience to command men,[8] George Washington eventually permitted Lafayette to enter the Battle of Brandywine. With Cornwallis on the attack, the American troops were in disarray. Arriving on horseback, Lafayette's training kicked in. Shouting from his horse, he rallied the troops. Then, he dismounted and physically pushed men towards the enemy. Seeing Cornwallis had the edge, Lafayette led the men in an organized retreat.[9]

It wasn't until the retreat that Lafayette noticed his boot filling with blood. He had been hit. His left calf had a musket ball sized hole in it. So severe was the wound that Lafayette needed help to get off his horse.[10]

A surgeon treated the Marquis in Chester, Pennsylvania. Lafayette had only been in America for a little over three months. He was a quick learner but would not become fluent in English until a year after his arrival.

During recovery, a young American lieutenant who spoke French stayed with him. The previous winter, the man had also received a wound and nearly lost his life during Washington's surprise attack on Trenton. This Virginian boosted Lafayette's spirits. The two would develop a lifelong friendship.[11]

That man's name was James Monroe, the future President of the United States.

Lafayette would recover to play an important role in America's ultimate victory over the British. He was at Valley Forge, where he helped clothe soldiers out of his own funds. He helped prevent the British from capturing Washington during the retreat from New York City. He quelled a potential American revolt against their French allies during a misunderstanding in Rhode Island. He returned to France (to a hero's welcome nonetheless) to solidify French support for the American patriots. Finally, his command was critical in the capture of Cornwallis at Yorktown, which signaled the beginning of the end of the Revolutionary War.

After the War, Lafayette returned to France, continuing to promote liberty. As an aristocrat advocating for the commoners during the French Revolution, he straddled the uncomfortable middle. Drawing suspicions from both the masses and European (as well as French) royals, Lafayette eventually had to flee France. His identity discovered in Austria, he was captured and held, ultimately imprisoned in Olmütz. He spent three years there, the last two with his wife and daughters.

Now President, George Washington tip-toed the precarious minefield of European diplomacy. Congress agreed to fund Lafayette with "back pay" for his service in the Revolutionary War. That helped Lafayette gain privilege while imprisoned. With the support of America, newly victorious Napoleon Bonaparte finally negotiated Lafayette's release. After more than five years in prison, Lafayette was again a free man.

Lafayette declined Napoleon's invitation to join his government. The hero of the American Revolution retreated to his estate upon the death of his wife in 1807. He returned to politics in 1815, continuing to fight for liberty. By 1823, when he began to receive the first informal invitations to visit America, he was serving in the Chamber of Deputies.

That didn't mean he wasn't ruffling feathers. The restored monarchy viewed him with suspicion. Lafayette still offered a beacon of hope to all those seeking liberty. They hoped he would not take up Monroe's invitation to visit America. They wanted him to stay in France and use his high-profile position in the Chamber of Deputies to continue to promote their cause.[12]

Meanwhile, Lafayette had legal troubles, too.

Chapter Three:
A Message From An Old Friend

By February of 1824, the foreign press had finally revealed the extent of Lafayette's legal troubles. He had already brought forth the wrath from the newly reinstated Bourbon monarchy.

In 1814, Napoleon was exiled to Elba. King Louis XVIII was restored to the crown his brother Louis XVI lost his head over during the French Revolution. Napoleon returned briefly in 1815, but quickly (after his defeat at Waterloo 100 days later) returned to exile, this time for good.

With that, the Bourbon Restoration commenced in full bloom. Lafayette, who had remained dormant following his wife's death, was convinced to return to politics. In 1818 he was elected to the Chamber of Deputies. Liberal advocates saw him as a leader of their cause.

However, as he sought to strengthen that cause in 1820, he and his allies came under the suspicion of the local police chief. When Lafayette visited Le Mans in September of 1820, local authorities banned pamphlets and prohibited gatherings of more than three people. Lafayette ignored these restrictions and held two banquets with over one hundred people each.[1]

As a result of this campaign, the government arrested a prominent journalist who backed Lafayette. Lafayette found himself embroiled in the trial through the early part of 1821.[2]

Two years later, Lafayette—and this time his son—became involved in another legal entanglement. Some French officers, under prosecution for conspiracy, were apprehended in Spain and returned to France. They escaped, but the wife of one of the conspirators remained in custody. Lafayette and several other "distinguished oppositionists" were subpoenaed as trial witnesses. They failed to show and were fined 100 francs (plus expenses). The trial was delayed until February 1824 with the stipulation that "if not forthcoming of their own accord," they would "be brought back by force before the tribunal."³

Between this legal issue and his duty as an elected official, Lafayette had reason to decline America's invitation.

That didn't dissuade his old friend James Monroe. The two had met in 1778 and had been friends ever since. They regularly wrote each other. This was not about to stop. On February 24, 1824, the President of the United States penned this letter to General Lafayette:

> *"My dear General,*
>
> *"I wrote you a letter about fifteen days since, by Mr. Brown, in which I expressed the wish to send to any port in France you should point out, a frigate to convey you hither, in case you should be able to visit the United States. Since then, Congress has passed a resolution on this subject, in which the sincere attachment of the whole nation to you is expressed, whose ardent desire is once more to see you amongst them. The period at which you may yield to this invitation is left entirely at your option, but believe me, whatever may be your decision, it will be sufficient that you should have the goodness to inform me of it, and immediate orders will be given for a government vessel to proceed to any port you will indicate, and convey you thence to the adopted country of your early youth, which has always preserved the most grateful recollection of your important services. I send you herewith the resolution of Congress, and add thereto the assurance of my high consideration and of my sentiments of affection.*
> *"JAMES MONROE"*⁴

Still, Lafayette felt duty-bound to remain in France. While a later published account stated, "It was impossible for Lafayette to refuse so honorable and so pressing an invitation,"⁵ clearly his position as an elected official prevented him from travelling.

At a celebration of George Washington's birthday in Paris, Lafayette said, "I request you, gentlemen, to accept my affectionate thanks for these new testimonies of your friendship. While every generous mind on this side of the Atlantic, has applauded the late noble and timely declaration of the United States, it could not but excite the pride of a heart glowing with all the feelings of an old American patriot and soldier—engaged, as I have been here from the beginning, & as I now am, in a great contest between the rights of mankind and the pretensions of European despotism and aristocracy. There are motives of duty and honor that must direct the time when it shall be my happy lot to revisit the shores of freedom, but that moment will be the most delightful I can ever enjoy."[6]

That all changed in April of 1824. With the establishment pulling out all the stops, Lafayette lost his reelection bid "by a considerable majority."[7] He was now free to accept America's invitation and make plans for an extensive tour. He decided to decline the offer for a free ride and sought his own transportation. He also turned down requests from his fellow countrymen to travel with him. Instead, he limited his traveling party to his son, George Washington Lafayette, and André-Nicolas Levasseur, who would serve as his secretary.[8]

Early May brought confirmation of what many had only mistakenly believed. While rumors of his death had circulated among "Eastern papers," a letter from Marietta, Ohio confirmed the death of General Rufus Putnam. With his passing at the age of 87, Lafayette was truly "now the only surviving general officer of the regular army of the United States which fought the battles of the revolution."[9]

Lafayette was about to revive American patriotic nostalgia in a tour worthy of the celebrity he was. James Monroe spent eight years in office priming his country for such an event. What made the American citizens ready for this veritable rock star visit?

Chapter Four: America In 1824

The year is 2024. Do you remember 2018? If you're a political junkie, you may recall it was the year Brett Kavanaugh won confirmation to the Supreme Court. If you enjoy reading *People Magazine*, then you'll note it was the year Meghan Markle married into the British royal family. If you prefer business, it was the year both Sears and Toys 'R' Us declared bankruptcy.

If you're an adult, each of those stories endure vividly in your memory. They don't seem that far distant. And if any of those subject areas carry emotional weight with you, those scars remain to this day.

Now imagine the year 1824. What major event happened in the year 1818 that sticks in your memory? For the typical citizen of the young country of America, the feelings of the War of 1812 are still with them. The Treaty of 1818 formally resolved the border dispute and other issues of that Anglo-American conflict.

Mind you, in the broader global context, while big in our country, the War of 1812 for the British represented just a mere skirmish. It stood as just one extended battle in the Sixty Years' War between Britian and France. Indeed, it was only a small part of the Napoleonic Wars that ended this generations-old conflict. In fact, it wasn't even the most famous "War of 1812." That would be France's invasion of Russia (which led to Tchaikovsky composing the *1812 Overture* in 1880).

America's War of 1812 also led to its own famous composition, although it would take several years for it to be put to music. That would be *The Star-Spangled Banner*.

It's appropriate that our national anthem derives from the Era of Good Feelings. Coming out of the War of 1812 ushered in a patriotic and confident America. The war itself proved America could hold its own against Britain. Subsequent treaties all but eliminated the British threat by creating the longest unprotected border in the world (between the United States and Canada).

There's more. And it was all part of James Monroe's strategy heading into his first term as presidency.

Politically, for the first and last time since George Washington, America became a one-party government. The opposition Federalist Party had lost much of its credibility by acting "disloyal" during the War of 1812.[1]

The war also opened up westward expansion. Six new states were added to the United States from 1816 to 1820.

Of course, one of the new states—Maine—wasn't from a new territory but came about as part of the Missouri Compromise. The Compromise revealed the growing national rift over slavery, but for the moment at least it appeased the two sides of the debate.

From an economic standpoint, things started slowly but picked up by the end of Monroe's term. The 1819 Panic marked the low point of an economic slowdown that began with the cessation of the War of 1812's hostilities. Despite the economic woes, America clearly felt it could survive on its own. To ensure this, Congress passed the first tariff act in 1816.

Still, financial doldrums didn't appear to dampen enthusiasm in the country. The nation certainly didn't take it out on the President. They happily reelected him as he ran unopposed in 1820.

Perhaps cultural changes might provide the ultimate evidence of the state of the United States in 1824. Daniel Webster was putting the finishing touches on his decades-long project, the *American Dictionary of the English Language*. It would place honor (not honour) in the center (not centre) of American nationalism.

In literature, James Fenimore Cooper published *The Pioneers* in 1823. It was the first of his five *Leatherstocking Tales* (the more famous one, *The Last of the Mohicans*, appeared in 1826). Cooper was part of an eclectic group of writers called the Knickerbocker Group. Among its members, Washington Irving also lent his talents to developing this new American ethos. His *Rip Van Winkle* (1819) and *The Legend of Sleepy Hollow* (1820) quickly became American classics.

For those who don't like to read, art offers a very good clue regarding American feelings. It started with the glorification of battles from the War of 1812. Thomas Birch painted *Perry's Victory on Lake Erie* in 1814.

As a painter, however, John Trumbull proved the best example of what was happening in America leading up to 1824. Known for his post-Revolutionary War depictions of the great battles for independence, he repeated the feat and then some in the years immediately after the War of 1812. Again, he focused on the events of the previous generation. Among these works include *The Declaration of Independence* (painted 1819 and placed in the United States Capitol rotunda in 1826), *Surrender of Lord Cornwallis* (1820), *Surrender of General Burgoyne* (1821), and *General George Washington Resigning His Commission* (1824).

It is this last painting the turns out to be most relevant to our story. It may have reminded both James Monroe and the American people to respect and honor (again, not "honour") the Father of Our Country. Monroe held true to Washington's self-imposed two-term limit.

It's quite possible he could have won a third election. With patriot fever at a high pitch, Monroe's countrymen idolized Monroe him. How popular was he? One way to measure this is by the number of counties within the states that were named in honor of him. There are seventeen, including Monroe County, New York, established on February 23, 1821, shortly after Monroe's uncontested reelection in 1820.

Do you know who else has seventeen counties named after him? James Monroe's good friend Lafayette.

With Lafayette's Tour of America confirmed to begin in the summer of 1824, people embraced the memory of America's war for independence. They glowed in the aura of greatness emanating from those who made their freedom possible. What better way to salute those long-gone heroes by praising those that remained?

Word quickly got out that Lafayette accepted the invitation. Ports across the eastern seaboard prepared to receive "America's Guest," now truly the last surviving general of the Revolutionary War. They lobbied aggressively for the honor.

But only one would earn that prize.

CHAPTER FIVE:
AND THE LUCKY WINNER IS...

The nation waited anxiously for a formal response to President James Monroe's invitation to General Lafayette. In March and April of 1824, newspapers across the country printed letters hinting that Lafayette had prior commitments.

To Major Joseph Wheaton of Washington came word from Lafayette that "...duties to the cause of freedom make it, if not a matter of hope, at least a point of honor, to keep his present post."[1] Similarly, Lafayette wrote to Dr. James Thatcher, "At this moment a sense of duty keeps me on the European side of the Atlantic."[2]

While the papers proclaimed these missives as "the latest communication from Lafayette,"[3] they were months old by the time they hit the press. It wasn't as if Lafayette disliked America. In truth, he loved his adopted country. He wrote his good friend William Eustis, Governor of Massachusetts, he was "as American patriot," and that "for political civilization, honesty and steadiness the United States hold a rank so superior to every other human aggregation."[4]

It wasn't until late April or early May that the nation learned Lafayette had lost his election to French parliament and was now free to accept Monroe's invitation. [5,6,7,8]

By early June, reports indicated Lafayette would arrive "before fall, or perhaps in a very short time." The source of this letter, "a gentleman now in Paris, who has lately visited Lafayette," had more to say. He said Lafayette "is the best person I ever came across in my life, and one of the most modest and distinguished men in the world. He is absolutely too good for Europe. America is the soil alone congenial to him, and may he soon be there to know and see how much we cherish and love him, and prove that republics are not, as was formerly said, always ungrateful."[9]

How's that for enthusiasm?

By late June, word got out the Secretary of the Navy had ordered the *North Carolina*, a ship of the line out of Norfolk, Virginia, to be ready to convey Lafayette to the United States.[10] These may have been outdated orders because by late April it was understood that Lafayette had declined the offer of the escort.[11]

Lafayette had decided to leave during the month of July. He hired out the American merchant ship *Cadmus* to sail from Havre. Together with his two travel companions and several unrelated passengers, he departed from that port at noon on July 13, 1824.[12] But where would he land in America?

Which American port would win the honor of becoming Lafayette's landing place? Would it be Norfolk, home of the Navy shipyard? Or how about that thriving port of New York, North America's largest city? Maybe it would be Boston, the birthplace of America's War of Independence.

Indeed, Boston was quick to jump at the opportunity. In early March, before the results of the French elections were even known, newspapers reported the Common Council of Boston had "appointed a committee to direct a letter in behalf of the City Council to Gen. Lafayette, requesting him, if not inconvenient, on his contemplated visit to the United States, to land in that place." As if it wasn't clear, they also sought to "assure him that his reception will be worthy of the city which has ever held in the highest estimation the services and sacrifices of the Adopted Son of Washington."[13]

That was from the City of Boston itself. The State of Massachusetts would later enter the fray when its Senate passed the following resolution: "Whereas the Marquis De Lafayette may be expected to arrive in this country during the present year; therefore, Resolved, by the Senate and the House of Representatives in General Court assembled, that His Excellency the Governor and the Hon. Council be requested to make such arrangements as will secure to this distinguished friend of our country an honorable reception on the part of this State; and that His Excellency be authorized to draw his warrants upon the Treasury for such sum as may be necessary for this purpose."[14]

Not to be outdone, a week later, New York City showed its muscle in a way only New York City can. Its board unanimously adopted:

> "Whereas the Senate and House of Representatives, have lately by a concurrent resolution, requested the President of the U. States to give the Marquis La Fayette, an invitation to visit this country, and to communicate to him the assurances of grateful and affectionate attachment still cherished towards him, by the government and the people.
>
> "And, as a further demonstration of respect, Congress directed that a national ship of the line, should be offered to the Marquis for the purpose of conveying him to the U. States.
>
> "And, it being understood that the invitation has been given and accepted, and that the distinguished visitor may, probably shortly arrive at our city— Influenced as this Board is by a respectful deference to the Constituted Authorities of the General Government, and animated by the highest esteem for the public and private virtues of the Marquis LaFayette. It is therefore Resolved, That the Corporation of the City of New York, acting in behalf [of] their fellow citizens, will receive and treat, the Marquis De La Fayette, as a guest of the nation.
>
> "Resolved, That a Committee of Five be appointed to prepare suitable apartments for his accommodation, and to furnish and supply them in a manner corresponding with the greatness and hospitality of our city, and the generous feelings of a free people.
>
> "Resolved, That his Honor, the Mayor is hereby requested, upon the first announcement of the arrival of the Marquis in this city, to convene the Common Council in the City Hall, for the purpose of receiving him, and of conducting him to the residence which shall have been provided for him by this Board.

"Resolved, That his Honor the Mayor is hereby requested, immediately upon the arrival of the Marquis in this city, to communicate to him a copy of these proceedings, and to inform him that a committee of the Common Council will wait upon him, to conduct him to the City Hall."[15]

And the winner was?

New York City!

No. Not really. Technically, Lafayette's first steps on American soil were on Staten Island.

The *Cadmus* had arrived in New York Harbor on a Sunday. A steamboat carrying Vice President Daniel Tompkins' son greeted Lafayette's ship. The younger Tompkins informed Lafayette and his party, that, since the City was "unwilling to break the Sabbath, and which moreover had still some preparations to make," would the Nation's Guest mind first being the Vice President's Guest by staying at his home on Staten Island until the next day?[16]

Soon after the three Frenchmen arrived at Vice President Tompkins residence, a brief shower passed through. As quickly as it appeared, the sun emerged once more, even before the rain had completely stopped. From the piazza of the Vice President's house, a brilliant rainbow materialized. Below the spectrum of effluent colors, as if a sign from heaven, stood the distant Fort Lafayette.

The scene had an enduring impact on Lafayette. After pausing to take in its splendor, the General turned to his host and remarked, "this day has been full of happy omens to me in arriving among those who have treated me with so much unmerited kindness."[17]

If Lafayette thought that day was special, just wait to see what he witnessed the next day.

CHAPTER SIX:
AMERICA WELCOMES THE NATION'S GUEST

The *Cadmus*, having departed from Havre on July 13, 1824, had been at sea for thirty-two days before seeing land on the horizon. On Saturday, August 14th, the passengers and crew spotted their destination.[1] New York Harbor would present the ideal place to make their inaugural landing. The *Cadmus* would reach that port early the next morning.

The Committee appointed by the Common Council of the City of New York was busy putting the finishing touches on the celebration to welcome Lafayette. It had arranged for a "suite of splendid apartments in the City Hotel" to be set aside for The Nation's Guest and his party. Besides the military display (anticipated to include 20,000 men), the City planned to host "a great civic feast, in the Banqueting Room in the City Hall, which will be illuminated at night, together with the whole City." To make a memorable first impression upon entering the Harbor, "a grand salute of 100 guns will be fired from Fort Lafayette, together with salutes from the Batteries and ships of war in the harbor, and the decoration of all the shipping."[2]

So, America's largest city was more than prepared to host The Nation's Guest. Only, not on a Sunday. And August 15, 1824, fell on the Sabbath Day.

Even before Vice President Daniel Tompkins' son arrived to greet them, the *Cadmus* found itself quickly surrounded by a fleet of "long, light, and narrow boats."[3] The men managing these boats eyed the incoming foreign vessel with tense anticipation.

One boat came aside the *Cadmus*. A sailor shouted, "Is Lafayette among you?" When the *Cadmus* confirmed he was, the faces of sailors on that boat beamed with delight. They enthusiastically shook hands and otherwise congratulated themselves. Quickly, that same feeling of excitement spread from boat to boat. It was as if "they had been the children of one family, rejoicing at the return of a much-loved and long-expected parent."[4]

Just as the young Tompkins' steamboat approached the *Cadmus*, the Harbor echoed with the roar of cannon. This report came from Fort Lafayette, officially signaling the arrival of its namesake.

The Fort was built during the War of 1812 on Hendricks Reef in New York Harbor. A casemated brick coastal fort, the 280-foot square sandstone structure contained 70 cannons mounted in three tiers within and atop its 8-foot thick 30-feet high walls. Originally named "Fort Diamond" (for its shape), the fortification was rechristened "Fort Lafayette" on March 26, 1823 to honor the Revolutionary War hero. Both Fort Lafayette and Hendricks Reef were razed in 1960 for the building of the North Tower of the Verrazano-Narrows Bridge.[5]

In case you're wondering, there was another Fort Lafayette. It was located just south of West Point and only lasted from 1779 until 1783, when it was abandoned.[6]

The cannons of the second Fort Lafayette—the one in New York Harbor—would boom again the next day at one o'clock in the afternoon. This time the thunderous sound announced the arrival of the *Chancellor Livingston*. The steamboat carried its honored passenger Lafayette from Staten Island along with "more than two hundred of the principal citizens of New York, among whom the general recognized many of his old fellow soldiers, who threw themselves into his arms, felicitating themselves on seeing him once more after so many years and dangers past."[7]

Led by the famed steamship *Robert Fulton*, a flotilla of boats accompanied the *Chancellor Livingston*, on that "clear, cool, and pleasant" day.[8] The *Cadmus* followed, as though it was being escorted in triumph. In the air flowed the French tune *Où peut-on être mieux qu'au sein de sa famille* ("Where can you be better than within your family?"). Lafayette's travel companion and private secretary André-Nicolas Levasseur notes that André Grétry, the composer of this nostalgic melody, describes this piece as reminiscent of "families reconciled who had been before at deadly variance."[9]

Ironically, *Où peut-on être mieux qu'au sein de sa famille* was also the unofficial national anthem of the Kingdom of France during the First Restoration and the Second Restoration from 1815 to 1830. This was the regime that essentially monitored Lafayette in the years he served on the Council of Directors.

Among those aboard the *Chancellor Livingston* was Colonel Marinus Willet, an 85-year-old veteran of the Revolutionary War. After heartfelt hugs, Willet turned to Lafayette, who had just sat down next to him, and asked, "Do you remember me at the battle of Monmouth? I was volunteer aid to Gen. Scott. I saw you in the heat of battle. You were but a boy, but you were a serious and sedate lad. Aye, aye; I remember well. And on the Mohawk, I sent you fifty Indians, and you wrote me, that they set up such a yell that they frightened the British horse, who ran one way and the Indians the other!"[10] Indeed, Lafayette remembered this and many other veterans he would meet.

General Lafayette disembarked at two o'clock to the cheers of a large crowd. A special group called the *Lafayette Guards*, sporting a portrait of the general on the chest of their uniforms, led him into the celebration. There, he was received with military honors, with several corps parading in front of his reviewing stand. Each soldier wore a ribband that bore the words "Welcome Lafayette."[11]

A soldier seated with Lafayette's party leaned into the group and proclaimed, 'Ah! Could this thundering welcome but resound to Europe, that it might inspire the powers which govern you with your love of virtue, and the people with the love of liberty!"[12]

After the reception, the hero of the American Revolution climbed into a waiting carriage led by four white horses. The general was then chauffeured through the dense crowd towards City Hall. All around him, he noticed the streets adorned with patriot displays—flags, bunting, flowers, wreaths, etc.[13]

Contemporary reports described the scene as "truly a jubilee—a more greater holiday than the Fourth of July. Business was suspended, stores were closed and streets thronged with well dressed people."[14]

Inside City Hall, Lafayette went to the common council chamber. There, he met with the Mayor, who offered cordial greetings on behalf of the citizens of New York. The General replied in kind with words to express his heartfelt feelings. He then met with each member of the board individually before being conducted to the City Hotel where the Board had approved a suite of rooms for his use.[15]

Before leaving City Hall, though, the General then had an opportunity to meet with the public for the first time. For two hours, "mothers surrounded him, presenting their children and asking his blessing, which having obtained, they embraced their offspring wither renewed tenderness; feeble old men appeared to become reanimated in talking to him of the numerous battles in which they had been engaged with him for the sake of liberty."[16]

At five o'clock, the travelers left for the City Hotel. Not only did that facility contain their accommodations, but it was also the location of the official welcoming dinner. During the next four days, Lafayette would find himself greeted by dignitaries and organizations. The New York Historical Society presented The Nation's Guest and his son with honorary memberships. Clad in their continental army uniforms, Revolutionary War veterans from the New York State Society of Cincinnati visited him and invited him to dinner. Next came members of the New York Bar, whose president delivered a message of greeting. Finally, French residents of New York City came to offer their respects.[17]

And so it would be throughout Lafayette's visit. These scenes would repeat themselves throughout the nation wherever Lafayette would visit, including during his travels through the Greater Western New York Region. Americans would welcome him not merely as the celebrity he was, but like a returning prodigal son.

What was it about this Frenchman that caused our nation to endear him so?

Chapter Seven:
Why Lafayette?

America stood poised on the cusp of celebrating the golden anniversary of its birth as a nation. With all the rising patriotism came a burst of nostalgia. America's first and greatest generation—the heroes of the Revolutionary War—were fast leaving their mortal coil. The heirs of that founding cohort desperately wanted one last chance to hear the tales of that victory from those that were there.

Of all the people they might select to focus on, why choose a Frenchman born to the aristocracy?

Well, for one thing, his life story shows he had long ago shorn off the mantle of gentry. Indeed, he not only had the physical scars of Brandywine to prove it, he also had the mental scars earned from the prison at Olmütz. But there was more to Lafayette than these undeniable badges of courage.

He was truly one of us.

It starts with his role in the American Revolution. You saw earlier of his exploits at Brandywine (see Chapter Two: "The Duty That Held Him Back"). He did more than that. Much more.

Though a teenager when he arrived on America's shores, Lafayette quickly established himself both in the eyes of the Continental Army and on the radar of the enemy. The British, and Cornwallis in particular, were keen to capture the young Frenchman.

One of the first documented attempts occurred at the Battle of Monmouth. According to a British report, "The enemy's cavalry, commanded it is said by M. LaFayette, having approached within our reach, they were charged with great spirit by the Queen's light dragoons. They did not wait for the shock, but fell back in confusion upon their own infantry."[1]

The Battle of Monmouth was a mess, apparently for both sides, although more for the Americans. This report appears to be a reference to an attempt to capture Lafayette. It was really a case of mistaken identity. Instead of Lafayette, it was Baron Friedrich Wilhelm von Steuben who led those troops. The baron barely escaped (but lost his hat in the process).

Not to be dismayed, a few years later during the early summer of 1781, Cornwallis did get the better of Lafayette. He still didn't catch him.

The Redcoats reported, "The attack was begun by the first line with great spirit there being nothing but militia opposed to the Light Infantry; the action was soon over on the right, but Lieut. Col. Dunda's brigade, consisting of the 43d, 76th, and 80th regiments, which formed the left wing, meeting the Pennsylvania line, and a detachment of the Marquis de la Fayette's Continentals, with two six pounders, a smart action ensued for some minutes, which the enemy gave way, and abandoned their cannon. The cavalry were ready to pursue, but the darkness of the evening prevented his Lordship making use of them."[2]

This was the famous incident where Cornwallis tricked Lafayette into thinking the British were retreating. Lafayette reported the false intelligence to his command before acting on it.[3]

Despite the setback, Lafayette kept his eyes on Cornwallis' movements. He was surprised when the British General left himself exposed at Yorktown. Lafayette convinced both the French and George Washington to exploit this vulnerability. They did, and the Franco-American victory at Yorktown sealed the fate of the American Revolution.

In a letter to his wife, Lafayette summarized the Virginia events thusly: "The end of this campaign is truly brilliant for the allied troops. There was a rare coordination in our movements, and I would be finicky indeed if I were not pleased with the end of my campaign in Virginia. You must have been informed of all the toil the superiority and talents of Lord Cornwallis gave me and of the advantage that we then gained in recovering lost ground, until at length we had Lord Cornwallis in the position we needed in order to capture him. It was then that everyone pounced on him."[4]

Between these two events, Lafayette proved himself a vigorous advocate for the American patriots. In 1780, the King of France issued a proclamation of the new Franco-American alliance. In that edict, he cited Lafayette's role.[5] America might have hated the English king, but they cheered the French king.

During the fight for independence, Lafayette developed a strong bond with George Washington. Evidence that Lafayette enjoyed a close friendship with the man destined to be dubbed "The Father of His Country" can be found in the number of letters our first President wrote to his Revolutionary War ally. From March 1778 through December 1798, Washington penned roughly seventy letters to Lafayette.[6]

In his last letter to Lafayette, Washington expressed the warm regards he had for his "dear friend." He closes the letter with this final line: "I shall now only add, what you knew well before, that, with the most sincere friendship and affectionate regard, I am always yours."[7]

Once the war was over, Lafayette proved his faith in the new country he helped create. He remained committed to American ideals. That commitment would get him in trouble when he espoused those ideals in Europe. He remained, however, adamant as to the source of those principles.

In 1818, he created a political club in Paris and served as its president. In one meeting, "the members discussed the advantages of a Republican Government, like that of the U. States, and it was unanimously agreed, that it was the best possible government, far superior to the highly boasted Government of Great Britain."[8]

While this was happening across the pond, people in the United States carefully crafted their origin story, beginning with the Revolutionary War. According to a home art exhibit in 1805, it became "a representation of figures of great characters." Among those characters you would find Lafayette.[9]

By the early 1820s, America was ripe to remember. Contemporary newspaper articles bluntly told this story. One paper summed this up when it printed, "every thing relating to the revolutionary war, is of deep interest to the generation, and the surviving patriots, together with every documentary evidence of their principle and services, are the property of the country."[10]

This nostalgic fervor and its ticking clock weren't limited to the American people. Lafayette felt it himself. His 1822 letter to Colonel Marinus Willet describes the feeling. In it, he wrote, "no time or distance can abate the patriotic remembrances and personal affections of our revolutionary times. We remain, but too few survivors of that glorious epoch, in which the fate of two hemispheres has been decided. It is an additional monitor to think more of the ties of brotherly friendship which united us. May it be in my power, before I join our departed companions, to visit such of them as are still inhabitants of the United States, and to tell you, personally, my dear Willet, how affectionately, I am your sincere friend."[11]

Lafayette's tour of 1824 and 1825 would result in his reunion and celebration with those surviving Revolutionary War Veterans. It also gave younger generations an opportunity to share in these deeply emotional meetings.

Before seeing what those events looked like in the Greater Western New York Region, we'll first give you a taste for how this tour grew from a quick four-month visit to a stay that saw him finally return to France sixteen months after he originally departed from Le Havre.

CHAPTER EIGHT:
OVERVIEW OF 1824-1825 AMERICAN VISIT (PART I)

When Lafayette arrived at the harbor in New York, he came with two traveling companions. They would remain with him for the entire journey. During this excursion, they would witness and experience the raw emotion of the reunion between old friends.

The most prominent of Lafayette's party was his son, Georges Washington Louis Gilbert de La Fayette. Contemporary American newspaper accounts refer to him as "George Washington Lafayette." This makes sense, given the patriotic zeal that enveloped the country.

Lafayette's son was born on Christmas Eve 1779. This was the year Lafayette was home in France in between his two war-time tours in America.

Think about that for a moment. Lafayette had only served under Washington for a little over a year. Still, the aura of that great man so impressed the young Marquis that Lafayette honored George Washington by naming his son after him.

Immediately after the American Revolution, Georges lived in Paris. Ben Franklin, John Jay, and John Adams would meet at the Lafayette's residence every Monday. Those weren't the only Revolutionary War icons Georges would meet.

The French Revolution ultimately forced the Lafayette family into exile. Georges was sent to the United States and studied at Harvard. He also was a house guest of his namesake, and now U.S. President George Washington. Georges spent time with George at both the presidential mansion in Philadelphia and at Mount Vernon.

The other member of the Lafayette travel party was Lafayette's secretary André-Nicolas Levasseur (also known as Auguste Levasseur). In 1829, after finishing his duties with Lafayette, Levasseur published

Lafayette en Amérique, en 1824 et 1825 ou Journal d'un voyage aux États-Uni. This book was immediately translated into English and published in America.

Many historians consider the two-volume set of *Lafayette in America in 1824 and 1825* the primary source of Lafayette's 1824-1825 American tour. Levasseur foresaw this as, in his Author's Preface, he wrote that his book "has a character of incontestable authenticity, for in addition to the testimony of several millions of witnesses, that might be adduced if necessary, I can also say, *all I relate I have seen*." (Author's emphasis.)[1]

Following the festivities marking his arrival in New York City, Lafayette departed for Boston. He traveled along the Long Island Sound on the shores of southern Connecticut, very close to the route of the current I-95. Along the way, he passed through cities like Greenwich, Stamford, and Norwalk.

They made a quick stop in New Haven to see Yale College before moving on to New London, where they turned North (think I-395) through Norwich and Providence before finally coming to Boston on August 24, 1824.[2] They stayed there about a week, visited Georges' alma mater (Harvard), meeting with the 89-year-old John Adams and reviewing the Massachusetts militia before leaving for Portsmouth, New Hampshire.

Lafayette and company meandered through southern New Hampshire and eastern Massachusetts before heading down what would become I-84 from Worcester, Massachusetts, to Hartford, Connecticut. Then it was on to New York again in time for the Society of Cincinnati's dinner on September 6, 1824 (coincidentally Lafayette's 67th birthday).[3]

For the next two weeks, Lafayette ambled about Manhattan. In the middle of his stay in that city, he headed up the Hudson to visit West Point, Poughkeepsie, and Albany, among others. On September 23, 1824, he left New York for Philadelphia. As was becoming his standard, he made several whistle stops in New Jersey before arriving in the City of Brotherly Love. He remained there for a little more than a week.

By October 7, 1824, the tourists arrived in Baltimore for a three-day stay. Then it was on to Washington, D.C. from the 12th of October through the 16th. On the 17th he visited Mount Vernon on his way to

Yorktown, Virginia. Lafayette's party remained in Virginia from October 18, 1824, until November 22, 1824. During that time, he visited Thomas Jefferson. He also stayed with James Madison for several days.

Next, Lafayette returned to Washington D.C. After taking a day's rest, the party left for Baltimore for the annual meeting of the farmers of Maryland. Lafayette took notes which he hoped "would prove useful on his farm at La Grange."[4]

A pleasant surprise awaited Lafayette when he came back to Washington, D.C. Dozens of messages from southern and western states invited him to visit. "The representatives of the different states who had come to sit in congress, daily came to see him, and spoke with enthusiasm of the preparations which their fellow citizens were already making to receive the nation's guest." So honored, Lafayette could not say no. He accepted the offers. The only caveat: he couldn't start what would become the second leg of his tour until the end of winter.[5]

After a 4-day diversion to Harrisburg, Pennsylvania in late January/early February 1825, Lafayette launched his southern tour from Washington D.C. the third week of February.

The civilized folk of the Nation's Capital expressed a certain lack of confidence in the Nation's Guest heading out into the hinterlands to the south and west of the coastal comforts. These new states—and parts of the original colonies, too—had a feral air to them.

At least in the minds of the civilized folk.

Lafayette had no compunction, though. He left it to his son George to work out a suitable itinerary that met with all the promises the father made. One of those promises was made to the City of Boston. Lafayette had agreed to participate in the dedication of the new Bunker Hill Monument. The celebration was scheduled to take place on June 17, 1825. The map would take Lafayette and his travel companions on a circuitous route—"twelve hundred leagues to pass over in less than four months."[6]

Still, the small crew did take precautions. One of their friends urged them to accept a "commodious and easy carriage."[2] Instead, they bought "good saddle-horses to substitute for the coach on very bad roads" and "reduced our baggage as much as possible." At nine o'clock in the evening of February 23, 1825, they set sail on the Potomac, into the Chesapeake Bay, and finally on the Atlantic Ocean. Their destination: Norfolk, Virginia.[7]

So began the second leg of Lafayette's Farewell tour across America. It signaled the start of a much different visit. The northeastern tour featured prominent cities, celebrity visits, and famous Revolutionary War battlefields. This next phase would herald hardship, but also the true heart of America.

Chapter Nine: Overview Of 1824-1825 American Visit (Part II)

Once again, only this time with greater speed, Lafayette marched through Virginia. That did not mean Lafayette didn't have spare time for the local folk. Levasseur provides the following anecdote from a few miles outside of Norfolk, Virginia. It expresses the feelings for the General shared by almost every American during his tour:

> "We were sitting in our carriage when the landlord presented himself, asked to see the general, and eagerly pressed him to alight for a moment and come into his house. 'If,' said he, 'you have only five minutes to stay, do not refuse them, since to me they will be so many minutes of happiness.' The general yielded to his entreaty, and we followed him into a lower room, where we observed a plainness bordering on poverty, but a remarkable degree of cleanliness. Welcome Lafayette, was inscribed with charcoal upon the white wall, enwreathed with boughs from the fir trees of the neighbouring wood. Near the fire-place, where pine wood was crackling, stood a small table covered with a very clean napkin, and covered with some decanters containing brandy and whiskey; by the side of a plate covered with glasses was another plate filled with neatly arranged slices of bread. These modest refreshments were tendered with a kindness and cordiality which greatly enhanced their value. Whilst we were partaking of them the landlord disappeared, but returned a moment after accompanied by his wife, carrying her little boy, about three or four years of age, whose fresh and plump cheeks evinced the tenderness and care with

which he had been cherished. The father, after first presenting his wife, next took his child in his arms, and, having placed one of his little hands in the hand of the general, made him repeat, with much emphasis, the following: 'General Lafayette, I thank you for the liberty which you have won for my father, for my mother, for myself, and for my country!!' While the child was speaking, the father and mother eyed the general with the most tender regard: their hearts responded to the words of their boy, and tears they were unable to suppress, proved that their gratitude was vivid and profound."[1]

Things slowed a bit in North Carolina as he spent a week visiting a dozen sites. While Lafayette may have made fewer stops in South Carolina, he spent nearly twice as much time there. A typical story (and maybe a reason for a longer stay) occurred in Camden, South Carolina on March 8, 1825.

This town of two hundred swelled as people from eighty miles away came to see the French hero lay the cornerstone of a monument dedicated to Baron de Kalb. De Kalb, a German, had served in France before, like Lafayette, joining the American fight for independence. Unfortunately, he was mortally wounded at the Battle of Camden. Though given little notice of his primary role in the ceremony, Lafayette performed with suitable honor and respect.[2]

The Grand Lodge of South Carolina led the ceremonial re-interment of de Kalb and the dedication of his monument. Lafayette, himself a Mason, was no doubt familiar with his duties for the occasion. Many, if not most, Revolutionary War veterans were Masons, including de Kalb, who was originally buried in Camden with Masonic honors. For the ceremony nearly a half century later, Lafayette was given a silver trowel made of Mexican coins. Now known as the "Lafayette Trowel," it remained the property of the Grand Lodge of South Carolina.[3]

Just over the border in Savannah, Georgia, the same thing occurred. This time to honor Casimir Pulaski, the "Father of the American Cavalry." Like Lafayette and de Kalb, Pulaski came from Europe to fight for the Patriots. The Polish native, however, suffered a fatal injury when grapeshot struck him while leading a charge to retake Savannah. He died two days later, just outside of Savannah in the town of Thunderbolt. He was buried there. As with de Kalb's monument, Lafayette laid the cornerstone for the Pulaski Monument on March 21, 1824.[4] (The site of the monument was later moved and the cornerstone was re-laid in 1853).

After three days in Savannah, Lafayette ambled through the rest of the most southern of the original colonies for another ten days. Of note, Lafayette did not travel through Florida. Florida Territory was formally annexed from Spain during President Madison's second term on March 30, 1822. It didn't become a state until March 3, 1845.

With no state of Florida on his tour map, Lafayette entered Alabama on March 31, 1825. Over the next nine days, he visited ten locations within that state.

On April 8, 1825, he took a steamship *Natchez* from Mobile, Alabama. The city of New Orleans provided the boat. A stormy night had the passengers of the *Natchez* fighting seasickness. At dawn, they spotted La Balize, the former French fort at the mouth of the Mississippi River. Later that morning, about 40 miles upstream, they spotted Fort St. Philip (formerly Fort Plaquemine), which honored them with a thirteen-gun salute. By midnight that same day, they could hear the batteries of New Orleans firing "a salute of a hundred guns" announcing their imminent arrival.[5]

As they awoke the morning of the 10th, they heard "cries of *Vive la liberté, vive l'ami de l'Amerique! vive Lafayette!* in the French language."[6] It was as though they had returned home. Lafayette remained in New Orleans until April 15th.

The following day he was in Baton Rouge from which he went directly to Natchez, Mississippi, for three days. From April 20, 1825 through April 27, 1825, Lafayette steamed up the Mississippi River. He stopped in St. Louis, where the former Missouri Territory Governor William Clark (of Lewis and Clark fame) escorted him.

The ship then turned back, heading south towards Kaskaskia, Illinois. At the insistence of the Illinois governor, Lafayette agreed to make an unscheduled stop there. It was one of the stops that didn't pull out all the stops to greet Lafayette. There was no carriage waiting for him (but one was quickly obtained), no ornate military parade to march for him, indeed, there was no triumph of any sort. Still "the accents of joy and republican gratitude which broke upon his ear, was grateful to his heart, since it proved to him that wherever American liberty had penetrated, there also the love and veneration of the people for its founders were perpetuated."[7]

Upon reaching the Ohio River on May 1, 1825, they parted ways with the *Natchez* and boarded the *Artizan*, the former being too big to navigate the shallow waters ahead.[8] In the next week, they traveled on the Ohio and Cumberland rivers. Along the way, they visited four states, but spent the most time (three days) in Nashville, Tennessee with Andrew Jackson as his escort. Like New Orleans, Nashville toasted Lafayette in the festive way of the east coast cities.

It was back on the Ohio River to Louisville, Kentucky, on board the *Mechanic*. That's when the unthinkable happened. The ship hit a snag. It went down in ten minutes. Lafayette lost everything but one or two trunks. He even lost a cane that belonged to George Washington, which he had just received as a gift.[9] Fortunately, Levasseur retrieved a snuffbox "ornamented with a picture of Washington" before escaping the sinking craft.[10] Later, a trunk believed to contain Lafayette's "valuable papers" was recovered and sent to meet the General during his visit to Boston.[11]

From May 12, 1825, through May 18, 1825, Lafayette's party, which since they had left Washington D.C. now included Francisque Alphonse de Syon, toured Kentucky via the overland route, arriving in Cincinnati, Ohio, on May 19, 1825. Then it was once again on the Ohio River, all the way to Pittsburgh on May 30, 1825. In those eleven days, Lafayette visited not fewer than thirteen separate towns in Ohio, Kentucky, West Virginia, and Pennsylvania.

Pittsburgh presented another big city celebration. It also offered reunions with more Revolutionary War veterans. One approached Lafayette and asked if the General remembered him. "No!" said Lafayette, "I have not forgotten Wilson, and it is a great happiness to be permitted to embrace him to-day!" Wilson was the soldier who carried the wounded Lafayette on a litter at the Battle of Brandywine.[12]

Once again, Lafayette takes the land route from Pittsburgh through Butler, Mercer, Franklin, Meadville, and Waterford before arriving at Erie, Pennsylvania.

CHAPTER TEN:
LAFAYETTE PREPARES TO ENTER THE GREATER WESTERN NEW YORK REGION

The sun rose the morning of Friday, June 3, 1825, at 4:05am local time in Waterford, Pennsylvania.[1] Lafayette had two weeks—14 days—to travel 550 miles and visit almost two dozen towns and villages before the June 17th dedication of the Bunker Hill Monument in Boston. He was determined to meet every community he promised to visit. Speed was of the essence.

But he couldn't show it.

At least not in a too obvious way.

Roughly three hours after the break of dawn, at about 7 o'clock, Lafayette's party left Waterford for the seat of the County, Erie, Pennsylvania.[2] Though technically still in the Quaker State, what Lafayette experienced there would prepare him for his travels through the Greater Western New York Region.

That made sense. It wasn't that long ago that New York State claimed what is known as the "Erie Triangle." And, like Western New York, most of the new settlers in Pennsylvania's western port came from New England.

It took a while, though.

The western boundaries of the interior colonies were always loosely defined. Well, technically, they were defined by the British royalty, but often in confusing and contradictory ways. Even still, the presence of indigenous inhabitants, who generally opposed western settlement, fuzzed up those technical boundaries. The end of the Revolutionary War failed to resolve this quandary. In a number of ways.

The Erie Triangle represents a prime example of this.

As the Revolutionary War began to turn to America's favor, the newly formed states began the process known as "cessation." States ceded western claims to the Federal government as a way to resolve the "sea to sea" boundaries declared by royal decree that created conflicting claims.

One of those became apparent when both New York State and Massachusetts ceded territory which now encompasses the Greater Western New York region. Much to the dismay of Pennsylvania, this included the Erie Triangle.[3]

Pennsylvania simply had no luck when it came to winning conflicting claims. Early colonial maps showed the northern border of Pennsylvania extended to a latitude just south of present-day Rochester, New York. With that, they claimed nearly the entire eastern coast of Lake Erie.

Given the New York and Massachusetts cessions, Pennsylvania wanted to get to the bottom of this claiming business. The state desired to secure its rights to Lake Erie. Unfortunately, Pennsylvania's hopes were dashed when, in 1783, its own state-sponsored commission found, instead of the hoped for thirty or forty miles of coastline, the State of Pennsylvania could only reasonably argue it had but two or three miles on the lake shore. The rest, including the much-desired former French harbor of Presqu' Isle (today, Erie) lay within the land ceded by New York and Massachusetts.[4]

The state rapidly put in place an effort to buy the Erie Triangle. After George Washington hired Andrew Ellicott (the older brother of Joseph), to formally measure the Triangle, the sale concluded in 1792.[5]

While the border definitions might have been secured, the western frontier was hardly considered safe. Not only did the Indians maintain an omnipresent threat, but the British, too, offered reason for trepidation. The population of the Triangle, with a little more land to the south added, now called Erie County, had but 1,468 inhabitants in 1800 and, just before the War of 1812, a meager 3,758. Following the end of hostilities, people poured into northwest Pennsylvania. The population swelled to 8,553 in 1820 and 17,041 in 1830.[6]

Where did all these people come from? The same place those who settled in the Greater Western New York Region came from. One author even says, "Erie County became more like New York than Pennsylvania, with its Connecticut, Rhode Island, and Maine settlers, several of whom had tried pioneering in New York."[7]

It makes sense that the greeting the citizens of Erie would offer to Lafayette would hint at what he would soon find once he crossed the border from the Keystone State into the Genesee Country.

With most of the short stops Lafayette would make, a committee from the next stop would arrive to escort the General. In the case of Waterford, Judah Colt, Esq., of the Erie committee arrived to welcome Lafayette. After an early breakfast, they left Waterford and began the 15-mile trek to Erie. About a mile outside their destination a uniformed battalion received them.[8]

Led by General B. Wallace, acting as Chief Marshal, they formed a procession that passed first down State Street to the public square, then down French to Third and back again to State Street. There, Lafayette and his party alighted and were received by Captain Budd, commanding officer of the naval station along with other naval and military officers. The group proceeded to the bank where, in full view of the harbor, the navy yard fired a national salute officially welcoming the Nation's Guest.[9]

Next they went to the home of Daniel Dobbins. Dobbins built the ships at the Erie shipyards that Oliver Hazard ("Don't Give Up The Ship") Perry used to win the Battle of Lake Erie in the War of 1812. It seemed the entire village, young and old, were at Dobbins to greet the famous French Revolutionary War hero. Those that Lafayette didn't meet at Dobbins' house he met immediately afterward at the home of Colt.[10]

Finally, a dinner was had by all at a table that nearly spanned the length of the one hundred- and seventy-feet long bridge on the Second Street bridge between French and State. With a picturesque vista of Lake Erie behind it, the table, "was covered by an awning of the sails of the British vessels taken by justly famed Commodore Perry during the last war, and tastefully decorated by the ladies with festoons of flowers and evergreens."[11]

The Americans toasted their guest: "General La Fayette—In youth a hero, in maturity a sage, in advanced life an example to the present and future generations." To which the General arose and replied, "Erie — A name which has a great share in American glory; may this town ever enjoy a proportionate share in American prosperity and happiness."[12]

Levasseur writes of this event: "The trophies suspended over our heads, the name of Perry and the view of lake Erie, necessarily directed the thoughts of the guests to the events of the last war; and in a short time the gallant deeds of the American navy became the subject of general conversation. As it was perceived that Lafayette took great pleasure in hearing a narration of the glory of the descendants of his former companions in arms, all the details of that memorable day were given him, in which, after a combat of three hours, an American squadron entirely captured a British fleet far superior in the number of guns. In hearing the recital of those noble actions, Lafayette cast his eyes alternately on the numerous English flags that floated over his head, on the lake, the theatre of such glorious events, and on the seamen who surrounded him; and his heart was filled with pride, on perceiving that the Americans of 1813 had shown themselves worthy sons of his old fellow soldiers, the immortal heroes of the revolution of 1776."[13]

After a few short hours it was time to say goodbye. The Erie committee escorted the General and his fellow travelers to their quarters where "affectionate" farewells were given to one and all. At three o'clock in the afternoon, Lafayette stepped into his carriage and the group was on its way to the next stop.[14]

Before the sun would set, Lafayette would once again step into New York State. Only this time, he would find himself in the Empire State's western region.

And that's where our real story begins.

Act Two:

– The Main Event –

Lafayette's Tour Of Western New York

ACT TWO:

CHAPTER ELEVEN:
THE STATE OF GREATER WESTERN NEW YORK IN 1825

Remember how excited you were when you began a new school year, started a new job, or moved to a new place? Life fills you with promise and anticipation. You can't wait to wake up and start the next day. Everything is sunshine and roses.

Then reality inevitably interrupts. Things get overwhelming. Despair and sometimes desperation set in. It seems as if you're trapped. You can't see a way out.

But, somehow, you find a way. You get over that hump. (Because, when you get over things, what once seemed like an overbearing mountain now appears as nothing more than a mere bothersome bump.)

Again, you look forward to tomorrow with an enthusiasm you thought you'd never again have.

Such was the state of Greater Western New York. It began as an enthusiastic rush into the undiscovered Genesee Country a few years after the Treaty of Paris ended the Revolutionary War in 1783. Then a new war reared its brutal head. Its aftermath, thanks to Mother Nature, left the survivors barely able to continue.

Thankfully, all bad things come to an end. By the beginning of 1825, the prospect of tomorrow elated the growing population of Greater Western New York. Like the rest of the country, Western New York felt that same Era of Good Feelings.

A blossoming confidence spread like wildfire. Gone was the uncertainty of war, the poverty of economic depression, the fear of an unrelenting nature. The pioneers of America's First Frontier outlasted the worst, and they were ready to succeed.

And celebrate.

Lafayette's arrival would coincide with the opening of the Erie Canal. Celebration and success were right around the corner.

And the people were ready.

Perhaps population growth represents the best way to demonstrate this roller-coaster affair. Before people could settle the land, governments had to agree who owned the land. Was it the Seneca Nation or The United States of America? Was it New York or Massachusetts? Or was it the British?

But let's not get ahead of ourselves. The story of the Greater Western New York Region begins in earnest on December 16, 1786, with the signing of the Treaty of Hartford. On that date, New York and Massachusetts settled their competing claims for the land west of what would henceforth be known as "Preemption Line."

But the negotiations didn't stop there. All the Treaty of Hartford did was confirm New York State had the political jurisdiction over the land, while Massachusetts kept the economic rights. That being said, paying Massachusetts only gave developers (in this case, Phelps and Gorham) the right to buy the land from the Iroquois Confederacy. In other words, you couldn't buy the land from the Confederacy without first paying Massachusetts. Before Phelps and Gorham could sit down with the Confederacy, however, two groups formed to jump ahead of the legitimate developers. They sought to exploit a loophole in the Treaty of Hartford.

The New York Genesee Land Company was comprised of wealthy New Yorkers ("mostly residing on the Hudson River"[1] and primarily from Columbia County[2]). Its counterpart, the Niagara Genesee Land Company, consisted of British and allied confederates who fled to Canada following the Revolutionary War. In November 1787, they met with the Six Nations and obtained a lease of 999 years.[3]

There was no doubt the lease was illegal. Still, this didn't stop these two companies from selling land. New York passed legislation voiding all these sales, but Phelps had to negotiate with the so-called "Lessees." Phelps and Gorham rewarded them with townships "for services rendered in facilitating the arrangement between the latter [Phelps and Gorham] and the Indians respecting the purchase of the *right of soil* in the land from which the *pre-emptive right* had been bought from Massachusetts."⁴

By 1789, settlers began to trickle into the new Ontario County, which included all the land west of the Preemption Line. Only a year later, according to the 1790 U.S. Census, Ontario County contained 205 families and 1,081 people.⁵ By 1800, the combined population of the towns of Geneva and Canandaigua was more than twice that figure.⁶

Despite this apparent gusto, settling the Greater Western New York Region came with a healthy dose of uncertainty. Remember those Lessees? They didn't give up. In November 1793, officials discovered disturbing circulars.⁷ These flyers referenced a convention held in Geneva that urged people to hold town meetings for purpose of creating a new state from the counties of Otsego, Tioga, Herkimer, and Ontario.⁸

This might seem frivolous today, but in 1793, New York State took this challenge of secession quite seriously. The state had just officially lost its northeastern colonies in 1790 to the independent state of Vermont. Such was the hatred of New Yorkers that Vermont secretly negotiated to return as a British Colony.⁹ Perhaps the fact that the notorious British Colonel John Butler headed up the Niagara Genesee Land Company suggested the British, and the Iroquois displaced to Canada hadn't quite given up on reacquiring the Greater Western New York Region.¹⁰

Complicating matters further, Connecticut refused to abide by a 1733 colonial era agreement and again laid claim to a narrow strip of land along New York's southern tier. The Constitution State didn't live up to its nickname and unilaterally decided to establish settlements in New York in the late 1790s. Remember, this aggressive behavior led to several short "wars" between Connecticut and Pennsylvania both immediately before and immediately after the Revolutionary War. The situation with New York, however, ended peacefully when the Federal government reached an agreement with Connecticut in 1800.¹¹

The War of 1812 confirmed those fears of British incursion, (the Seneca sided with the Americans). The situation produced different reactions among Western New Yorkers. Some joined the militia. Others fled east. Joseph Ellicott sought to address concerns of settlers, saying the "lines were well guarded and the country safe from invasion."¹²

That didn't quite turn out to be true. Following the Americans burning Newark (today it's called Niagara-on-the-Lake), the British and their Indian allies crossed the border to burn Lewiston and Buffalo. Rumors plagued Western New York settlers. Aaron Miller of Byron remembered one such scare. "A neighbor who came from Batavia brought home the report that 1,500 Indians were at Black Rock, and would come down through here to butcher us all." The report turned out not to be true.[13]

In his 1846 book, Judge E.F. Warren described the scene of the extreme western portion of our region thusly:

> "At this period, the frontier presented a scene of desolation rarely witnessed. The inhabitants who had escaped the tomahawk, fled into the interior, in the depth of winter, without shelter or means of support, and subsisted on the charity of their friends. The panic was general, and pervaded this county, though in a degree somewhat less than in the section of country in the immediate vicinity of the point of attack. The only buildings remaining in Buffalo were the jail, which was built of stone, a small framed house, and an armorer's shop. All the houses and almost every building between Buffalo and Niagara Falls were destroyed, as were also many of those on the Batavia road, for several miles beyond Buffalo."[14]

Finally, in 1815, the war with Britain was over and America could begin to relax. Not so much for those that remained in Western New York. Called "the year without a summer," (likely because of the eruption of Mount Tambora in Indonesia), 1816 was an unusually cold year. Orsamus Turner described it as "Peace had but just been concluded, when the cold and untoward season of 1816, came upon them, its biting frosts upon hill and valley, destroying all their hopes of sustenance, creating distress and want, driving, in many instances, men to the game in the forest, the fish in the streams, and wild roots and herbs, as their only resources toward off a famine."[-5]

For the Greater Western New York Region, the War of 1812 and its immediate aftermath took its toll on the population growth of the western counties (although the eastern counties saw some growth).[16]

But the best was yet to come. By 1825, Western New Yorkers had much to look forward to. For one thing, the Erie Canal would open later that year. Emigration was picking up, but the Canal would open the floodgates.

The census of 1830 had Rochester as the twenty-first largest city in America (and bigger than Buffalo). Ten years later, in 1840, the city on the Genesee had grown to rank 15th among cities,[17] still bigger than Buffalo. The Queen City would finally pass the Flour City in the 1850 Census.[18]

The state of the Greater Western New York Region was one of growing exuberance heading into 1825. Add to that the knowledge that The Nation's Guest—General Lafayette—was soon to arrive only raised the level of excitement to puffing patriotic pride.

Chapter Twelve:
The Buffalo and Erie Road

At the turn of the 19th century, a dense forest covered the southwest corner of New York State—what is now Chautauqua County. A rough trail that followed the Lake Erie shore represented the only visible evidence of human occupation. Except for what appeared to be remnants of a chimney right on the lake.[1] The trail was brutal. Settlers journeying to Connecticut's lands in the future state of Ohio preferred to take the water route over Lake Erie from Black Rock, just off Buffalo Creek.[2]

That chimney might well have been the ruins of what Sir William Johnson described as a French "baking place."[3] During the French and Indian War, France had designs on using the mouth of the Chautauqua Creek (a.k.a. "Barcelona") as the start of a portage between Lake Erie and Chautauqua Lake. This provided a connection to the Alleghany River and ultimately to the Ohio River. The Marquis Duquesne, Governor General of New France, decided against this in the summer of 1753, opting instead to use a portage beginning at the harbor of Presqu'isle (now called Erie, Pennsylvania).[4]

In October of that same year, Duquesne decided to hedge his bets and build the portage from Barcelona to Mayville at the head of Chautauqua Lake. (Of course, he didn't use those names at the time.) Shortly after beginning construction of this "Portage Road," British intelligence became aware of its existence.

The French had been holding British soldier Stephen Coffen prisoner for some time before agreeing to have him travel with a group that eventually built the road. He escaped immediately after. In his deposition to Sir William Johnson, Coffen testified, "the 30th [of October] arrived at Chadakoin, where they staid four days, during which Mons Peon with 200 Men, cut a Waggon Road over the carrying place from Lake Erie to Lake Chadakoin, being 15 Miles, viewed the situation which proved to their liking."[5]

If the British were skeptical of Coffen's account, they needn't be for long. By coincidence, they had sent a team to observe French activity in the Chautauqua area. Lieutenant-Governor James De Lancey wrote to the Lords of Trade saying Coffen's "deposition is fully confirmed by intelligence we have received several ways."[6]

One man in that scouting party, Samuel Shattuck, then only 13, would afterwards tell the story of his life as a spy in the French and Indian War. Shattuck later served in the Revolutionary War (fighting at such venues as Bunker Hill, Bennington, Yorktown, etc.). Once his military duties ended, Shattuck went back to the place of his birth in Deerfield, Massachusetts. Ultimately, however, he returned to live at the site of his noteworthy act of surveillance (the Town of Portland in Chautauqua County) in November 1823.[7]

After the Revolutionary War, George Washington recognized the strategic significance of the "Old French Road," (as the old Portage Road has been referred to). In a Letter to General Irvine dated October 31, 1788, Washington wrote, "If the Chataughque Lake, at the head of Canewango River, approximates Lake Erie as nearly as is laid down in the draught you have sent me it presents a very short Portage indeed between the two and an access to all those above the latter."[8]

Yet, Portage Road remained unused. Vegetation slowly devoured it. In fact, an old Indian trail it crossed in what is now the Village of Westfield saw more use as the 18th century gave way to the 19th.

Remember that land claim conflict New York had with Connecticut? Though these two states resolved their issue, Connecticut continued to claim lands in present day northeast Ohio. Called the "Connecticut Reserve" or the "Western Reserve," (and sometimes the "Connecticut Fire Lands," or "New Connecticut"),[9] the Connecticut Land Company bought the rights to settle this land from the state of Connecticut.

There were two ways to get from Connecticut to the Western Reserve. The southern path passed through Pennsylvania (and Pittsburgh). The northern route went through Buffalo. From Buffalo, travelers had two choices, hugging the shore of Lake Erie either on land or on water (preferably in the form of ice).[10]

It is the land route that interests us here. This was the Indian path that following along the geological landform called the "Portage Escarpment." As Indian paths go, it was a major thoroughfare. Alas, what was good for the Seneca and their Confederacy allies wasn't too kind to New England settlers (and, in particular, their wagons).

The Connecticut Land Company was hot to settle its Western Reserve. The state incentivized settlers. To address the sorry state of the rugged trail from Buffalo to Erie, the Company hired General Edward Paine in 1801 to assemble a team to cut through the nearly impassable path. He got as far south from Buffalo as the old Portage Road before others eventually extended "Paine's Road" to the Pennsylvania state line.[11]

Paine didn't survey the route. Also, he didn't erect any bridges. Still, after its completion in 1802, it became the primary road used by settlers of the Connecticut Reserve.[12] In his memoir, one such settler—Reverend Joseph Badger—pokes fun at Paine (from whom the town of Painesville, Ohio gets its name). One night while traveling on the trail in October 1801, Badger noted "At evening General Payne (sic) and two or three hands came in from pretending to cut and open a road through from Buffalo to Pennsylvania line."[13]

While the Connecticut Reserve was getting its fair share of settlers, nothing was happening in the southwestern corner of New York State. Badger observed, "from Buffalo to Pennsylvania line, seventy miles, there being no cabin on the route, we cut our path by day, pitched our tent by night, 'and slept safely in the woods.'"[14]

Things were about to change. In the spring of 1802, James McMahan bought and cleared a plot of land near the present village of Westfield where he built a modest dwelling.[15] Edward McHenry came immediately after and constructed a tavern at the "Cross Roads."[16]

If you haven't figured this out by now, this would have been the intersection of Paine's Road and the old Portage Road. McHenry had an entrepreneur's flair as he built the tavern to entertain all those Connecticut Yankees emigrating over Paine's Road in route to the

Western Reserve. Quickly, though, we see settlers coming to what would eventually become Chautauqua County.[17]

(In 1802, it was still part of Ontario County as Genesee County was not fully organized and detached from Ontario County until March 1803. Chautauqua County, while created from Genesee County in 1808, was initially attached to Niagara County and not detached until February 1811.)[18] Confused? The Western New York merry-go-round of counties could merit its own book!

The horrid condition of Paine's Road called for action. Joseph Ellicott, the man in charge of seeing people settle in Western New York's Holland Land Purchase, wasn't pleased. He had long sought to build a road from Buffalo to Erie. When he proposed to the proprietors of the Holland Land Company that he approach Connecticut about jointly building the road from Buffalo to Erie, the Company rebuffed him.[19]

Seeing the debacle of Paine's "road" enabled Ellicott to finally convince his bosses to build the road. James McMahan had the honors of surveying the route.[20] It was completed in 1805, where it met with a Pennsylvania road being cleared by David Ellicott at the state line.[21] Surveyors didn't measure the roads on either side (along the lake shore and the ridge) until later.

The road was known as the "Erie Road," "Ellicott Road,"[22] as well as the "Buffalo and Erie Road" and the "Main Road."[23] Initially, New York State assigned it "Route 18" before changing it to "Route 5."[24] In 1927, the Federal government labeled it "U.S. Route 20," which it remains to this day.[25] Oddly enough, the current Route 5 along the lake shore was originally designated "20A."[26]

The mail service initially used Paine's Road to travel between Erie and Buffalo. It later switched to the road surveyed by McMahan. At first, residents of Chautauqua County had to pick up their mail in either Erie or Buffalo, for there was no post office in their county. When it came time to build the County's first post office, where did they build it? Why, at the Cross Roads in Westfield, of course.[27]

Or not.

You see, when Lafayette's secretary wrote the journal of their trip, he makes no mention of "Westfield." Why? Because there was no Westfield in 1825. It was called Portland. The Town of Westfield wasn't formed until 1829, four years after Lafayette's visit.[28]

And it would be the first stop by the Nation's Guest in Western New York.

Chapter Thirteen: Special Delivery To Westfield, A Fitting First

Was Lafayette supposed to depart Erie by land or by sea? As late as May 31, 1825, organizers in Erie, Pennsylvania tried to arrange steamboat accommodations for the General. The ship was to convey the Nation's Guest from Erie directly to Buffalo.[1]

Confusion reigned over Lafayette's exact itinerary. You see, he had promised to attend the dedication ceremonies for the Bunker Hill Monument on the anniversary date of that battle. That meant he had to be in Boston by June 17th. Initial reports said he would not visit Western New York until after laying the cornerstone on the Bunker Hill Monument.[2] The newspaper corrected this misinformation the following week, just a day before Lafayette would cross the state line into Chautauqua County.[3]

What firmed Lafayette's travel plans? Olive Risley Seward's grandfather commanded the militia for the Lafayette reception in Fredonia. In addition, her then eleven-year-old father and nine-year-old mother also attended—and remembered—Lafayette's 1825 visit to Fredonia. Based on the stories from her family, she wrote the following in 1904: "An enterprising-young citizen of Fredonia, Walter Smith, made the suggestion which decided his course." Despite the abortive machinations in Erie a few days later, word reached Chautauqua County that Lafayette would travel from Erie to Buffalo on the mail route.[4]

That would be the Main road, a.k.a. the Buffalo and Erie Road, today's U.S. Route 20.

Actually, the plan had Lafayette traveling by both land and sea from Erie to Buffalo. The first leg of the journey, from Erie to Dunkirk, would require a horse-drawn carriage. The second half, from the harbor at Dunkirk to Buffalo, necessitated the use of a steamship.

Using the mail route, however, presented an opportunity to the citizens of Chautauqua County. They could partake first-hand in the great American experience. They could meet General Lafayette face-to-face. Veterans could relive their war experience. Women could realize their dream of hobnobbing in the air of French aristocracy. Children could see with their own eyes what they learned in history class.

But they had to act fast.

On the evening of June 2, 1825, the day before Lafayette's expected arrival, an ad hoc committee met to plan for the village of Westfield's reception of the French General. This "committee of arrangements" consisted of Jonathan Cass, Joseph Farnsworth, Henry Abell, Oliver Lee, Joshua R. Babcock, Fenn Demming, E.L. Tinker, Silas Spencer, Thomas B. Campbell, L. Averill, John Dexter, E.P. Upham, William Peacock, and T.A. Osborne. Peacock offered his carriage to carry Lafayette from State Line (in the Town of Ripley) to Westfield (in the Town of Portland). Campbell, Spencer, Upham and Demming formed the welcoming committee and set out with Peacock's carriage to greet Lafayette at the Pennsylvania border.[5]

We don't know what time the Westfield delegation left, but we know Lafayette departed from Erie at 3 o'clock in the afternoon.[6] Unfortunately, we have yet to unearth a definitive record of the time the two groups met at State Line. And neither did the people of Westfield. The military had been in the village all day in anticipation of Lafayette's arrival. By late in the day, an "immense concourse of citizens from the neighboring towns were likewise waiting, with intense anxiety the signals of his approach."[7]

Meanwhile, at State Line, the two parties approached each other. While we don't know the exact time, we do know what Campbell offered on behalf of his committee by way of introduction upon meeting Lafayette:

> *"General La Fayette:—With hearts full of gratitude from services rendered our country, we, as a committee, in behalf of the citizens of Westfield, have come to meet you and welcome your return to the state of New York. We assure*

> *you, General, that the same grateful feelings which have been so unanimously expressed to you by the people of this republic, influence and animate the citizens of this part of our state; and although unable to receive you with the splendor which accompanied your reception on landing upon our shores, yet we do receive you with no less affectionate and grateful hearts."*[8]

Ever the proper gentleman, Lafayette replied:

> *"Gentlemen:—I am fully sensible of the kindness and affection thus expressed to me by the people of this part of your state; and I assure you, sir, it affords me much pleasure to take you by the hand and return you, and, through you, the citizens of Westfield, my hearty thanks for the respectful manner in which they have been pleased to communicate their feelings towards me. I am very happy to find myself again in the patriotic state of New York. Accept, sir, for yourself and the other gentlemen of the committee, the assurance of my best wishes for your health and happiness."*[9]

Shortly after sunset on Friday, June 3, 1825, the anxious citizens received the exciting news. Lafayette approached. Escorting him were men on horseback. These men came from the nearby towns of Ellery, Chautauqua, Portland, and Ripley. Signal guns announced the General's arrival. Though not quite twilight, brightly lit public houses provided an impressive runway for the Nation's Guest. Crackling flames from an immense bonfire danced to the sky from the town square.[10]

This was only the beginning of the pageantry. As Lafayette stepped down from Peacock's ornate carriage, the soldiers let loose a gigantic boom from the cannon. Captain Towle led the Light Infantry, which helped escort Lafayette and his party to a room set aside for the event. Campbell made the introductions.[11]

Obsorne quickly stood to make the following statement:

"General:—Permit our feeble notes of congratulating Welcome to swell the general anthem of the American nation. Taught from earliest infancy to lisp the venerated name of LaFayette, which now trembles upon our tongues with gratitude and joy, we greet thee as the champion of freedom, the friend of Washington, of our country and her institutions, and the benefactor of mankind.

"While the burst of grateful acclamation which hailed your landing upon our shores has been borne on the tide of hearts, until the remotest parts of the Union have vibrated with its influence, we of the Western New York have cause for deep and peculiar emotions.

"At the period of your valuable labors for the establishment of our republic, the spot upon which you stand was only tenanted by the howling inhabitants of the wilderness. Until a long subsequent period, our country was with a name and without a population. Now, within its borders the hearts of more than twenty thousand freemen beat your welcome. It is to you, whom we now address, that, more than to any other, this important change is to attributed. The councils of your wisdom were felt in the cabinet, and your youthful arm lent vigor to their execution in the field. Animated by your spirit and fired by your example, your king and your country stepped forth in the cause of liberty and man, and forever sealed the fate of tyranny in this western hemisphere. The life giving energies of the triumph of liberty were felt in the rapid increase of population and settlement. Had a state of colonial servitude and dependence continued, your eye would not now have witnessed our fields covered with golden grain, waving their undulating shadows with sportive playfulness in the breeze. Compare, as you traverse the mighty Niagara, the colonial and independent shores, and by their contrast test the influence of liberty on the improvement and settlement of

> the country, and the promotion of the social happiness of man.
>
> "Finally, General, in behalf of the citizens of the vicinity, we tender to you their most cordial congratulations upon your arrival among them, and the anxious aspirations of their hearts, that the evening of your days may be as serene and tranquil as your life has been constant in the pursuit of freedom. That they have enjoyed the felicity of meeting and welcoming you among them, will ever be among the most gratifying of their recollections, while the remembrance of the affectionate farewell which they must shortly bid you, their father and their friend, cannot fail to awaken the liveliest sensibilities of their natures, and call forth the most poignant grief."[12]

While the burst of grateful acclamation which hailed your landing upon our shores has been borne on the tide of hearts, until the remotest parts of the Union have vibrated with its influence, we of the Western New York have cause for deep and peculiar emotions.

At the period of your valuable labors for the establishment of our republic, the spot upon which you stand was only tenanted by the howling inhabitants of the wilderness. Until a long subsequent period, our country was with a name and without a population. Now, within its borders the hearts of more than twenty thousand freemen beat your welcome. It is to you, whom we now address, that, more than to any other, this important change is to attributed. The councils of your wisdom were felt in the cabinet, and your youthful arm lent vigor to their execution in the field. Animated by your spirit and fired by your example, your king and your country stepped forth in the cause of liberty and man, and forever sealed the fate of tyranny in this western hemisphere. The life giving energies of the triumph of liberty were felt in the rapid increase of population and settlement. Had a state of colonial servitude and dependence continued, your eye would not now have witnessed our fields covered with golden grain, waving their undulating shadows with sportive playfulness in the breeze. Compare, as you traverse the mighty Niagara, the colonial and independent shores, and by their contrast test the influence of liberty on the improvement and settlement of the country, and the promotion of the social happiness of man.

Finally, General, in behalf of the citizens of the vicinity, we tender to you their most cordial congratulations upon your arrival among them, and the anxious aspirations of their hearts, that the evening of your days may be as serene and tranquil as your life has been constant in the pursuit of freedom. That they have enjoyed the felicity of meeting and welcoming you among them, will ever be among the most gratifying of their recollections, while the remembrance of the affectionate farewell which they must shortly bid you, their father and their friend, cannot fail to awaken the liveliest sensibilities of their natures, and call forth the most poignant grief."[13]

Again, with heartfelt emotion, Lafayette answered:

> *"Gentlemen:—I cannot express to you my happiness at the kindness of your reception. When about ten months since I first landed upon your shores, I was received in a manner which can never be forgotten. The impression then received has been heightened by every subsequent event. Wherever I have been, I have received the kindest welcome. But it affords me peculiar pleasure to be thus received here in Western New York, and to witness the astonishing rapidity of its progress in improvement and settlement. Accept, sir, of my best wishes for your personal happiness, and, gentlemen, for the happiness of you all. I am happy to enjoy the interview; to see you all assembled; and most sincerely regret that circumstances render it necessary that my stay with you should be short."*[14]

Indeed, this visit was short. It contained no documented toasts or other fanciful orations. But it did have a common feature. After the brief formalities, Lafayette dove into the crowd, greeting each person—ladies and gentlemen—as the long-lost friends both believed they really were.

Lafayette worked the crowd with "cordial, animating, and affecting" sincerity.[15]

As usual, he met many Revolutionary War soldiers. Could one of these veterans have been Samuel Shattuck?

No sooner had the visit begun than it was over. At ten o'clock that same evening, after only roughly a two-hour stay, the Fredonia delegation took the reins from Westfield's committee of arrangements. And with the sound of twenty-four artillery rounds, Westfield said goodbye to the hero, proud to now have been a part of those lucky few whose lives he had literally touched.[16]

With that, Lafayette left the hamlet of the first permanent settlers of Chautauqua County, a fitting first step into Western New York.

Back on the Main road went the Nation's Guest for what was hoped to be a quick trot to Fredonia.

CHAPTER FOURTEEN: GASLIGHTING THE GENERAL

The first week of June in 1925 saw unusually warm temperatures across the northeast.[1] Nearby Jamestown had record-breaking highs in the low 90s.[2] You can imagine the temperature on Main Street in Fredonia at 2:45 in the afternoon on Thursday, June 4. Still, the crowds came. So many, in fact, that the village had to redirect traffic away from the primary road running through its downtown.[3]

The ceremony was spear-headed and organized by the Benjamin Prescott Chapter of the Daughters of the American Revolution. Citizens marched down the flag-decorated streets and assembled to see the unveiling of a new marker dedicated to memorializing two major events in this small rural community.[4] One hundred years to the day earlier, General Lafayette set foot on that same main road. Just as citizens in 1825 went out of their way to see the Revolutionary War hero, so too did their descendants gather a century later to mark the anniversary.

And, oh, what a celebration they had! It seemed like everyone was there. Well, everyone except Arthur R. Maytum, President of the Village Trustees. He was off in Syracuse for a conference of New York State village officials.[5]

The people merged onto the corner of West Main Street by the bridge over Canadaway creek. The flag-covered object they surrounded drew their attention and anticipation. Onlookers quieted as the Reverend Walter A. Henricks of the Fredonia Presbyterian church read the opening prayer. The high school orchestra and choir followed that with a heartfelt rendition of "America." High School Principal Claude R. Dye gave the welcoming address. He urged the audience to live by those ideals responsible for making our country great.[6]

He then introduced the keynote speaker, Mrs. Charles White Nash, state Regent of the D.A.R. She gave an inspiring speech that began with, "To keep alive the history of a nation by the placing of markers, the preservation of buildings and relics or by the rehearsing of deeds and the holding of ceremonies is not merely to perform a laudable task but to thus preserve a record of past events and achievements is to develop a realization of human progress which should bring an appreciation to each succeeding generation of what it owes to its predecessors. For no generation is great of itself alone nor its any nation or individual living up to its highest and best if it fails to learn the lessons its past has taught."[7]

As Mrs. Nash closed by dedicating the memorial, Edith Gardiner and Clarence Cato, dressed in colonial costumes, removed the flag covering the boulder to reveal the attached bronze plaque. All sang "America the Beautiful" before closing remarks by Dr. Howard G. Burdge, President of the Fredonia Normal School (predecessor to SUNY @ Fredonia). Dr. Burdge, in keeping with the theme of the previous speakers, said not only should we laud history, but we can't stop there. We need to also follow through on the advances made by those who preceded us. Harriet Ross (from Rochester) conducted an intricate flag drill before Mrs. A.J. Gardiner, regent of the local chapter of the D.A.R., formally presented the boulder to the village. Trustee William L. Hart accepted, seeing that President Maytum was in Syracuse. The exercise ended with all singing the national anthem.[8]

Here's what the plaque on the boulder reads:

> "The site of the first gas well in the
> United States
> Lighted
> In honor of General Lafayette's
> visit June 4, 1825
> Placed by Benjamin Prescott Chapter,
> Daughters of the American
> Revolution
> June 4, 1925"

Take a closer look at this inscription. Doesn't it imply the first gas well was lit on the day of Lafayette's visit to Fredonia—June 4, 1825?

It sure seems that way.

There's only one problem with this. The earliest record of the use of natural gas (and specifically from the well the plaque recognized—the first natural gas well ever dug in America) wasn't until August 31, 1825.[9] This was more than two months after Lafayette left Fredonia.

What gives? How did they get the history of this so wrong?

It gets worse.

In January 1925, *The Fredonia Censor* ran a page one story titled "The Story Of Natural Gas Is Here Recorded." It offers a rather detailed chronicle of how a group of young boys accidentally discovered the "inflamable (sic) air" in 1821. Without giving any other dates, the article describes the location and the building of the first well. It then reports Lafayette, when visiting Fredonia, toured the gaslit house with a local clergyman who could speak French. The General "expressed satisfactory astonishment and is said to have told the clergyman that he was afraid that Fredonia must be pretty near hell, in a upward direction, and he thought he would hasten his departure."[10]

This certainly wasn't the first instance of the 1821 date. An industry journal cited this date in 1886. It said, "A correspondent of the *Tribune* states that the first natural gas well was bored in 1821, by a man named Hart, at Fredonia, at the crossing of Main street and Canadaway Creek. The well was one and a half inches in diameter, was twenty-seven feet deep, and yielded enough gas to use in thirty burners. Natural gas has been used there ever since."[11] There was no citation for this "correspondent of the *Tribune*," nor does it say which "*Tribune*" it's referring to.

The earliest reference found (so far) that ties the natural gas well with Lafayette occurs in 1873. It states, "The use of natural gas at Fredonia was begun in 1821, when experiments were made to determine its illuminating value and it was introduced into a few of the public places, among which was the hotel which then occupied the site of the Taylor House, and which was thus illuminated when Lafayette passed through the village."[12]

This story, in varying forms, was repeated throughout the many history books covering Chautauqua County.[13,14,15]

Even industry chronologies from as recently as the 1960s repeat these falsehoods. One has these entries (citing as its source "Diary of an Industry," published by the *American Gas Journal*, Dallas, Texas, October 1959):

> "1821 - Natural gas discovered at Fredonia, New York, in the form of a 'burning spring.' Residents drill a 27-foot deep well and 'log-pipe' gas to nearby houses for lighting."[16]

> "1825 - June 4-At Fredonia, New York, during a visit to the United States, General Lafayette arrives by stagecoach at the old Taylor House at 2 a.m. to find the city and the inn brilliantly illuminated in his honor by natural gas."[17]

Post World War II newspaper accounts weren't that reliable, either. Their elaborate (some might say fanciful) stories even went so far as to say the Abell Tavern (where Lafayette briefly sat while in Fredonia) was the first to receive the gas and was lit for the French guest.[18] Of course, one newspaper identifies the owner of the tavern as Col. Thomas G. Abell[19] but fails to mention his then co-owner and brother Mosley W. Abell who figures prominently as host to the dinner for Lafayette (Mosley sold his share to Thomas in 1828[20]).

So, what really happened in Fredonia in 1825?

Sometime that summer, William A. Hart successfully tapped a well very near to the Main Street bridge over Canadaway Creek and, by the end of August, "2 stores, (one a grocery) 2 shops and one mill that are every evening lighted up with as brilliant gas lights as are to be found in any city in this or any other country."[21]

In November, Hart had built a reservoir large enough to hold 1200 gallons, enough to light 150 lights.[22] The Abell Tavern was connected to the gas line a year later in November 1926.[23]

And what of Lafayette? If he even saw a demonstration of the gas in Fredonia, it didn't leave an impression. The gas lights during the ball held in his honor in Baltimore drew much attention. His secretary André-Nicolas Levasseur noted "the gas blazing abundantly from numerous pipes, and throwing floods of dazzling light over the hall, discovered to our delighted eyes the most ravishing picture I ever beheld."[24]

Note that, unlike the natural gas lights in Fredonia, the Baltimore lights utilized a man-made gas, initially using tar or wood before moving to coal in the mid-nineteenth century.[25]

It's not, as we shall see, that Levasseur had nothing to say about Fredonia. He did. Just nothing about natural gas. Indeed, you might say Lafayette was just as likely to see natural gas in Fredonia (he missed by about two months) than he was to see the Buffalo Bills (he missed by almost two centuries).

And don't even start about whether he thought Groucho Marx used the village as the model for his most acclaimed movie. (He didn't. The country in the movie *Duck Soup* had two e's, as in "Freedonia.")

And speaking of something easy to accomplish, the road from Westfield to Fredonia certainly wasn't duck soup.
But, in the end, the ride was worth the "violent jolting."

Chapter Fifteen:
Fast Fredonia Frenzy

The trot to Fredonia was anything but quick. The Buffalo and Erie Road turned out to be less "finished" than Joseph Ellicott had hoped. André-Nicolas Levasseur, one of Lafayette's traveling party who would eventually publish an extensive journal of the General's American Farewell Tour, went out of his way to point out the poor condition of the Main road between "Portland" (a.k.a. "Westfield") and Fredonia.

"On leaving Portland," wrote Levasseur, "yielding to the fatigue of the preceding days, we were sleeping in the carriage notwithstanding the violent jolting occasioned by the trunks of the trees forming the road over which we were rapidly passing."[1]

Ellicott had rather strict guidelines for those he hired to clear roads, especially when it came to those jolting tree trunks. "He required that all the main roads should be opened forty feet wide, all trees and saplings to be cut level with the ground if twelve inches or less in diameter; if more than that, they might be cut at the usual height unless standing within eight feet of the center of the road in which case they too were to be cut level with the ground."[2]

Meanwhile, in Fredonia, the people waited. According to Olive Risley Seward, "Before midday every road leading to Fredonia was lined with wagons, carts, and carriages; and people came pouring in from over the hills and up and down the Lake and Main roads, on foot and on horse, and in every vehicle that could be found to bring them to greet Lafayette." She then goes on to imply Lafayette was greatly delayed in arriving at Fredonia.[3]

Mention of this delay failed to appear in contemporary reports (although it may be inferred by his widely reported 2:00 AM arrival). Still, in an 1886 lecture titled 'Men of Note Whom I Have Met," Fredonia native Hanson A. Risley recalls "The committee appointed to meet him, being delayed in returning, he did not reach the place until late in the night…"[4] Of course, since Hanson was Olive's father, he can hardly be considered an independent second source. About all we can conclude is that Olive appears to faithfully retell the story her father told her.

Both Olive Risley Seward[5] and Edson[6] suggest Lafayette's carriage suffered an accident on the way to Fredonia, but this cannot be corroborated by Levasseur's journal. He only mentions the "violent jolting," until…

> "On a sudden the startling explosion of a piece of artillery awoke us, and our eyes were immediately dazzled by the glare of a thousand lights, suspended to the houses and trees that surrounded us."[7]

That "startling explosion" would be the sound of Capt. Brown's thirteen artillery guns firing to salute Lafayette's arrival in Fredonia. He, along with Capt. Whitcomb's Rifle Rangers and portions of the 169th regiment stood ready at the west hill to receive the Nation's Guest.[8]

It may have been two o'clock in the morning, but the patient citizens weren't tired. As the carriage pulled up to the Abell Tavern, its riders noticed two distinct lines to the platform in front of the hotel. What they didn't notice was the edge of the creek by the bridge where the first natural gas well would soon appear.

The reception could not have been better choreographed. On one side stood the women and girls, and on the other side stood the men and boys. "Struck by so touching a reception, the general was unable for some time to subdue his emotions; at last, he advanced slowly through the crowd, at every step shaking affectionately the hands that were stretched out to him, and replying with tenderness to the sweet salutation of the children who accompanied his progress with cries of 'Welcome, Lafayette.'"[9]

Lafayette made his way up to the platform, where the Reverend David Brown greeted him and pronounced:

"*General LaFayette:— Gen. LaFayette:—We rejoice to see you. We greet you welcome to our rural hospitalities, and thank you for the great pleasure thus to sale a man most high and most dear in the estimation of every American. It pains me, sir, to add the least possible degree to your fatigue at this late hour of night, but my fellow citizens having appointed me to the honor of addressing you, expect from me a passing remark on the motives which have prompted the little attentions within our very limited powers, dwelling as we do, where shortly since dwelt the beasts of the forest.*

"*It will suffice to tell how much and for what we admire you; but, sire, our admiration is qualified by a dearer sentiment. We greatly admire your character, as standing in the front rank of the true and disinterested champions of the universal Republic, whose citizens comprise all the friends of liberty on earth. We admire the brilliant lustre of your early heroism, by which you were inspired to read the strongest and dearest ties to nature, and as a disinterested volunteer in the righteous cause of liberty, to burst from the attractions of all that was splendid and all that was lovely. In this act of your youth, sir, as in many that followed, we behold an eminent illustration of the much admired virtue, which enabled a great chief of sacred antiquity to look down with indifference on all the splendors and glories of the royal court of Egypt when the cause of freedom and of God called him to the privations and toil and dangers of a hostile wilderness.*

"*That, at every earthly hazard, through a life devoted to the vindication of liberty, you have uniformly asserted the rights of man, we admire you; and we rejoice in an opportunity to acknowledge your undisputed claims to the gratitude and admiration of the world.*

"*We are almost lost in admiration, sire, as we look forward to the transcendant eminence that you will hereafter occupy in history above all the princes and potentates of the earth, however shining may have their virtues, for, with our* won Washington, you have shown that *"a man is greater than a monarch."*

"But it is not so much by our admiration for what is illustrious in the character of Gen. LaFayette that we are moved and animated on this occasion, as by our veneration and love for what is excellent and amiable. Most sincerity and deeply do we appreciate the respect and admiration due to you exalted character; yet, the sentiment which predominates over even these, if not in general estimation more highly honorable, we feel as not less your due, as our benefactor and friend, nor less worthy ourselves as Americans. We love you, sire, as our own friend and our fathers' friend—we love you and can never forsake you. Never can our heats beat with sentiments become men and Americans, when they shall have ceased to glow with filial affection for Gen. LaFayette.

"It would be needless to speak of the origin and strength and warmth of affection entertained for you by those who took part with you in the liberation of our country from a foreign yoke. It may not however be unpleasing, we hope, to be reminded of the means by which, in the bosoms of the generation that have since come on the stage of life, this sentiment has been implanted and made to grow with our growth and to strengthen with our strength.

"For almost a half a century, sir, your name, associated with all that is amiable in the philanthropist, as well as with all that us chivalrous in the soldier of liberty, has been on of our most favorite "household words,"

"When, in your tour through our country, our hearts have followed you, and witnessed your emotions while embracing your old comrades in arms—especially when our sympathies were roused by the sublime and affecting scene at the sepulchre of our Washington, the interested fire-side scenes of our early days were again brought home to our *bosoms, when our fathers and our mothers taught us to venerate—to love the name of LaFayette.*

"I have seen and I have felt the tear standing in the eye of childhood, when the tale has been told of your youthful disinterestedness, in devoting your fortune, your life and your honor to the cause of our country—and of your sufferings and wrongs and of your unbending virtues that no sufferings nor wrongs could subdue.

"When the fires of persecution assailed you, sire, our hearts were taught to burn with indignation, and to shiver at the name of Olmutz when its prison damps were settling on the beloved brow of our hero and friend. God be thanked, we trust those scenes of sufferings and wrongs and persecutions, will no more be renewed. If a rampart of American hearts may be allowed to defend you they never can be renewed. But, on this spirit-stirring subject I must not dwell.

"In behalf of my beloved fellow citizens, most cordially do I welcome you, where thro' the influence of our free institutions, which you yourself, sir, so greatly contributed to rear, the wilderness as of yesterday, is now blossoming as a rose.

"As our country's friend and benefactor with heartfelt sincerity and gratitude do I salute you. May that ever gracious Being by whom we are thus favored, strew the path of your pilgrimage with his richest blessings, until at some far distant day He may please to receive you to himself in glory everlasting."[10]

There was much more to the speech than that, to which Lafayette replied:

"My Dear Sir:—Accept my most sincere thanks for your most affectionate address. Your allusion to my early visit to America, to my services here and to my sufferings since, are

very kind, and, as I must frankly confess, are very gratifying to my feelings. The manner of my reception here, my very dear sir, this place so shortly since a wilderness, as you have said, surprises me as much as it pleases me. Surely, I am very much obliged. And I beg you, sir, with the committee, who have shown me every kindness, to accept my grateful acknowledgments."[11]

With that, the General then turned to greet everyone individually, first the ladies, who impressed him by staying up so late. "That the ladies, too," he repeated for emphasis, "That the ladies, too, should remain up all night to receive me, surely it is too much." and then the veterans. There were so many people there that he had to stand on the platform as the crowd paraded by him.[12]

One story involving the ladies was told by Olive Risley Seward: "The ladies were presented individually by a master of ceremonies equal to the occasion, Mr. David J. Matteson, and he has often recalled to me his care to choose the prettiest lady in the village, who happened to be my grandmother, Doctor Crosby's wife, for the first presentation, and how he noted with pride the elegance of her plum colored satin shawl and the enormous size of her fashionable bonnet. Mr. Matteson said he was somewhat surprised, however, as lady after lady came forward arrayed as she in a plum colored shawl and flaring bonnet, and how he never would have understood the mystery had not his own wife explained to him the next day that the doctor's wife who possessed a new bonnet and shawl from Boston, the mart of fashion, had loaned her finery in turn to each less fortunate friend and neighbor, as they passed in to be presented."[13]

With the introductions complete, it was now time to partake of the entertainment and repast prepared by Mosley Abell. John M. Edson had traveled all the way from Sinclairville to see Lafayette. He was lucky enough to sit down at the same table as Lafayette. He would later describe the General as "a man less than six feet in height and somewhat corpulent. He wore a wig of dark hair, was of dark complexion and had full cheeks. He talked English well and freely with the soldiers; was very affable and courteous. He sat at the head of one of the tables, at which, besides others, there were thirty soldiers of the Revolution, twelve of whom were at Yorktown."[14]

All this occurred within sixty minutes. His travel on the Main (a.k.a. "Buffalo and Erie") road may have been slow and bumpy, but his whirlwind visit with Fredonia was fast and furious. It was three o'clock. "Notwithstanding the striking character of this scene, the general felt himself obliged to abridge it, that he might not expose to the cold, for a longer time, the women and young girls, who, slightly clad, had passed all the night in the open air, waiting for him."[15]

The sun was just beginning to paint the forests to their right as they made their way out of Dunkirk.

If they thought the Main road was bad, just wait until they discover what something that isn't the main road is like!

Chapter Sixteen:
Dunkirk, The Last Frontier

It was three o'clock in the morning when Lafayette and his travel partners left Fredonia. They weren't alone. A horde of enthusiastic citizens accompanied the nation's guest to the *Superior*, the famous Great Lakes steamer that had been waiting offshore in the Dunkirk harbor from the previous day.

The late (or early) hour had no impact on the escort. They gladly trudged through the dew and mud. It would be something they would remember for the rest of their lives. There they were. Side by side with the Revolutionary War hero, the friend of George Washington, an icon they could only dream of meeting.

After all, who were they, these pioneers of Western New York? Sure, a few were surviving veterans of the War for Independence. The rest were their children and grandchildren. They worked hard each day not just to survive, but to build a community. In doing so, they would also build a nation.

Just like so many others living on the edge of the nation's frontier.

That General Lafayette would honor them by spending even a few minutes with these citizens of the nascent Chautauqua County meant the world to them. They just couldn't let the moment go.

And they didn't.

They sloshed their way through the sludge with the General on the barely beaten path to Dunkirk.

But which path did they take?

To answer that question, you need to answer this question "What did Dunkirk look like in 1825?"

Unlike Barcelona at the mouth of Chautauqua Creek, Dunkirk had a less auspicious beginning. The French no doubt sailed by it. As stated before, they bypassed Dunkirk's bay, preferring to first explore the mouth of Chautauqua Creek (which led to the creation of Portage

Road). Ultimately, they chose Presque' Isle (today's Erie, Pa,) as their harbor site.[1]

Still, while not "harbor" material, the cove no doubt offered protection for sailors looking to ride out a storm or otherwise find a safe port.[2] The bay had one big problem: it offered no stream to travel inland. Settlers instead looked just to the south to take advantage of Canadaway creek. That's the creek that leads to Fredonia.

Worse. The bay didn't offer much of a landing spot. While the early nineteenth century saw small villages like Fredonia and Westfield grow at the intersection of the Buffalo and Erie Road, the future city of Dunkirk "remained covered by a dense and unbroken forest."[3]

You can get an idea if you consider how Canadaway creek got its name. According to famed Rochester historian Lewis Morgan, it's derived from the Seneca word "Gä-na' -da-wa-o." Translated, it means "Running through the hemlocks."[4] That's a lot of trees.

How bad was it? Heman Ely migrated to Dunkirk with his wife Emma in February 1810. They traveled from Buffalo over the lake because, as you might expect, the ice was a lot smoother than the Buffalo and Erie Road. They stuck it out as long as they could, but decided to move to Portland in the spring of 1816.[5]

Such was the disappointment of Dunkirk. After having lost its bid to become the western terminus of the Erie Canal, interest in the area dropped off. By 1825, the struggling settlement had only 50 families living by the bay.[6] One of those was John Brigham, who first arrived in 1808. He built a road. It's called—wait for it—"Brigham Road." It was the second road from Dunkirk to Fredonia. The first snaked along Canadaway creek. The third one has had many names. Today we call it Central Avenue.[7]

Central Avenue was a lonely road. In 1816, it was "merely a path marked by blazed trees, with the underbrush cut out."[8] Four years later in 1820 it was still "a continuous forest from Third Street to Fredonia.[9] In the summer of 1823, Mary Ann Drake taught in one of the few log houses on it.[10]

Of all the places Lafayette would visit in the Greater Western New York Region, Dunkirk most retained the character of the frontier. In a few months, the Erie Canal would open. With that would come an influx of settlers, a different breed of people.

The people Lafayette would see in Dunkirk represented the last of the true pioneers. They were the frontiersmen that made the "Niagara Frontier" America's first frontier. They came most directly from nearby settlements of New York and Pennsylvania. After the canal opened, settlers were wealthier (or at least the less poor) and better suited for the transition from "frontierland" to "farmland."[11]

So, let's return to the question of which road Lafayette took from Fredonia to the harbor at Dunkirk. We know two things about it. First, it was "improved and prepared for the occasion." This should have helped because the procession of military and civilians in carriages, on horseback, and on foot stretched a mile long.[12]

Second, the route was described as being "three miles to the shore of the lake."[13]

Do these clues give us enough evidence to determine the road travelled on that early morning of June 4, 1825. Mapquest tells us the Central Avenue route—the shortest route—measures 3.5 miles. The Brigham Road comes in a little longer at 4.2 miles. The path down Canadaway creek (today's Temple Street) is even longer.

Whatever the road taken, Lafayette's carriage was not alone.

Chapter Seventeen:
To The Dunkirk Dinghy By The Dawn's Early Light

Walter Smith was there, no doubt in front of the crowd of people riding along with Lafayette. Unlike the fawning civilians eager to not let go of the Nation's Guest, Smith wore the uniform of a Colonel, confidently in command of the militia regiment that received Lafayette. He even had an elegant sword draped from his belt.[1]

Major General Elijah Risley, Jr., father of nine-year-old Hiram (and future grandfather of Olive) strode with his military staff alongside Smith. With little notice, Smith was tabbed as marshal of the day.[2] Both were businessmen, not full-time soldiers. Today, or rather this night turning into early morning, they faithfully presented all the martial pomp and circumstance proper in honoring the last surviving general of the American Revolution.

But there may have been more on the mind of Walter Smith. He wasn't just a businessman; he was the leading businessman of the town. He came to Fredonia in 1819 still a teenager. He set up a business and sold more than $20,000 in goods the first year. That was enough to buy out his partner. Now, a mere six years later, he was well on his way to grossing $75,000.[3]

He put his money to good use. Whether farmer or merchant, Walter Smith was the hub that connected everyone to everything. It is attributed[4] that Hiram Risley would later cite Smith for "the timely aid he gave to struggling settlers," and describe him as "this remarkable man, who for almost half a century occupied so large a space in the business affairs of Western New York. Throughout this long career, marked with patient endeavor and noble enterprise, he always maintained a reputation for generosity, courage, energy and fidelity."[5]

In a way, those 1825 profits helped subsidize Lafayette's travels through Chautauqua County. The whole scheme came from Smith. He suggested the route Lafayette would take upon entering New York State from his travels in the Midwest. He would bear the expense of chartering the *Superior* to ferry Lafayette from Dunkirk to Buffalo.[6] Perhaps that's why he had the honor of being asked to serve as marshal of the day.

At twenty-five years old, Smith was already a visionary.

It would be another decade before he would, much to the derision of others, predict about the coming thing—railroads—that "the day would come when cattle fattened in Indiana, Illinois and Ohio would be brought to the New York Market."[7]

It would be another year before he would move from Fredonia to Dunkirk and virtually build that city from scratch. In doing so, Walter Smith would become "at once the controlling power in Dunkirk, and soon the most influential, public spirited and capable business man in the county."[8]

Oddly, though, for all his popularity and success, and unlike many of his peers, Smith never sought higher office. He only served in one official position: that of "path master."[9] This was one of the lowest state positions but most important at the time of settlement. The job of the path master was to make the new roads for all those incoming settlers.

Could it be that's what Smith considered as he rode to Dunkirk? Sure, the road they traveled was "improved and prepared for the occasion."[10] Still, if it was to become Central Avenue, it left much to be desired. The desolate road was still in a dense forest with few if any homes.

The dawning sun barely touched that forest as the parade approached the bay. The air was clear and calm. Soon, Smith and Risley and all the others could see the pier. On it stood the exuberant Buffalo committee, ready to accept the baton in the form of Lafayette.[11]

The *Superior* stood about a mile offshore. A small dinghy was at the ready to take the General to the famous steamship. Now, put yourself in Lafayette's shoes. He just spent an all-nighter in a carriage making two stops where the good citizens of Westfield and Fredonia had feted him with huge frontier parties. Was he tired? What do you think?

The last thing he probably wanted was a long, drawn-out, formal exchange on the pier. The two committees obliged. They offered each other a "mutual exchange of civilities"[12] then led the General and his party to the small boat. And with that, Lafayette rowed away from shore. The crowd, as they say, roared.

That wasn't the only thing that roared. As the dinghy pushed off, the *Superior* offered a 24-gun salute. The militia on shore answered the same with a *feu de joie*, their rifles firing in rapid succession along their line.[13]

Through it all, the band played on, courtesy of Colonel Abell's regiment.[14] Close your eyes for a moment and imagine the atmosphere in Dunkirk Bay that fresh summer-like morning as you face the *Superior*. Lafayette grows increasingly smaller with each stroke of the oar. You hear the soft sounds of Lake Erie's waves caressing the pier around you. The muffled sounds of the rifles echo from the forest wall behind you. To your delight, the music wraps it all up in an audio bow.

If you're smiling at the contentment this thought evokes, you are not alone. Levasseur wrote in his journal they arrived on board the *Superior* "to the sound of music, the delightful harmony of which accorded deliciously with the beauty of the morning, and the romantic aspect of the bay in which we were."[15]

And Levasseur was not alone, either. For, accompanying Lafayette and the Buffalo committee was a contingent from the Chautauqua committee, including Walter Smith and Major General Elijah Risley, Jr.

Chapter Eighteen:
Rebuilt Buffalo

Cyrenius Chapin stood where no sane man dare stand. He knew exactly what he was doing. He also knew it was all McClure's fault.

Nonetheless, there he was. He measured his pace as he approached the British line. Despite the noise and excitement about him, he could hear his feet crunch through the snow. Or maybe he imagined his cold ears picking up the sound.

Certainly, he could feel his feet crush the white blanket as he made his way up Schimmelpenninck Avenue (it didn't get the name Niagara Street until July 12, 1826[1]). The excitement of the night and now early morning kept his blood flowing to his extremities. His medical training taught him that would help prevent the onset of frostbite.

Cyrenius fully understood the consequences of his actions. With the cannon behind him blown off its makeshift perch by an overzealous (and perhaps inexpert) volunteer squad, parley represented the best hope to offer the woman and children, as well as the militia, time to escape. If he were lucky, he might just save the village he helped build.[2]

The good doctor first came to the mouth of Buffalo Creek in 1801. He put in a bid for the whole lot to Joseph Ellicott, the local agent for the Holland Land Purchase. Chapin promised "forty respectable citizens that are men of good property have signed articles of agreement to take a township if it can be purchased."[3] Ellicott, noting that the lands had not yet been surveyed, declined the offer.[4]

Two years later, after the Holland Company completed its survey, on October 11, 1803, Chapin purchased Lot No. 41, Township 11, 8th Range. He paid $346.50 for the ninety acres, making Cyrenius Chapin one of the first permanent settlers in what would become the City of Buffalo.[5]

Chapin would soon develop a life-long friendship with Louis Stephen Le Couteulx, who came to Buffalo in 1804. His wife, Madame

Le Couteulx was a niece of General Touzard, who accompanied General Lafayette during the Revolutionary War (and lost an arm as a result). Le Couteulx would eventually become the first clerk of Niagara County.[6]

That same year, Yale President Timothy Dwight traveled to Buffalo. He described the place as "about twenty indifferent houses." As far as the people he met there, Dwight saw them as "a casual collection of adventurers; and have the usual character of such adventurers, thus collected, when remote from regular society, retaining but little sense of government or religion."[7]

Did that description also apply to Cyrenius Chapin? In the ensuing decade, he had built a home, brought his family over and set up a successful medical practice in both Buffalo and Fort Erie on the Canadian side.[8] In April of 1813, Chapin (along with Eli Hart, Zenas W. Barker, Ebenezer Walden, and Oliver Forward) was nominated by act of legislature to serves as one of the trustees for the newly incorporated Village of Buffalo.[9]

He even helped build the first school in Buffalo.[10] By 1811, it was among the fewer than one hundred buildings in Buffalo. Set on the corner of Pearl and Swan Streets, the schoolhouse also served the nearly 500 residents as a town hall, a church (for all denominations), and for any other public purpose.[11]

And the last thing Dr. Chapin wanted was to see the British burn that school, or any other building, in retaliation for General George McClure's callous misdeeds in Newark The American press vilified McClure's uncalled for burning of the innocent town of 100 homes.

Still, the Tories felt compelled to punish, and punish they did. They had already captured Fort Niagara. They had already burned and massacred every settlement along the Niagara River. Buffalo was their last stop. It didn't help that McClure abandoned the Niagara frontier for safer confines in the interior of New York State.

He left in a huff, chased out by the citizens of Buffalo after arresting and trying to imprison Chapin on charges of "mutiny if not treason," calling the Buffalonian an unprincipled disorganizer."[12]

Asa Ransom, who lost a slander suit against Cyrenius Chapin prior to the start of hostilities,[13] would later come to the doctor's defense.

Ransom testified McClure and Chapin had "quarrelled violently about the burning of Newark and that he believed that animosity continued to exist." In his official deposition, Ransom said the notorious McClure, when asked to confront the British in Buffalo, said "I will stay and defend you if the inhabitants will arrest and bind that damned rascal (Chapin) and bring him to me; if they will not do that they may all be destroyed and I don't care how soon."[14]

McClure made his feelings formal when he wrote to Governor Tompkins, "I this day ordered Colonel Chapin into confinement for treason and mutiny. There is not a greater rascal exists than Chapin, and he is supported by a pack of tories and enemies to our Government. Such is (sic) the men of Buffalo. They don't deserve protection."[15]

The British themselves were not unfamiliar with the rascally Doctor. They had captured him once already, in the summer of 1813. While transporting him by boat, he rallied the other prisoners and, unarmed, wrestled control of the boat, capturing his guards in the process. He made his escape to Fort Niagara with 16 prisoners of his own as well as two boats.[16] The event was widely covered in the national press.[17]

So, as the erect, six-foot tall man walked towards his enemy, he knew what he was doing, His thin face featured arching eyebrows, piercing eyes, and a dominant Roman nose.[18] His dignified, firm, military bearing halted the British advance. He was about to fulfill McClure's wish that he be "taken by the enemy."[19]

It tells you something about the nature of the battle that, despite Lieutenant-General Sir Gordon Drummond's contention that Chapin "considerably annoyed our troops with round and grape shot from a six-pounder," the British respected the Doctor's "self-constituted flag of truce."[20] For a moment, all stopped, and it appeared Buffalo would be spared.

However, no sooner had the truce been agreed to than the burning began. It's not clear if there was ever any intent on the part of the British to spare Buffalo. In a January 1814 proclamation, Sir George Prevost, Governor-in-Chief of British North America, declared, "the opportunity of punishment has occurred, and a full measure of retribution has taken place." Still, he also stated he had every intention of "pursuing no further a system of warfare so revolting to his own feelings, and so little congenial to the British character."[21]

That being said, eight months later the British would burn Washington, D.C.

As for Chapin, Lieutenant-General Drummond reported "the famous Dr. or Colonel Chapin, whom, in consequence of his former escape, I have sent off towards Quebec by an officer and two dragoons."[22] The Canadian papers echoed these sentiments.[23] For them, the capture of Cyrenius Chapin was a prize worth repeating.

Chapin would be held for nine months and eventually return to Buffalo. Among the many things he'd do was help create the Niagara County Agricultural Society. He was its first president, and as such, presided over its Fair in 1820.[24] Today we recognize that event as the first ever "Erie County Fair" (because, in 1820, there was no Erie County and Buffalo was part of Niagara County). The U.S. Census counted more than 2,000 people living in Buffalo/Black Rock/Tonnewanta Buffalo (up from 1,500 in 1810).[25] The village also surpassed 150 dwellings in 1820, also surpassing its pre-war level.[26]

Buffalo, however, still had a problem. It was a problem even Timothy Dwight noticed. He noted that Buffalo Creek, while "a considerable mill-stream," had a considerable obstacle. "A bar at the mouth prevents all vessels, larger than boats, from ascending its waters."[27]

Solving that problem would result in a future for Buffalo that Chapin (and others) dreamed of.

And, at noon on Saturday, June 4, 1825, General Lafayette would find himself heading straight toward it.

Chapter Nineteen:
Regal Reception In Buffalo's Blossoming Queen City

Thousands crowded the shore near Buffalo's new harbor. Oliver Forward couldn't help but gloat. It had been a slugfest. Whether Joseph Ellicott or Peter B. Porter, it seemed like those who could help his struggling village didn't. But he and his friends succeeded. And now, just as the clock struck noon, the Nation's Guest – General Lafayette – appeared on Lake Erie's horizon.

The big show was about to begin.

But the impetus for it almost didn't. There almost wasn't a harbor. And without a harbor, there would be no canal. And without a canal, well, Peter Porter would have been the one gloating right about now.

A dozen years earlier, Buffalo, once "a little scattered village of about one hundred houses and stores," had been reduced by the British torch to all but one house, one blacksmith shop, and one jail. And lots of naked chimney rising like oh-so-many solitary obelisks from the blackened ashes below. Beside these ruins snaked "a sinuous creek, navigable for small vessels only, winding its way through marshy ground into the lake, its low banks fringed with trees and tangled shrubbery."[1]

The canal represented the key to prosperity. With it, Buffalo would attract more settlers, more businesses, and more money.

Ah, money. There's the rub. For it was money that was needed to create the one thing that would set everything in motion: a navigable harbor.

Black Rock, then a competing village a couple miles up the Niagara River, had several distinct advantages. It possessed a superior natural harbor thank to – you guessed it – that big black rock that protected the inlet from stormy lake waters and nasty river currents.

Black Rock also had a powerful advocate in Peter Porter. The former Congressman had connections galore. And ambition. The combination represented a one-two punch that had the potential to knock Buffalo out of contention in the fight for which harbor would become the western terminus of the fast-approaching Erie Canal.

In 1818, Buffalo was able to convince the state to authorize a survey of Buffalo Creek, but with the caveat that Niagara County pay for it. (Remember, Erie County had not yet been created from Niagara County). William Peacock, the Holland Company's agent located in Mayville, agreed to do the survey without charge. In 1819, the state agreed to provide a loan for the construction of the harbor. This loan would convert to a grant if Buffalo became the terminus of the Erie Canal. In the meantime, private individuals had to back the loan.[2]

The village was still a relatively small community. It didn't possess men of great wealth. So, it turned to the one entity that would most benefit from the canal: the Holland Land Company. They had been contemplating a canal for some time now. Indeed, Joseph Ellicott pushed the idea. Surprising, when Buffalo asked the Company to back the loan, General Agent Busti rejected the request because the work would not be completed by the public authorities.[3]

Not to be denied, Oliver Forward and a handful of others (Charles Townsend, Samuel Wilkeson, and George Coit, under the superintendence of Judge Wilkeson) agreed to secure the loan. They put up their own money, took personal risk, all for the benefit of the entire community.[4]

The plan worked. The harbor was finished and the state selected Buffalo as the western terminus of the Erie Canal. The state paid the loan.[5] On August 9, 1822, Oliver Forward, turned over the first shovel of dirt signaling the start of local construction of the Erie Canal. He was joined by Cyrenius Chapin and other prominent citizens.[6]

And now the village would reap its first reward for this endeavor.

Meanwhile, on board the *Superior*, a "violent and contrary" wind slowed the ship's entry into port. It took two hours from the time their eyes first spotted the shore until they pulled up to port. Levasseur says they were "struck by the air of prosperity, and the bustle in its port." They also couldn't help but notice what they saw before them. Only months earlier, and five hundred miles to the east, they had seen the eastern terminus of the Erie Canal. Now, before them, stood its western counterpart.[7]

Once again the roar of guns greeted the travelers. First, a round of 18 announced to the large crowd gathered on the shore that Lafayette had arrived. On cue, another 24 artillery units answered from the hill.[8]

With that, the show was about to begin. No doubt this was much to the relief of Colonel H.B. Potter's several companies of the military. They had been in a constant state of readiness for almost two days. But now, the time for the grand reception had come. General Lafayette had arrived. As contemporary reports said, "the immense multitude of spectators had collected to witness an event which had been so long and so devotedly wished for."[9]

Upon disembarking, Lafayette and his suite were received by the military under Col. Storrs, Marshal of the day. The throng of citizens present also received him.[10] A detachment of Capt. Vosburgh's company of Cavalry, and the Frontier Guards, under Capt. Rathbun immediately escorted them to the Eagle Tavern. In front of the tavern sat an ornate pavilion, constructed specifically for the event.[11]

In no time, the familiar face of Le Couteulx introduced the visitors to the village corporation. Oliver Forward, on behalf of the village trustees and the entire citizenry, offered the following formal welcome:

> *"In behalf of the citizens of this village and its vicinity, I have the honor of welcoming you among them and of tendering to you that regard which has been again reiterated, from the centre to the remotest extremity of the Union. This regard we are unable to testify to you amidst the splendor and magnificence of a state or national emporium: but to you we are aware that it will not be less acceptable if presented in the unimposing forms of republican simplicity. We are not less mindful than the whole people of this extended empire, or the services you have rendered our common country, nor less conscious of the gratification the patriot and the philanthropist must feel in passing the declivities of life, carrying with him the richest of*

all earthly rewards, a nation's love and a nation's gratitude. But few of us were among those who participated with you in the toils and the dangers of the revolution, which established not only the liberties of the confederacy, but what the world had never before seen, a welcome, a happy, and a protected home, for the oppressed of all nations. But we alike revere the memory of the brave, cherish with the same zeal the principles for which you and our fathers bled; and with all the grateful recollections which a love of liberty can inspire, of the voluntary sacrifices you have made in support of her cause, we beg you to accept the humble tribute of our respect, in conjunction with what has been and will continue to be proffered not only by every citizen of the American nation, but by every friend of liberty and of mankind."[12]

To which, Lafayette replied:

"It would have sufficed to my high gratification, Sir, to visit this frontier on the state of New York, to admire its wonderful improvements, and to meet the affectionate welcome which I have received from the people of Buffalo, and which in their behalf you are please most kindly to express. But here additional sources of delight are opened to me: after having lately seen the lines of Orleans, I now have approached those parts of the union, where in the last war the rights and honor of the nation have been gloriously supported by the sons of my revolutionary contemporaries; the account of which achievements have excited in my breast proud and patriotic emotions long before the principal leaders in that war had become my personal friends. I have this morning navigated the lake the name of which is forever associated to the illustrious name of Perry, as being the theatre where has been so conspicuously evinced the superiority that in every instance of two wars against Great

> *Britain has attended the American flag. Be pleased, Sir, to accept my personal thanks, and to receive the tribute of my grateful respect to the citizens of Buffalo."*[13]

Upon conclusion of these pleasantries, Lafayette met with the people. There is a famous interaction between Lafayette and Red Jacket, much chronicled by the press at the time and repeated in the historical annals. While the event may have occurred as written, its premise may be false. It involves a story that Lafayette had previously met Red Jacket at Fort Stanwix during the treaty negotiations of 1784. There is some question if Red Jacket actually attended the Fort Stanwix negotiations.[14]

We'll close this with an account of the dinner at Buffalo from the June 15, 1825, *Fredonia Censor*. [N.B.: The *Buffalo Emporium and General Advertiser* wrote the dinner began at five o'clock, an hour later than reported by the *Censor*.] Reprinted here is the *Censor's* account in full:

> "At 4 o'clock the General and suite, (his son George Washington La Fayette, and secretary, Mr. La Vasseur,) sat down to dinner, with the corporation, committee of arrangement, and as many citizens as could be conveniently accommodated. C. Townsend, Esq., presided, assisted by Col. H.B. Potter, and E. Walden, Esq. as vice presidents. On the removal of the cloth, the president expressed to Gen. La Fayette the gratification he felt in common with his fellow citizens, in beholding one of the founders of the republic, and gave:
>
> "Our Illustrious Guest – The efficient defender of Liberty in both hemispheres.
>
> "By the 1st Vice President, H.B. Potter, Esq. – The surviving patriots and soldiers of the American revolution.

"By the 2ᵈ Vice President, Capt. M.M. Dox – The pillar of American Glory – On its column are engraved the names of Washington, La Fayette, and Bolivar.

"By the President of the Corporation – Our Country – Her majesty is her laws, her sovereign, her people.

"Gen. La Fayette's Toast.

"Buffalo – May this young city, rapidly improved from its ashes, more and more exhibit in example of republican prosperity and happiness.

"By G. W. La Fayette. – Lake Erie – One of the Theatres of American Glory.

"By Mr. La Vasseur. – Liberty – May its principles pervade the world.

"By the President. – The health of our Guest, George Washington La Fayette.

"By Hon. W.C. Bouck. – History does not present a more brilliant example of virtue and heroism, or one more worthy of imitation, than is offered in the biography of our illustrious Guest.

"By Maj. Gen. Risley. – The Prisoner of Olmutz – He now receives the homage of freedom's friends throughout the world.

"By a Stranger. – Amid our national prosperity and happiness, let us bear in mind suffering Greece. Heaven send a Washington to her councils, and a La Fayette to lead her armies.

"By Mr. Le Couteulx. – His Excellency the Governor of the State of New York."[15]

With that, "the evening was spent pleasantly, and the village handsomely illuminated."[16]

Then it was off to sleep. In a bed. Not moving. For the first time in two days.

And rest would be important, for tomorrow would be a big day.

Chapter Twenty:
Peter B. Porter's Home Sweet Home

Peter Buell Porter woke up early that morning. Yesterday, despite all its pomp and circumstance, was just a prelude to today. For it was on this day, Sunday, June 5th, 1825, the General would host the General. General Porter would soon entertain General Lafayette for breakfast at his Black Rock house.

For nearly a quarter of a century, Peter Porter had lived in the Greater Western New York Region. During the last fifteen years, he had fought—both literally and figuratively—for his beloved home of Black Rock.[1]

Born in Litchfield, Connecticut in 1773, Peter Porter graduated from Yale College before studying law in his hometown with Judge Reeves (who, incidentally, was the brother-in-law of Aaron Burr)[2]. He couldn't, however, resist the lure of "the far famed 'Genesee Country' — of its fertile soil, its genial climate, of its beautiful lakes and rivers." In 1793, he and a friend first visited Western New York.[3]

To give you a flavor of what it was like for a pioneer exploring America's first frontier in the late eighteenth century, here is how Porter himself described it:

> "We entered the interminable forests of the west, at the German Flatts, on the Mohawk, which was then the extreme verge of civilized improvements, and plodded our weary way, day after day, to the Genesee river. The only evidences of civilization, at that time, consisted of some half a dozen log huts at Utica, as many more at this place, and the same again at Canandaigua. Beside these, there were a few miserable cabins, sprinkled along the road, at a distance of five to fifteen miles apart, where the traveler might look, not as now, for comfort or for rest, but for the sheer necessaries for continuing his journey."[4]

In 1795, Peter Porter settled in Canandaigua, New York, joining his older brother Augustus. Two years later, he was appointed Ontario County Clerk. He made Augustus his deputy a year later. In 1802, he served in the New York Assembly representing the counties of Ontario and Steuben.[5] In this, he was following in the footsteps of his father Joshua Porter, who served in the Connecticut Assembly.[6]

Those weren't the only shoes he shared with his dad. Peter served as a general in the War of 1812. Joshua commanded a regiment during the Revolutionary War and witnessed the surrender of Burgoyne on October 16, 1777.[7] This victory helped convince the French to come to the aid of the American Patriots. Among those to come to help: the Marquis de Lafayette.[8]

The father may have never met the French General, but the son just had dinner with him last night. And now, he was preparing to have breakfast with Lafayette in his storied and finally decorated home.

Ah, yes, about that home.

While his brother Augustus took responsibility for the upper Niagara River close to the falls, Peter settled on the Lake Erie end in Black Rock. There, he built a home on the cliffs overlooking the river. That was a blessing and a curse. On one hand, it offered a spectacular vista of not only the river, but of nearby Canada, only a stone's throw away. On the other hand, Black Rock was well within range of the British field artillery used during the War of 1812.[9]

Chairing the Committee of the House on Foreign Relations, Congressman Peter B. Porter introduced resolutions couched in "great ability, firm and energetic in its tone, yet temperate and judicious" to deal with the rising British aggressions. Congress adopted the resolutions on December 19, 1811, and Porter immediately resigned his seat.[10]

After declining a Brigadier's commission from the U.S. Army, Porter opted instead to serve as Quartermaster-General in the New York State militia.[11] In command of a body of New York militia following the Battle of Queenston Heights, Porter used his home as headquarters. In October 1812, the British attacked Black Rock, its cannons hitting Porter's home. A 25-pounder dropped through his roof while he was eating dinner. The

British stopped firing when they hit their intended target, the east barracks, exploding the magazine within it.[12]

Porter apparently didn't learn his lesson, or, more likely, remained defiant of the British. He was sleeping in his house when the British attacked again in July 1813. This time they came ashore and seized the building, gathering there for breakfast. The general barely escaped capture. When he returned with troops, he recaptured his homestead, severely injuring the British second in command. Porter brought the soldier to his home until he had recovered.[13]

Before the end of the year, however, Porter's house would meet its end. When the British marched down the Niagara River burning almost all in their path, Peter's home would not survive. But not because the Tories burned it. No. They blew it up.[14] Apparently, they wanted to make a statement.

Following this fiery conflagration, the Committee of Safety and Relief at Canandaigua also wanted to make a statement. And they did. They wrote to the citizens of New York in an openly published letter, "Niagara county, and that part of Genesee which lies west of Batavia, are completely depopulated. All the settlements in a section of country forty miles square, and which contained more than twelve thousand souls, are effectively broken up."[15]

Once the war was over, Porter returned to Black Rock. He built a new home in 1816 on its original foundation.[16] A few years later, he married Letitia Grayson. Widowed since 1811, she was the daughter of John Breckinridge, of Kentucky, formerly the Attorney General of the United States, under President Jefferson. She brought her southern charm to Western New York and immediately impressed. She was described as "her amiable temper, her buoyant spirits, her varied information, her playful wit, and her unaffected, ingenuous and fascinating manners, never failed to win the love and admiration of all, and render her the centre of attraction, and the life-spring of the circles in which she moved."[17]

On the morning of Sunday, June 5, 1825, General Lafayette would get his chance to experience Mrs. Porter's magic in her own home.

But that's not all the French visitors would experience. Despite all he had done to encourage the creation of it, Peter Porter lost the battle with Buffalo to make Black Rock the western terminus of the Erie Canal. Yet, it would be he, along with acting Canal Commissioner William C. Bouck, who would first introduce Lafayette to the portion of the new waterway that had just opened.

Chapter Twenty-One:
Breakfast At Black Rock
Then On To Tonawanda

The gates of the grand lock at the foot of the harbor opened for the first time on Thursday evening, June 2, 1825. Water from Lake Erie came gushing in. Slowly, but steadily, water flowed into the newly opened portion of the Erie Canal from Black Rock to "Tonnewanta" (present day Tonawanda). By nine o'clock Friday morning, the water filled the nine-mile length to a depth of three and a half feet. The celebratory committee launched the inaugural fleet of five elaborately decorated packet boats.[1]

Upon their return to Black Rock at three o'clock, a procession of 150 people led by Marshal of the day J.L. Marshall, Esq. marched to the Steam Boat Hotel. As the news reported of the event: "The day was marked by great hilarity and good feeling and not the least incident occurred to mar its pleasures."[2]

After partaking of a fine dinner provided with usual aplomb by Mr. Thayer, the round of toasts began. General Peter B. Porter, officiating the event as President of the committee, offered the first toast: "The event we celebrate – the tapping of Lake Erie. Seven years of patient and patriotic labor expended in perforating the earth and rock to introduce and stanch the faucet, will be amply repaid by the rich and never-failing stream of water and wealth, destined to flow from this copious reservoir."[3]

Indeed, General Porter had led the fight for the canal. He had hoped his hometown of Black Rock would serve as the western terminus, but clever maneuvering by his competitors in Buffalo took that prize. Still, Black Rock received the honor of being an appendage, at the cost of sacrificing the geological formation that gave it its name.

After the first half dozen or so toasts, Mr. Jackson of Black Rock rose and rendered: "Black Rock and Buffalo – never more worthily employed than at present. One in paying homage to a great event and to those who have consummated it – the other waiting with open arms the arrival of their country's best friend."⁴

Indeed, General Lafayette would arrive in Buffalo the next day and spend Saturday night there.

The Nation's Guest arose early Sunday Morning, June 5. The military units that had greeted him the previous day rose with him, along with the Buffalo committee. The entire entourage left the village at six o'clock AM. At least says the *Buffalo Emporium*, which also wrote the General arrived at Black Rock when the clock struck seven.⁵

The *Black Rock Gazette* had a slightly different interpretation of events. This rival newspaper claimed Lafayette didn't arrive in Black Rock until "half past eight o'clock" at which point the Buffalo committee handed him off to Peter Porter, chairman of the Black Rock Committee. A few other folks, including acting canal commissioner William C. Bouck, accompanied the committee to Thayer's Hotel.⁶

Levasseur noted that Black Rock was "a small but handsome port which rivals that of Buffalo in bustle."⁷ Things were sure bustling those couple of days, and that Sunday morning in particular.

After exchanging the usual pleasantries at Thayer's Hotel, General Porter took the travelers and a few others, (including acting canal commissioner William C. Bouck) to his house for breakfast with his wife and family. As they approached the home, they passed through the elegantly decorated gate that led to the courtyard. While no doubt Mrs. Porter had a hand in this, the entire citizenry gets credit for this festive display. At the top of the arch sat a live eagle. The columns on either side featured two flags, each held in place by "spiral wreaths of variegated cloth."⁸

After breakfast, Lafayette emerged from the house to find a very orderly line of men and women to offer him their greetings and good tidings. As usual, he returned their politeness with more of his own, making sure to shake each hand in a sincere manner.⁹

At ten o'clock, the committee led the guests down to the new steamboat wharf and they boarded the canal boat *Seneca Chief*. Three barges, replete with flags and with four oarsmen each, towed the brand-new packet boat through the harbor for more than a mile before it reached the entrance of the canal. There, the rowers handed off the *Seneca Chief* to a pair of teams of horses. One team attached itself to the flagged boats, the other to the *Seneca Chief*. The small fleet included a number of other boats filled with eager citizens. Off they floated towards Tonnewanta.[10]

At noon, the boats began to arrive at Tonnewanta. The General disembarked with the Black Rock committee. Waiting for them there was the Niagara County committee. As before with the Buffalo committee, the two committees exchange formalities. Lafayette and his party climbed into the waiting carriages.[11]

The carriages quickly rolled on their way. Soon, the guests heard "a deep roaring, which shook the earth." In the distance, they could see "a thick column of vapour... rising towards heaven."[12]

They were about to enjoy one of the most unforgettable sights ever.

Chapter Twenty-Two: Augustus Porter Could Have Danced All Night

Anna Spencer Foster loved the Genessee Country. Born in East Haddam, Connecticut in 1777,[1] by the time she was nineteen in 1796 she was living in Palmyra (then in Ontario County) with her first husband Moody Stone.[2] The young couple traveled freely through the challenging frontier of Greater Western New York. That year, the young couple forded the Genesee River above the falls to visit her sister and brother-in-law. On the way, they passed through Irondequoit and Rochester (where "there was but one house").[3]

Late in the fall of 1796, Nathan Harris hosted a "husking frolic" at his home in that growing settlement.[4] In general, these social events allowed neighbors to gather to work on a particular task, then party upon the completion of that task. The tasks could range anywhere and included "husking bees, raisings, quiltings, and pumpkin pearings."[5]

Harris, known as "Uncle Nathan," as the jolly newcomer soon became known as, had emigrated to "Township No. Twelve in the Second Range" within the Phelps and Gorham Purchase. This would later be known as Palmyra. Harris built a log home from the timber on his property. Only a crooked trail led to his isolated cabin.[6]

This is where Anna attended the husking frolic. There, she says, "We had a pot pie baked in a five pail kettle, composed of 13 fowls, as many squirrels, and due proportions of beef, mutton and venison; baked meats, beans and huge pumpkin pies, hunting stories, singing, dancing on a split basswood floor, snap and catch 'em, jumping the broom stick, and hunt the squirrel, followed the feast. All joined in the rustic sports, there was no aristocracy in those days."[7]

The real fun, however, took place in Canandaigua. Anna recalled "the dances were more fashionable, but there was no aristocracy there." She really gives the sense that, no matter what one's position or title is, everyone met on the same level. Even a half century later, Anna remembered dancing with many prominent men. Among her dance partners were the Porter brothers—Peter B. Porter and Augustus Porter.[8]

We already know the impact Peter Porter had on Black Rock and his role in Lafayette's visit there. But what of his older brother Augustus?

"Among the men firm of purpose and of indomitable courage who, before the dawn of the last century, strode down the rugged hillsides and crossed the pleasant valleys of New England and, coming to the borders of the river Hudson crossed to explore the country beyond, few names stand out with greater prominence than that of Augustus Porter." So begins the biography of Judge Augustus Porter as written by his great-grandson.[9]

Lest you think the preceding represents familial hyperbole, an earlier assessment from another author writes, "Few names were earlier, have been more intimately, and none more honorably, associated with the entire history of settlement and progress in Western New York, than that of Augustus Porter."[10]

Augustus was both on January 18, 1769, in Salisbury Connecticut. Unlike his father and younger brother Peter, he did not attend Yale College. In fact, he did not attend college at all. Instead, he studied surveying. Bored with farm life in Connecticut, in 1789 the twenty-year-old ventured out to survey the nearly created Ontario County in Western New York. Remember, at this time, Ontario County included everything west of the Preemption Line (all or part of the twenty western-most counties in New York State today). His first assignment: That section of the Phelps and Gorham Purchase that would eventually become East Bloomfield.[11] He later became a surveyor for the Holland Land Company under the supervision of Joseph Ellicott.[12]

Augustus would spend his summers surveying the uncharted territory of Western New York, returning to his father's home in Connecticut to write his reports.[13] As he rose through the ranks, Augustus located to Canandaigua. Peter joined him there in 1795. One wonders why the married Anna Spencer Foster found herself dancing with these extremely eligible bachelors. Augustus married a year later and brought his new wife with him to Canandaigua. Presumably, all the dancing stopped (at least with other women).

In 1796, while Anna was husking corn at Nathan Harris' place, Augustus Porter was surveying the Connecticut Reserve as principal surveyor of the Connecticut Land Company. For this, they paid him five dollars a day. He was at the time described as "full middling in height, stout built, with a full face and dark, or rather brown, complexion. In a woodman's dress, anyone would see by his appearance that he was capable and determined to go through thick and thin in whatever business he was engaged." He was also missing the thumb on his left hand, on account of the accidental misfiring of a gun.[14]

Sadly, Augustus' first wife passed away in 1800. A year later he remarried the sister of a "long time" (six years) resident of Canandaigua. He was slowing down on the surveying side of things, taking up a career that allowed him to be closer to his growing family. In 1802 he was awarded the contract to carry the mail from Utica to Fort Niagara. That same year, he was elected to serve in the New York State Assembly.[15]

Despite leaving the surveying business, he didn't forget what he learned. Using the knowledge and contacts he accumulated, he and several others bought the "mile strip" along the Niagara River. According to Albert H. Porter, "In the year 1805 the state of New York first offered the lands along the Niagara river for sale, and Augustus and Peter B. Porter, and Benjamin Barton, and Joseph Annin, jointly, purchased largely of the lands at Lewiston, Niagara Falls, Black Rock, and elsewhere along the river."[16]

Some might have thought this a risky investment as it lay smack dab on disputed territory. But Porter wasn't afraid of the British, having outmaneuvered them early when he traveled to survey Connecticut.[17]

In early June 1806, he relocated to Niagara Falls, having sold his Canandaigua home to John Greig, a partner of his wife's brother.[18] Remember that name. It figures into our story later on.

While Peter Porter was busy with Black Rock, Augustus Porter focused on Niagara Falls, with an eye especially on Goat Island. Together, all four partners created various companies, specializing in transportation. They had a State sanctioned exclusive monopoly on portage and transport along the Niagara River. Their clients included John Jacob Astor.[19] At one point, they controlled nearly all the trading vessels on the two lakes and river. Unfortunately, the British reduced all of Augustus' buildings to ashes in December 1813.[20]

Augustus was away from home when the attack came. Luckily, he sent word to his wife to evacuate. She took the children and a few precious goods. She arrived in Canandaigua and stayed with her brother… for four years.[21]

During that time, as his brother Peter was leading the troops against the Tories, Augustus used his expertise in logistics to keep the supply lines flowing. He was rewarded for his good deeds. The State finally deeded him Goat Island, and he promptly gave Peter half of it. The family returned in 1815 and Augustus Porter rebuilt his house—twice as big as it was before![22]

Augustus Porter, who would become the first judge of Erie County, had quite a dance card, beyond Anna Spencer Foster, of course. Among the visitors to his home included Seneca leaders Red Jacket, Corn Planter, and Farmer's Brother, as well as Washington and Albany luminaries such as Senator Henry Clay, Governor De Witt Clinton, and sitting President James Monroe.

And on the afternoon of June 4, 1825, shortly after three o'clock, Judge Augustus Porter was about to host his most famous guest: the Nation's Guest.

But only after the distinguished Frenchman offered pleasantries at a dinner across the street.

Chapter Twenty-Three:
The Natural Wonder Of Niagara Falls, Goat Island, And Lewiston

Another day, another carriage. Another carriage, another bumpy ride. And the road from Tonnewanta to Manchester took a slow, lazy curve following the east fork of the Niagara River as it arcs around Grand Island. Today, driving from Tonawanda to Niagara Falls—the names that have since replaced those 1825 names—would take about twenty-five minutes. But during the time of Lafayette's tour, it took much longer. And the ride was definitely not as smooth.

The fleet of canal boats arrived in Tonnewanta at noon on Friday, June 5, 1825. As he had now become accustomed to, the French guest was greeted by far more people than lived in this small hamlet. Very quickly, however, a convoy of carriages and horses departed for Manchester. It wasn't until two o'clock that Lafayette's party could be seen on the main road heading into the future city of Niagara Falls.

Waiting for him were the citizens of that village of 1,807. They gathered in front of the Eagle Hotel. Originally a thirty or forty square foot log cabin, it was one of three buildings that survived the British flames of 1814. It's owner, General Parkhurst Whitney, built an addition that allowed him to open it as the first hotel in 1815.[1] During the Battle of Chippewa in 1813, Whitney had been captured by the British while carrying a dispatch to the American commander at Queenston Heights. He was later released in a prisoner exchange.[2] From POW to local luminary, Whitney was about to greet a hero of the American Revolution. He could barely contain his joy.

One story of Lafayette's arrival in Manchester reports that, as he approached his destination, he could hear a band playing music to greet him. His ride slowed to a stop outside the Eagle Hotel. The building's hewn oak log walls only added to the rustic character of the frontier Lafayette was travelling through. Suddenly, the door to his carriage unexpectedly swung open with gusto. There, outside the door, stood owner and proprietor Whitney. The burly man reached in with his arms to scoop up his guest. With Lafayette's feet dangling in the air, Parkhurst proceeded to carry him into the hotel. While Whitney no doubt considered this a most appropriate gesture, there's some question whether Lafayette shared this view.[3]

Indeed, Levasseur's account of the event leaves little to question. He writes rather curtly, "Full of an impatience that may readily be conceived, we abridged as much as possible, the duration of a public dinner, of which we were obliged to partake on arriving."[4] Remember, Levasseur wrote this in French, the "diplomatic" language. To be as blunt as he was leaves one to wonder how well Whitney's stunt was received.

Not that Whitney picked up on any of this. Years later, (more than seventy, to be precise), his son still spoke of Lafayette's visit to his father's hotel in the most glowing of terms. Solon Whitney, who was only eight years old at the time, said Parkhurst Whitney, with all the bluster one could imagine might come from a major general in the state militia, proudly introduced Lafayette to the many guests that gathered in his ballroom. He even escorted the Nation's guest to his next stop. (Solon followed riding his pony.)[5]

Perhaps Levasseur was being a bit harsh. After all, it was much later revealed that Lafayette, so impressed with Parkhurst's hospitality (or perhaps feeling guilty for displaying "an impatience that may readily be conceived"), sent the hotelier a pewter chandelier from France.[6]

The original log cabin may have survived the burning of the settlements along the Niagara River when the British crossed the border in 1813. The hotel, under a new name, would itself fall victim to fire in 1918. So large was the fire that it threatened to consume the entire business block. Ironically, Canadian fire companies crossed the border to help stymie the blaze and protect those other buildings.[7]

Parkhurst bought the nearby Cataract Hotel across the street (initially to handle overflow from the Eagle Hotel). He ended up selling the Eagle Hotel in 1835. The good news is he moved Lafayette's gift to the Cataract. He even built a new extension and placed the pewter chandelier in the River Boat Room within that addition. Unfortunately, in 1945 that hotel was also destroyed by fire. The bad news is that the fire started in that new wing that housed Lafayette's pewter chandelier.[8]

In either case, by 3:30 PM Lafayette and crew were about to experience possibly the biggest highlight of their tour through Western New York. They came to Judge Augustus Porter's home. Coincidentally, they had just come from his brother Peter's house earlier that morning. While they might have been impressed with the European-designed mansion that Augustus built to replace his first house that was burned by the British, it was what was beyond the house that really left an indelible mark.

There, in front of their eyes, lay Augustus' prize: Goat Island. He had struggled for years to acquire it. When he finally obtained the island, he built the first bridge to it. That didn't last, so he learned from his mistakes and built a second bridge. Stronger. Steadier. Superior in every way.

Once again, we need to trust Levasseur's words on this: "The sight of the bridge which leads to this island, called Goat Island, admirably prepares the mind for the contemplation of the imposing scene that presents itself, and gives a nigh idea of the boldness and skill of those who constructed it. Built on a bed of rocks, whose numerous points are elevated above the water, and by opposing the current only increase its violence, its wooden pillars are agitated by a continued vibration, which seems to announce that the moment approaches when it will give way and be precipitated in the abyss; some minutes after having passed the bridge we found ourselves in presence of the great fall."[9]

So in awe of the nature before him, Lafayette spent more time in the tranquil white noise of the rushing current and roaring falls than he did at the Eagle Hotel dinner. He embraced the warm solitude of the natural beauty around him. When it was time to leave, he hesitated. Sensing this, Porter told Lafayette he would soon put the island up for sale. The French general inquired as to the asking price. "$1,000," said Porter. With a sigh, Lafayette left, wondering what it would have been like if France wasn't so far away.[10]

At five thirty they were on the road again, this time heading to Lewiston. Once again, they'd snake along the Niagara River. This time, however, they wouldn't travel abreast of the current. No, they'd experience the amazing vista of the Niagara Gorge. When he finally finished the roughly eight-mile journey, he arrived at Lewiston. He alit from his carriage with a face of astonishment upon seeing nearly all of the more than twelve hundred residents waiting to greet him. The newspaper reporting the event said he confessed he felt as if he were "at home."[11]

He had only one more item on his to-do list for this day. The good folks of Lewiston had arranged for a reception in the west parlor of Thomas Kelsey's Tavern in the center of town. Built around 1820 to replace another tavern burnt by the British, it appeared as a modest two-story home with clapboard siding.[12]

In fact, it served as both a family home and a tavern. One story says, when Lafayette saw Martha Kelsey, Thomas' eight-year-old daughter, he kissed her on both cheeks. It's said he also embraced Tuscarora Indian Chief Nicholas Cusick on the steps of the building. Cusick had been one of his scouts during the war. After the reception, he had his evening meal and slept in the best bedroom at the front of the building.[13]

Then it was off to a quiet sleep—the first one in many nights. Tomorrow would start early but involve only two stops. One would look back in time. The other to a future that would awe Lafayette.

Chapter Twenty-Four: Riding The Ridge (Road)

Over the eons, what would become the North American continent heaved and hoed. Rock strata, once flat with the earth when created, now undulated in waves. Each layer born in a different geological epoch bore their own unique properties. Some too loose and soft to sustain the onslaught of wind, water, and ice; others stubbornly sturdy, able to withstand those same powerful forces.

As the most recent period of glaciation receded into Canada and further north, the melting ice revealed the natural formations known as cuestas. These landforms represent a gentle upward slope on one side and dramatic fall—often evidenced by a face of rock on the frontslope.

This precipitous cliff is called an escarpment. Western New York contains three such formations. The Portage Escarpment defines the southern tips of the Finger Lakes and runs along the eastern shore of Lake Erie. Thirty-five miles to the north, the Onondaga Escarpment traverses the northern tips of the Finger Lakes before heading into Lake Erie just south of Buffalo. Another twenty-five miles to the north you'll find the star of today's show, the Niagara Escarpment, which parallels the shore of Lake Ontario and goes through Niagara Falls (and well beyond).

These escarpments define long ridges in the landscape. These ridges make great paths for animals, trails for migrating Paleo-Indian hunters and their less itinerant descendants, and roads for modern times. The Portage Escarpment outlined the Indian trail that became the Main Road between Buffalo and Erie which in turn became Route 20. The Onondaga Escarpment once defined the Great Central Trail of the Iroquois Confederacy. Today Routes 5&20 align with it.

The Niagara Escarpment, the lowest in elevation and most northern of the three, comes into play in the next chapter. In the meantime, it is another rise (though not as tall), further north of the Niagara Escarpment, which drives our current interest. This ridge represents the ancient shoreline of the glacial Lake Iroquois, the predecessor of Lake Ontario.

What of this winding geological formation?

Once the old "Iroquois Trail," you now know it as Ridge Road. Back in the early 1800s, it was simply known as "the Ridge road" (as in, "the road on the Ridge"). In case you missed it, it follows along the northern (lower) side of the ridge on the Niagara Escarpment.

Here's the odd thing about escarpments: they have an upside (great ready-made travel corridor) and a downside (if you want to travel through them). Yep, if you think it's hard for nature to erode that hard rock away, imagine what it's like for civil engineers. Luckily, we have TNT today to blast our way through them. That wasn't always the case.

In case you're curious, when you're riding along the Thruway you might notice driving through a rock faced cut just east of Batavia. On the Batavia (west) side of that cut, the land is higher and more level. On the LeRoy (east) side of the cut, the land drops down quite quickly (and faster than the elevated roadbed of the Thruway). That's the Onondaga Escarpment.

Here's the really exciting news: that dramatic drop in elevation isn't just your run-of-the-mill cuesta. It's due to the Clarendon-Linden Fault System. That's right. The stuff that causes earthquakes. Right here in Western New York. We've known this since at least 1920. That's when George H. Chadwick reported that the Niagara and Onondaga Escarpments both "jogged northward."[1]

In 1806, William Howell didn't care about any of that. In 1810, DeWitt Clinton did.

In an 1878 interview, William Howell's daughter Harriet tells the story of her parents' migration from New Jersey to the newly formed town of Cambria in the newly formed county of Niagara. She was born after her parents had settled, so her story represents a retelling of what her parents no doubt told her. They took four horses, bedding, clothing, and the necessary provisions over Indian trails through Painted Post to Batavia. From there, the Howells took the path to the Iroquois Trail past Lewiston and into Canada. They saw no home west of the Genesee River until they reached the Niagara River. After a short while, they returned to the American side.²

It wasn't unusual for settlers coming from the east to head into Canada. That was the closest location for supplies and provisions.³ You could only travel with so much, so having a "convenience store" nearby was always good.

A series of land trades ultimately led William Howell to his homestead on what is today Route 104 (a.k.a. Ridge Road). It was a lonely, isolated place. Harriet's mother told her "When on the mountain months would pass away without seeing a white man or woman." Still, her father made use of the resources around him. He built a sawmill (the first in the area). More important, he built a tavern.⁴

We've already seen the importance of taverns during the pioneer days of Western New York. With very few dwellings over far distances on main "roads" (they were actually paths), these taverns offered a haven for weary travelers…

…and commissioners appointed by the New York State Legislature to explore possible canal routes. That's where DeWitt Clinton enters the story. In 1810, the future governor, along with Governor Morris, Stephen Van Rensselaer, Simeon DeWitt, William North, Thomas Eddy, and Peter B. Porter (remember him?). Clinton traveled to Lewiston along "on the Ridge road without seeing but very few houses." Clinton was aware of the condition of the road and its future development.⁵

As he traveled on the Ridge road, Clinton stopped at various taverns. Wouldn't you know it, but one of those was Howell's Tavern. There he spoke to William Howell. The tavern keeper informed Clinton of what he found when he dug into the earth to build his sawmill. It gave Clinton a greater sense of the makeup of the soils.⁶

But it was the road on the Ridge that so greatly impressed Clinton. The following year, before the New York Historical Society, he would say of it:

"From the Genesee near Rochester to Lewiston on the Niagara, there is a remarkable ridge or elevation of land running almost the whole distance, which is seventy-eight miles, and in a direction from east to west. Its general altitude above the neighbouring land is thirty feet, and its width varies considerably; in some places it is not more than forty yards. Its elevation above the level of Lake Ontario is perhaps 160 feet, to which it descends with a gradual slope; and its distance from that water is between six and ten miles. This remarkable strip of land would appear as if intended by nature for the purpose of an easy communication. It is, in fact, a stupendous natural turnpike, descending gently on each side, and covered with gravel; and but little labour is requisite to make it the best road in the United States. When the forests between it and the lake are cleared, the prospect and scenery which will be afforded from a tour on this route to the Cataract of Niagara will surpass all competition for sublimity and beauty, variety and number."[7]

Once leaving the inn, Clinton proceeded up to the "mountain" above the Ridge road. What he saw awed him. Here's how he described the Niagara Escarpment in his journal:

"After leaving Howell's Tavern we turned from Ridge road and ascended the great slope (mountain ridge) which approaches it here. The bottom of it is composed of a ledge of limestone, and its elevation is two hundred feet. On this hill we had a sublime view of immense forests towards the lake like on prodigious carpet of green and a distant glimpse of the great expanse of waters."[8]

More than a decade later, Howell would entertain his most famous visitor. He would be awed by what engineers had done to that same Niagara Escarpment.

Chapter Twenty-Five:
Fort Niagara And The Man-Made Wonder Of Lockport

Monday, June 6, 1825, began bright and early all across Niagara County. Excitement, anticipation, and the coming relief following a job well done swirled in the minds of many. For the young, it presented a chance to build memories that would last a lifetime (whether or not they are true). For the old, the day meant the culmination of a grand adventure in coordination, dedication, and ultimately respect for an older generation. For that older generation, their thoughts delighted in remembering the glories of their past.

So, yes, Monday, June 6, 1825, began bright and early.

At Fort Niagara, Major Alexander Ramsay Thompson, with his officers and their wives, rose early to prepare for a proper breakfast banquet.

In the town of Cambria on the Ridge road, William Howell woke early to make sure everything in his tavern was in order for the meeting of the two local committees escorting Lafayette.

Just south of Howell, John Gould readied his Red Tavern for yet another meeting of escorts.

Lockport was abuzz. Like many other small villages on Lafayette's itinerary, it seemed like the entire population of 3,007 people were part of the set-up committee. Alfred Barritt woke up knowing he'd be the one to lead his brothers and companions in ceremonies that were destined to rank as the biggest in their lives. Col. Asher B. Saxton, the rugged Revolutionary War veteran, groomed his horse for the day's long ride which he would lead. Stephen Van Rensselaer got up knowing it was now his turn to perform the same task fellow canal commissioner William C. Bouck performed at Black Rock.

Finally, in Lewiston, the impetus for all these early risers himself rose early. Thomas Kelsey made sure of that, although he probably didn't have to. Lafayette and his crew were well accustomed to the rigors of their ambitious schedule.

At 5 o'clock in the morning, General Lafayette bid adieu to Kelsey's Tavern. He was quickly on his way to breakfast with Major Thompson (or "Thomson," as Levasseur incorrectly calls him). The major commanded the garrison at Fort Niagara, having been placed there only a month before. He and his men had been moving from frontier fort to frontier fort the past year. Their mission: repair old forts or establish new forts.[1] They were the janitors of the army and they were about to meet a military legend.

In a way, it was a homecoming for Lafayette.

The Fort Niagara Lafayette would soon visit represented the third attempt by New France to build a fortress at the mouth of the Niagara River. The French meant to use the edifice to protect their interests on both the River and Lake Ontario. It didn't quite work out for them, but the site of his countrymen's handiwork must have pleased Lafayette.

Thompson and his officers met Lafayette's party in advance of the Fort itself. As they entered the compound, the troops stationed there greeted them with an 18-gun salute from the long eighteens. Guests and hosts then sat down for breakfast.[2] Officers, their wives assisting, provided the entertainment. But Lafayette was on the clock and he had to cut his visit short.[3] After a quick view of the lake from the lighthouse, it was back on the road. By 10 o'clock he was on his way to Lockport.[4]

Some reports suggest Parkhurst Whitney provided his carriage for the ride to Lockport, with his ten-year-old son Solon following on his pony.[5] As these reports came out years after the event and don't appear in any contemporary reporting, we'll leave it to the reader to decide if they can be taken at face value. That being said, there was a "Whitney" listed in the June 6, 1825 meeting minutes for the Ames Royal Arch Chapter's meeting with Lafayette in Lockport.[6]

Of course, that might have been "Warham Whitney" from Rochester, who became a member of Hamilton Royal Arch Mason, number 62 on February 1, 1819.[7] Warham Whitney served two terms as a trustee of the Village of Rochester[8] prior to Lafayette's visit and may very well have been part of the delegation sent to convey the General from Lockport to Rochester.

But let's not get ahead of ourselves.

Based on what you know about Western New York topography, note how Levasseur described what happened next. "On a height near Lockport we met a troop of from seventy to eighty citizens on horseback…"[9] That "height" refers to the "Ridge" upon which they travelled. The stop was at William Howell's Tavern and the horsemen were led there by none other than Col. Asher B. Saxton.

It's at Howell's Tavern that we find another of these "oh, by the way" stories involving then young people only telling the story in their older years. This one involves Howell's daughter Harriet. Said to be between 10-12 at the time of Lafayette's visit, the story goes the General took a liking to her and while all the other men sated themselves with adult beverages, he asked young Harriet to share her lemonade with him.[10]

Harriet may have told this story a time or two, but when she gave her family's migration story to Sanford & Co for its 1878 edition of the *History of Niagara County*, there was no mention of lemonade. Or Lafayette for that matter. In fact, it said she was sixty-nine years old, meaning (if she was that age in 1878), she would have been born in 1809. When Lafayette visited in 1825, she would have been sweet sixteen. Furthermore, the story as printed in that volume says she was married in December 1824 – before Lafayette's visit.[11] You do the math. It kind of makes you wonder if there really was lemonade that day.

Almost immediately after leaving Howell's Tavern the convoy left the Ridge road, heading south on what is today Route 425. After hanging left on Lower Mountain Road, they made a quick stop at Gould's Red Tavern. There "old people remember seeing Lafayette standing in the west room, greeted by all ages and both sexes, the landlord's animated bearing showing his appreciation of being honored by so distinguished a guest."[12]

From there, it was a straight shot into the Village of Lockport. As they entered the village, before them loomed an ominous rock wall. Seemingly impenetrable, it screamed "Halt!" to all those who graced its presence. This was the famed Niagara Escarpment. It stood as the greatest challenge to the engineers building the Erie Canal.

But it was far from impenetrable.

The eyes of French visitors continued to gaze in awe at this natural edifice. Suddenly, a tremendous explosion occurred in the rocks above them. Shattered fragments of the Niagara Escarpment rained down from the ensuing cloud of dust. The workmen had set up a series of powder-infused explosives that all ignited at the same time. This, together with the constant sound of the hatchet and the hammer, spoke to the industriousness of this young community.[13]

Levasseur describes what immediately followed this display of pyrotechnics:

> "Our carriages stopped opposite to an arch of green branches, and General Lafayette was conducted to a platform, where he had the satisfaction of being welcomed by one of his old fellow soldiers, the venerable Stephen Van Rensselaer, now president of the board of canal commissioners. After having been officially presented to the deputation from Monroe county, as well as to a great number of citizens, we sat down to a public dinner, presided over by Colonel Asher Saxton, at the end of which the general, induced by the feelings awakened in him by the sight of so many wonders, gave the following toast: "To Lockport and the county of Niagara—they contain the greatest wonders of art and nature, prodigies only to be surpassed by those of liberty and equal rights."[14]

The dinner occurred at the Washington House on the corner of Main and Transit. Before they could leave Lockport, General Lafayette, his son, and Levasseur were hosted by the Ames Chapter No. 88 Royal Arch Masons in their Masonic Temple. Although that event was held in private, the minutes of that meeting became public decades later. Here they are:

> "An extra communication of Ames Chapter, No. 88, was held at the Masonic Hall in Lockport on the 6th June, A. L. *5825, pursuant to special notice to the companions.
>
> "Present—Companions Alfred Barritt, M.E.W.P.; H. Gardner, King; S. Scoville, Scribe; Ladd, Tyler, P.T., and Companions Ganson, Bounds, Brown, Draper, Pomeroy, Judd, Parks, Gooding, Maynard, Danone, Taylor, Wright, Turner, Shepard, Haigh, and Haines, and visiting Companions Rochester, Weed, Whitney, Cobb, Armstrong, and Whitmore, and opened in the Royal Arch degree for the dispatch of business.
>
> "Resolved. That a committee be appointed to introduce our worthy friend and companion, Gen. La Fayette, whereupon companions Kind and Rochester were appointed for that purpose, who retired and introduced and presented him to the Grand Council and to the Companions, who welcomed him by a short address from Companion Rochester.
>
> "Resolved. That another committee be appointed to introduce the son of Companion La Fayette, vix., Companion George Washington Lafayette, and Companion Bond, Whitney, and Millard were appointed as said committee, who retired and introduced the same, together with the General's private secretary, who were respectively presented to the Grand Council and to the Companions.
>
> "Minutes read and accepted, and chapter closed in due form.
>
> "Joel M. Parks, Secretary"[15]
>
> *A.D. 1825

Once they concluded their meeting, the Masons led Lafayette to the basin above the unfinished five flights of locks. At 7 o'clock they boarded a packet boat "much more convenient and better provided with the comforts of life than could have been supposed."[16]

On that slow boat to Rochester, they had probably the best night's sleep in Western New York.

Too good a sleep if you ask the horde of people unfortunately waiting for them at King's Basin outside their next stop.

Chapter Twenty-Six:
Remembering Silvius Hoard

Think of history as a mosaic containing thousands of tiny stones. When you get up close, they appear unremarkable. Except for a few, often minor, variations in color or a slightly different shape, they look nearly identical. Sure, for any number of reasons, a few stand out and pique your curiosity. But all in all, they're all the same.

Until you back away. Farther away, you see the small rocks begin to transform into a series of patterns. It's as though each stone represents a dot connected to its neighbors. From a more distant perspective, you no longer see individual stones. You see a compelling picture. As if it was always there.

That's history. It's a picture you see, far removed from the original source, the original data points, the human stones that actually created the picture. It's too easy to forget those people. But you shouldn't. Without them, you wouldn't have history.

But it's more than just history. Without them, you wouldn't have a country. You wouldn't have a stable community. Indeed, you maybe wouldn't even be here.

It's important to remember that. You, your community, your nation, owe much to these people. Not all of them, but many of them. Every community starts off as a settlement. Not all settlements survive. Not all settlements thrive. Some remain villages. Others grow into cities.

Rochester began as a small settlement, grew into a village, then blossomed into a city. For decades following the establishment of the Erie Canal, it stood out as the largest city in Western New York. (As mentioned earlier, Buffalo only surpassed it in 1850.)

We are all familiar with the name Nathaniel Rochester. He's the man credited with starting the community that would earn his name. He was a big stone. When Lafayette visited in 1825, Nathaniel Rochester had the honor of riding in the carriage with the French general.[1]

But there were other stones present on that day. Each played a role in creating the historic mosaic you see before you. When you learn about their lives—not only what they did on Tuesday, June 7, 1825, but the entirety of their lives—you learn a little bit more about how our nation was built, how our state was built, and how Western New York was built.

If you're lucky, you even learn a little bit about how you are built. How do you measure up to those people? How do your parents, your family, and your friends measure up to those early settlers? Do you have the fortitude to confront a pioneering life, or do you seek the path of least resistance? Do you have the confidence to step in and make a difference, or do you defer to others? Are you brave enough to tackle new challenges, or do you prefer to avoid them?

In other words, are you made of the same stuff as those who made America? Or are you merely a pebble that has decided to go along for the ride, satisfied to not earn a spot on and be left off the mosaic of history?

It's a hard question to answer, because times today are so much different. In some ways, it was easier to make a difference 200 years ago. There were fewer people. This meant each person was under more pressure to help others. Life was tough, and if you wanted your settlement to do more than survive, you had to chip in. There was really very little choice otherwise.

Which brings us back to one of those stones on the Tuesday in Rochester. He represents not only all that was good about our ancestors, but also the happy fortune of the confluence of coincidence.

Silvius Hoar was born in Springfield, Vermont on July 23, 1789. At least we think so. Several sources say that.[2,3] One source says he was born in Massachusetts on September 23, 1789.[4] This is the problem with relying on secondary source information.

It's very possible that the fact there's a more famous Springfield in that state confused the Massachusetts source. Indeed, that same source states that Silvius' brother Charles Brooks Hoard was born in Springfield, Massachusetts. We know, however, from his congressional biography (Charles B. served in the U.S. House of Representatives) that he was in fact born in Springfield, Windsor County, Vermont.[5] It is reasonable to assume Silvius was also born at that location.

Speaking of errors, yet another secondary source misidentified Charles Brooks Hoard as Silvius' son.[6] That's incorrect. Silvius's son was named "Charles Alexander Hoard."[7]

And lest you think the first mention of "Silvius Hoar" is a typo, it isn't. That's the name he (and his brothers) were born with. After they moved to New York, they petitioned the New York State Legislature to legally add a "d" to their original name, making their new last name "Hoard."[8]

One would presume it would be difficult to run for Congress when your last name sounds like "hoar frost." Or it might be they didn't like the fact that, in Old English, "hoar" refers to showing signs of aging. Or... well, we won't go there. In either case, the name change occurred well before Charles ran for Congress, and Silvius may have instigated it.

You might ask, "Why did these Vermont boys get an act passed by the New York Legislature?" Well, the answer is simple. The family moved to Northern New York prior to the War of 1812. Silvius and his older brother Daniel were hired by David Parish as agents. Daniel was assigned Parishville in St. Lawrence County and Silvius got Antwerp in Jefferson County.[9]

Silvius made quite a name for himself in Antwerp (and not just literally by changing his name, but by his proactive nature). In 1816, he became a commissioner for the Jefferson County Bank.[10] That same year, David Parrish built a brick meeting house and put Silvius on the committee in charge of it.[11] A year later, he was selected as the Antwerp director for the Jefferson County Agricultural Society.[12] In 1819, he was named trustee when the first Presbyterian Society was formed.[13]

The busy Mr. Hoard also served in a more official civic capacity. Actually, more than one. He was elected Town Supervisor in 1818-19 and again in 1823-24.[14] In 1819, when a 184 Regiment was newly formed, Silvius became second in command, serving as Lieutenant colonel.[15] He became a full colonel in 1820.[16]

On February 24, 1814, he married Nancy Mary DeVillers.[17] This would play a key role in his prominence (and relevance) in Rochester on June 7, 1825. You see, Nancy was the daughter of Louis Charles Aime LeFebvre, (American name: Lewis DeVillers). DeVillers, a French nobleman like Lafayette, came to fight in the American Revolutionary War. After the peace, he decided to make America his home.[17]

Would you be surprised to hear that DeVillers and Lafayette were friends? It makes sense. They were. And that gave reason for Lafayette to visit Hoard's Tavern when he arrived in Rochester. Or so says one source written a century after the event.[18]

How certain can we be that this connection is true? It's tough to say as there is no contemporary reporting on this. It's also difficult to determine how, why and when Hoard came to Rochester. That same century-later source says he arrived in 1820 after he "lost both his money and his health in an attempt to float the Ogdensburg Turnpike Company."[19] This could not be independently confirmed.

One contradiction we know of is that Silvius Hoard appears on the 1820 census for Antwerp, Jefferson County, New York.[20] served as supervisor of the Town of Antwerp in 1823-1824. That makes it difficult to place him in Rochester during that time period. Two things are certain: First, on November 30, 1824 (presumably after his time of office in Antwerp had expired), he was in Canada turning over the first ceremonial sod of the Welland Canal, the construction of which he was hired to supervise.[21] Second, Hoard definitely owned the tavern and Lafayette definitely visited there.[22] Beyond that, who knows?

Oddly enough, that same article states Hoard sold the tavern the day after Lafayette's visit. No reason was given. How long did he stay in Rochester? Well, someone thought he was there as late as March 1826 because the Rochester Post Office advertised he had a letter waiting for him.[23] We do know Hoard died at age 39 on September 23, 1828 in Niagara Falls, New York while working on the Welland Canal. He's buried with his wife in Ogdensburg.[24]

Yet, in that brief life, he accomplished much in all the communities he served. He most assuredly earned his spot on the mosaic of history. Yet, like the Rochester tavern he operated in 1825, Silvius Hoard has disappeared into the foggy mists of time.

Let's remember him.

And his tavern.

Chapter Twenty-Seven: Competing Memories Turn Lafayette's Rochester Visit From History To Mystery

You've heard the expression "the sands of time," right? Well, sometimes the expression reads better as "the sandblaster of time." The march of time has a way of eroding all in its past, leaving no trace behind. Spoiler Alert: Nearly every single landmark you are about to read of here no longer exists.

Worse, those same sands often erode memories as well. We often remember what we think is true, even if it's not. That's why if you ask two people who witnessed the same event, you'll often get two different descriptions of what happened. At least two. Because if you ask the same person a week later to describe what happened, there's no guarantee the story will remain the same.

These are the challenges when recounting history. That's why it's better to rely on primary witnesses (the people who were actually there). It's even better to rely on multiple primary witnesses, because you can "average" their stories to get a more reliable understanding of what really happened. Finally, it's best you hear from these primary witnesses immediately after the event occurs. That way the memory is freshest and less prone to error.

Such are the issues with retelling the tale of Lafayette's visit to Rochester on Tuesday, June 7, 1825. Everything is gone and even firsthand witnesses, years later, tell conflicting stories. Fortunately, we do have one contemporary newspaper report. That forms a solid foundation from which to build on. Unfortunately, after that we just can't be sure which version of the story is true.

Complicating matters, as we've seen previously, history writers often omit the second story or fail to identify sources so readers can "fact check" as the investigation reveals new evidence.

Nonetheless, we begin with a certain set of somewhat reliable facts, based on the contemporary reporting.

The citizens of Rochesterville, as the Village was called then (we'll continue to call it "Rochester" to keep things simple), found out Lafayette was on his way to them on Monday, June 6, 1825. They sent a delegation of eighteen to Lockport to meet the French General there.[1]

Indeed, as mentioned in the Lockport story, there were at least two names in the Ames Royal Arch Masons listed under visitors that could have been in that delegation. One of those visitors was listed as "Rochester."[2] Could this have been Judge William Beatty Rochester, former Congressman and son of Nathaniel Rochester? The Honorable W.B. Rochester gave the welcome speech when Lafayette arrived in Rochester.[3]

We also know that, on Tuesday morning, the committee of arrangements provided eleven boats and located them at the basin near Fitzhugh Street. The boats were "fitted up for the conveyance of those ladies and citizens who wish to accompany the expedition to King's Basin, to meet Gen. La Fayette." The boats were to leave at "6 o'clock precisely."[4]

In case you don't have a map of the original Erie Canal handy, King's Basin was located in Greece about 1½ miles south of Ridge Road and 6½ canal miles from Rochester.[5] Basins were spread along the canal the way rest areas and exits are spread along the Thruway. They give boats a chance to get out of the way of through traffic.

Here's where things start to get dicey in terms of the history of Lafayette's visit to Rochester. It's not clear where Lafayette first met the villagers. According to his secretary Levasseur, they didn't leave the cabin and go on deck until they had reached the aqueduct over the Genesee River.[6]

Judge Ashley Sampson, a member of the reception committee, told his version of the events when he was 65 years old on the 30th anniversary of Lafayette's visit in 1855. Sampson, among the first judges in Monroe County, offers far greater detail in his narrative than either the contemporary newspaper reports or Levasseur. There are, however, some discrepancies in his story with both these other stories.

Sampson was able to recall only two members of the delegation sent to Lockport to meet Lafayette: Dr. Levi Ward and James K. Livingston. He mentions the delegation didn't just go to pick up Lafayette, but to ask the Nation's Guest to consent to visit Rochester. He, as chairman, and Jacob Gould, a Mason like Lafayette, were among the members of the reception committee (a.k.a. "committee of arrangements") responsible for making the necessary preparations to greet and host the French party.[7]

Although Sampson did not recall the name, we know Palmer Cleveland was on the committee of arrangements. Cleveland wrote a letter to Nathaniel Rochester dated June 6, 1825. In it, he invited the 73-year-old founder of the city that bears his name, to join Lafayette in his carriage at the boat landing at Gilbert's Basin.[8]

At this point, Sampson's account begins to differ from Levasseur's. The Judge says, as chairman of the reception committee, it was his job to be the first to greet the General. He and his committee walked down the towpath about "one or two miles" from the aqueduct when he saw "a beautiful procession consisting of 13 canal boats, with banners flying and a band of music on board approaching us."[9]

Apparently, the 11 boats that left Fitzhugh basin had joined Lafayette somewhere earlier (perhaps even at the appointed spot at King's Basin in Greece.) Contemporary reporting, in contrast to Levasseur's journal, said the General had actually left the cabin to greet them at that time. The boats then formed a nautical Congo Line convoy to make the final approach to the city.[10]

Once the boats caught up to Sampson, they stopped for the reception committee to go on board. There, Sampson was introduced to the General. He was too excited to prepare a speech and was only able to get out a feeble, "General Lafayette, our country's benefactor, in behalf of the citizens of Rochester, I bid you a cordial welcome to our village." To which, the Frenchman replied, "Sir, you are very I kind; I thank you." Sampson thought Lafayette delivered the response "in a bland and rather subdued tone, evidently evincing a little emotion."[11]

The convoy once again started for the village. You must remember that in 1825, Rochester was still a small village. The canal cut its way through thick undeveloped forest. Once near the village shortly before noon, both sides of the canal were covered with people from all around, not just Rochester but the adjoining counties. While everyone else wore their hats, Sampson said Lafayette insisted on standing on the bow without a hat. This allowed the many spectators to more easily recognize him.[12]

Sampson relayed a story of two little girls, dressed in white, boarding the boat just as it cleared the trees in front of a young ladies' school. They offered a polite bow to the General before dropping a beautiful bouquet of flowers at his feet. Without saying another word, they quickly left. Sampson pick up the bouquet and handed it to his guest who then read the hand-written words, "Welcome LaFayette."[13] So touched was the General that he passed it to his son and said, "Take that, put it in your trunk, and preserve it."[14]

Here Sampson diverges greatly from the contemporary reporting. He says Lafayette first stopped at "The Clinton House" before proceeding to the aqueduct.[15] The newspaper report at the time, and most (but not all) subsequent historical writings say the first formal stop was at the aqueduct after which Lafayette finally disembarked from the canal boat and was led by carriage to subsequent meeting places. We'll depart from Sampson at this point and pick things up from the other primary sources.

Unlike Levasseur, both Sampson and the contemporary reporting agree that Lafayette appeared on deck well before the Aqueduct. The *Rochester Telegraph* wrote immediately after the event, "As they passed the crowded bridges he presented himself on deck and was hailed with demonstrations of joy; and, as he approached the village, the sides of the canal, the bridges, the windows and tops of houses, in short, every point from which the coming boats could be seen, was thronged with spectators, who sent forth, at intervals, shouts of joyful acclamation. The number collected was variously estimated at from eight to ten thousand persons."[16]

What happened next, we'll let Levasseur describe: Once Lafayette returned to deck from the cabin, "we followed him, and what was our astonishment and admiration at the scene that presented itself! We were apparently suspended in the air, in the centre of an immense crowd which lined both sides of the canal; several cataracts fell rumbling around us, the river Genessee rolled below our feet at a distance of fifty feet; we were some moments without comprehending our situation, which appeared the effect of magic: at last we found, that the part of the canal on which we were, was carried with an inconceivable boldness across the Genessee river, by means of an aqueduct of upwards of four hundred yards in length, supported by arches of hewn stone."[17]

What the visitors saw was a temporary stage specially built for this event. It sat above the center arch in the middle of the aqueduct for this event. That's where Lafayette's boat stopped. There, William Beatty Rochester formally greeted Lafayette with a lengthy speech (see appendix "Rochester Speeches and Toasts"). Lafayette responded in an equally elegant fashion. Sampson liked this response better than the earlier one. He said it was conveyed "in a very happy manner, expressing his admiration of the rapid improvements which had been made since he left the country more than 40 years before."[18]

After these pleasantries, the artillery guns offered a salute, and the boat made a hard right on the east end of the aqueduct. They proceeded about a half mile down the canal along the banks of the Genesee River until they reached Gilbert's Basin, where the canal meets a feeder. This is where Colonel Nathaniel Rochester joined them for a carriage tour of the village streets.

The *Rochester Democrat and Chronicle* article, a century after the fact, and with no citation, described the vehicle as "an elaborate 'Brewster wagon,' seating four persons, manned by four outriders and drawn by six white horses."[19] All stories say the parade at taverns where the General first met with Revolutionary War veterans was followed by a 200-person dinner. Exactly which taverns they were is a bit confusing.

Sampson says both events occurred at the Clinton House.[20,21] We know he got the order wrong regarding the timing of the first meeting (with the veterans). Could he have gotten the name wrong, too? Later histories repeat that he met the veterans at the Clinton House (or Clinton Hotel), including a relatively new (1969) account by then Rochester City Historian Blake McKelvey.[22]

Contemporary reports say, "he arrived at Col. Hoard's, where a suite of apartments had been previously prepared for his use by the committee of arrangements." And, afterwards, "He was escorted to Christopher's Mansion House, where, after a repast, of which more than two hundred partook… toasts were drank."[23]

It's possible Hoard's Tavern and the Clinton House are one in the same, as one researcher speculates.[24] One later report says Hoard sold the tavern the day after Lafayette's visit.[25] To date, no records have been found. So, this remains a mystery.

Less of a mystery is the location of the second meeting. Rochester's first substantial tavern, the Mansion House, was built in 1817 on the east side of what was then Carroll (now State) Street. John G. Christopher bought the tavern from its original proprietor Daniel Mack. In 1821, he built a three-story addition. When it opened, he advertised it as "a very commodious and extensive establishment containing in a whole, 33 Sitting and Lodging Rooms, besides a very large and airy Dining Room."[26] It was destined to become the "go-to" place for all important functions. Nearby establishments advertised their location in terms of their distance from "Christopher's Mansion House."

The event most assuredly occurred at the Mansion House, as it was the only facility capable of handling such a large crowd. After dinner, and after the toasts, Lafayette took a moment to rest. Sampson tells the story Jacob Gould told him. Quite by accident, Gould happened into the room where Lafayette lay prone on the floor. When asked if he was OK, Lafayette responded, "This is the way I always rest in the daytime! I am an old soldier and used to a hard bed!"[27]

At 4:00 in the afternoon, Lafayette and his traveling companions boarded a carriage and took the stage route to Canandaigua. But they'd have to make one quick stop before reaching that destination.

Chapter Twenty-Eight:
Timothy Barnard, A Soldier's Story

"Another Revolutionary Patriot Gone." That was the lead, buried at the very bottom of the third of seven dense columns on page two in the Tuesday, April 13, 1847, edition of the *Geneva Courier*. Three perfunctory sentences followed.

> "Hon. TIMOTHY BARNARD, father of Hon. DANIEL D. BARNARD, the distinguished ex-member of Congress of the Albany district, died at Mendon on the 29th inst. Judge Barnard took an active part in the revolutionary struggle, and for his services he drew a pension until his death. For many years judge Barnard was associate judge of the old county of Ontario, and after Monroe county was set off; he held the same office in the latter county."[1]

That was it. That was the sum total of nearly 91 years of life.

But there was more to Timothy Barnard. He represented all that made America great; that first generation of rebels turned heroes turned pioneers turned nation-builders. In a way, he was like the Forrest Gump of America's founding. He was in all the right places at all the right times.

And, for him, ultimately the right place was a home in a small rural town called Mendon in Monroe County.

Actually, at first it was neither Mendon nor Monroe County. It was Bloomfield and Ontario County. The home, however, remained firmly planted in the same location, roughly the corner of what is now West Bloomfield and Canfield roads just south of the Thruway.

But let's not get ahead of ourselves.

Timothy's father, Ebenezer Barnard, was born on January 9, 1725, in Hartford, Connecticut Colony. Ebenezer's mother Sarah Williamson, originally from Barnstable, Massachusetts Colony, died the next day, likely because of complications of childbirth.[2] Not much is known about

Ebenezer's father, Samuel Barnard, although it's felt that he came to Hartford from England sometime after 1700 and before marrying Sarah in 1714.³

What is clear is that, when the time came to decide between the Tory and the Patriot, Ebenezer Barnard knew where he stood. And so did his son, Timothy.

When 1776 called, Ebenezer Barnard answered. He served as Captain in a militia regiment led by Major Roger Newberry of Windsor, Connecticut. His son Timothy, then only 20 years old, served beside him as Drum Major.⁴

Much of what we know about Timothy Barnard's military record comes from depositions taken six decades later when he applied for his veteran's pension. These records were compiled and summarized by Anah Babcock Yates in a 1920 article published by the *Honeoye Falls Times*.

According to the GenWeb Monroe County, NY website, "Yates was one of the founders of the Rochester Historical Society and an active member of the Daughters of the American Revolution. She also was state genealogist of the New York Historical Society for many years. She died in August 1932. Mrs. Yates was a good genealogist but she didn't include many references. You should check for primary sources to verify this information."⁵

Yates' account of Timothy Barnard appears to be based on source material obtained through military records. She doesn't cite the exact source but given that the basic story is consistent with other accounts, including those of family members, it is reasonable to assume her article contains factual information.

In a nutshell, Timothy Barnard, born June 19, 1756, began his Revolutionary War service in July 1776 at the age of twenty. He was with Washington's troops at Valentine Hill when they retreated from New York City. He recalled "the Americans lost many in their retreat in crossing a marsh and creek near some mill."⁶

Later, Washington tasked him with carrying the soldiers' payroll in saddle bags from New York to Valley Forge. In a 1915 letter to *Daughters of the American Revolution Magazine*, Mrs. Fran. H. Barnard, wife of

Timothy's grandson, stated, "Washington thought that there was less danger of the money being stolen if it was carried in a casual manner; and Judge Timothy Barnard was never known to have had any lost while under his care."[7]

Speaking of "Judge," we'll get to that in a moment. Speaking of Valley Forge, some historians state Barnard was George Washington's "bodyguard" at Valley Forge, but there is no reliable source for that claim.

Continuing with his Revolutionary War record, it appears he worked with the French army during its time in America. He was at Yorktown when the British surrendered. Afterwards, Barnard was assigned to Jeremiah Wadsworth's Commissary Department. As a "principal conductor," he was given command of the third division of that group with the rank and pay of Major. Wadsworth left extensive accounting books and Barnard's name appears in them frequently.[8]

Barnard must have not been aware of these books because, when applying for his pension, he said he had no physical evidence or documentation of his service. He did rely on testimonials of fellow soldiers, though.

After the War, Barnard remained in Hartford until moving to the Genesee Country. In 1809, he came to Ontario County.[9] He built a house in Township 11, R. 5 on a portion of the "Eleven Thousand Acre Tract" owned by his father and Jeremiah Wadsworth.[10]

At the time, that was part of the Town of Bloomfield in Ontario County. Barnard became a judge in Ontario County, as his obituary says. In that capacity, he took an active role in creating the Town of Mendon. On Tuesday, April 6, 1813, he presided over Mendon's first town meeting.[11]

He was very active in the Ontario County Agricultural Society. He was named one of the first town managers for the newly formed group in 1819.[12] On October 3, 1820, at the Society's second annual fair, he won ten dollars as a farm owner cited for "best cultivation."[13]

He was involved in at least one meeting addressing the creation of Monroe County.[14] He became one of the first judges when that new county was created from Ontario County. By the time Lafayette came to visit in 1825, Timothy Barnard and his family were well placed in the broader community.

Ironically, a little more than a decade later in 1837 when he was applying for his pension and feeling he was short on "proof" of his service, Barnard would have benefited from recalling what Judge Ashley Sampson remembered about Lafayette's visit.

Sampson recalled, in a long piece published by the *Greece Press* in 1855, how Lafayette had met Revolutionary War veterans at Hoard's Tavern in the village of Rochester. The French general seemed to remember many of them, but Sampson felt, "that sometimes his memory was a little aided by his kindness of heart and his determination to recognize them."[15]

But one man stood out. Lafayette couldn't take his eyes off of him. He stared intensely for several moments before saying, "Sir it seems to me I have seen you before."[16]

It was Timothy Barnard. Sampson recalled the Judge's reply:

"Yes, General, you have seen me more than once. During the war I was engaged in the commissary department, and was often at headquarters, where I saw General Washington and yourself. By special permission from- Washington, I was present as a spectator at the Battle of Yorktown. I saw General Hamilton, under your command, sword in hand, with his brave followers storm one of the enemy's redoubts and with the bayonet, compel a surrender, 'without firing a gun. I saw the whole army, under the command of Washington, immediately afterwards pouring into the enemy's fort one broadside after another of cannon and grape shot, until I began to feel quite sure that the enemy must surrender. Very soon I saw a white flag arise and move towards the American quarters. Almost instantly the roar of cannon ceased. All was still for perhaps half an hour. Then I saw the whole of Lord Cornwallis' army march out and ground arms! Then I felt sure that the long struggle was over. Very soon afterwards I started North for my residence in Hartford, on horseback. On my route, I was often asked, are you from the

South? Upon my answering in the affirmative, the next inquiry was, 'What news?' My reply was, 'Glorious news! The whole army of Lord Cornwallis has surrendered!' Upon this announcement often would gray headed old men swing their hats in the air and exclaim, 'Glorious news! Now we shall have peace.' And so it turned out. And how much, General, we owe you."[17]

The sincerity of the emotion on Lafayette's face could not help but have affected all those in the room.

CHAPTER TWENTY-NINE:
DISPELLING MENDON MYTHS

By 1825, the road from Rochester to Canandaigua was a well-travelled road. Samuel Hildreth saw to that, although he didn't live long enough to see it first-hand.

Hildreth might be considered a first generation Western New Yorker. He was born on March 20, 1778, in what would become the town of Phelps in Ontario County. His parents had moved there from New Hampshire.[1] He moved to Pittsford in November 1814. There, he quickly established himself as a mover and shaker. He ran a store, rented to others, and operated a tavern. More important, he set up the first stage line from Rochester to Canandaigua.[2]

This was just part of a larger network of stages using his horse barn in Pittsford as a center of operations. He served as postmaster for the Town of Pittsford.[3] In 1815 he began running mail twice a week between Rochester and Canandaigua.[4] By August 1817, the Rochester to Canandaigua stage line had stops in Pittsford, Mendon, and East Bloomfield.[5]

Because this was the standard stagecoach route, it's reasonable to assume this is the route Lafayette took from Rochester to Canandaigua. We also know that, if Lafayette took this route, the man who blazed this trail wasn't there to see him. Samuel Hildreth died on April 20, 1824, more than a year before Lafayette passed through this road on Tuesday, June 7, 1825.

The exact route was not recorded in contemporary newspapers. The best report we have comes from the *Ontario Repository*, which wrote, "After receiving the hospitality of the citizens of Rochester, he was escorted to Mendon, where he was met by a deputation from the committee of Canandaigua, who, with a number of other gentlemen, accompanied him to this village, where he arrived last evening."[6]

An article published more than a century later claims, without citing sources, "General Lafayette was escorted to an awaiting carriage by

Colonels Brown and Riley and driven, with these officers, by Main Street and East Avenue, to Mendon Village, where a relay coach waited to carry the General as far as Canandaigua on his journey eastward. A repair job on the canal, east of Rochester, with no available water detour, made necessary the carriage ride from Rochester to Syracuse."[7]

Again, no contemporary report confirms either the exact route or who accompanied Lafayette in the carriage once it left Rochester. It would have been standard practice for the committee of arrangements to accompany Lafayette to a transfer point between any two destinations. They would then present the General and his travelling companions to the committee representing the next stop upon reaching this midpoint.

The small hamlet of Mendon was that midpoint between Rochester and Canandaigua. The entire town of Mendon had only 2,777 inhabitants, and most of them lived in the growing community of West Mendon, soon to be incorporated as the Village of Honeoye Falls. This was the original Ball Tract of Township 11, R.5, which had been purchased by Augustus and Peter B. Porter, (remember them?) and Zebulon Norton.[8] Norton would be the first to establish a homestead there, along with building some mills. Early on, this part of Mendon was called "Norton's Mills."

Ebenezer Barnard, who with Jeremiah Wadsworth owned half of a big chunk of that township called the "Eleven Thousand Acre Tract," never settled there.[9] Barnard's son Timothy, however, located to this tract and became a prominent citizen by the time Lafayette passed through. In fact, the Barnard family became and remained prominent for generations. Besides his progeny serving as supervisor of the Town of Mendon and as a U.S. Congressman, his great-great-grandson Kenneth Barnard Keating of Lima served a term as U.S. Senator before losing his bid for reelection to Robert F. Kennedy.

Being so prominent, it's easy to understand how later Lafayette stories stretched the truth to include people, places, and things that didn't really happen. These historical errors come at the hands of otherwise well-respected historians. To be honest, not all can be classified as "errors." They may merely be the result of lack of source citation with the original sources no longer readily available.

Timothy Barnard figures into one of these faux pas. A prolific writer of local history once penned a piece with his son telling a tale of Lafayette's visit to Mendon.[10] In it, they had Lafayette casually recognizing Barnard in the crowd. Granted, the authors cite their cousin (Kenneth Keating's grandmother) as the source. Apparently, she told them this story just before she died at age 100. Unfortunately, that may explain the inconsistency with eyewitness reports. We know, from Ashley Sampson's 1855 recollections, that Lafayette met Barnard at Hoard's Tavern in Rochester, not in the Hamlet of Mendon.[11]

Along the road to Canandaigua, there are other questionable calls of "Lafayette stopped here" (a riff on the equally dubious claims of "George Washington slept here"). Nearly all these accounts did not surface until a century or more after Lafayette's visit.

For example, the same article referenced above goes on to state that Lafayette stopped at Wangum Mills in Fishers, NY and met with Silas Pardee where he spoke from the porch of Beach's Tavern in Victor. This implies the carriages turned east at Mendon rather than go the usual south. There's no contemporary record stating that Lafayette visited either of these locations and the authors fail to cite their sources.

Closer to Rochester, two articles make the claim that Lafayette stayed at the Stone-Tolan House, then a tavern, in Brighton[12] and was a guest at the Phoenix Hotel in Pittsford.[13] He most certainly didn't stay at either of these locations. While it is certainly possible Lafayette may have passed by these two buildings (assuming he did exit Rochester via East Avenue), the most he could have done was pause and shake a few hands in the vicinity of those taverns.

Finally, there's the mistaken report that Lafayette dined in the Mendon Hotel.[14] This popular stagecoach stop was located in the Hamlet of Mendon. It's very likely Lafayette stopped near or at that location to change carriages. The story was repeated several times over the years.

It's false. You can attribute it to a misunderstanding of the contemporaneous report in the *Albany Argus* what, after mentioning Mendon, reported "After receiving the hospitality of the citizens of Rochester, he was escorted to Mendon, where he was met by a deputation from the committee of Canandaigua, who, with a number of other gentlemen, accompanied him to this village, where he arrived last evening. Here he partook of a supper, which was served up in a handsome style, at the Hotel."[15]

It's a bit misleading and one can easily see where a reader might mistake "this village" to mean Mendon instead of Canandaigua. Had one read the original article, which appeared in the *Ontario Repository*, (see above), then the reference to "this village" might have been more obvious.

Here's what we do know: what happened when Lafayette's carriage arrived in the Hamlet of Mendon. It comes from the diary of a young man who was in the "Ontario Brass Band" and who went to Mendon to receive the General.

"The General was received from the Rochester committee at Mendon, and placed in the finest coach that could be obtained, and drawn by four grey horses under the hands of Mr. Samuel Greenleaf. A lengthy procession of carriages and horsemen, with the multitude on foot, and was finally formed, and escorted by the band and martial music (alternating), they marched down Main street [in Canandaigua]."[16]

Like so many small communities, the Hamlet of Mendon didn't offer much more than a passing fancy on Lafayette's farewell tour. But unlike the others, we know that Lafayette did stop there.

If only to change carriages.

Chapter Thirty:
John Greig Lives The American Dream

The sun rose on Tuesday, June 7, 1825, signaling the start of a new day. For John Greig, it would prove among the most momentous days of his life—so far. It would prove anyone can attain their American dream.

By that morning, Greig had lived a tad more than a quarter of a century in his adopted home country. Born in Moffat, Dumfries and Galloway, Scotland on August 6, 1779,[1] he immigrated to the United States in 1797 after attending the Edinburgh High School.[2] Only eighteen when he sailed to America, no doubt like many his age, Greig sought to make his mark.

He certainly did.

But not immediately.

Greig spent his first few months living in New York City before moving to Albany. He relocated to Canandaigua in April 1800. It's likely this move came about because of John Johnstone, assistant to Charles Williamson. Williamson, a native of Balgray, Scotland, was hired as agent for the Sir William Pulteney, John Hornby and Patrick Colquhoun (later just the Hornby portion) Estate in the Genesee Country. When Johnstone returned to Scotland, he met Greig and convinced the latter to go back to America with him.[3]

Upon arriving in Canandaigua, Greig became a student at law in the office of Nathaniel W. Howell (who would later become Judge Howell). In 1804, at the age of twenty-five, John Greig was admitted to the bar and formed a partnership with Howell. Two years later, upon the death of Williamson, he was appointed agent of the Estate of Hornby and Colquhoun.[4]

What happened next was nothing less than remarkable. It was summed up as follows in a biography written a century later:

"Mingling with his professional duties the arduous ones consequent upon the sale and settlement of large contracts of wild lands, professional eminence could hardly be expected, yet in early days, when there were 'giants in the land,' when the bar of Western New York had in its front rank a class of men hardly equaled today, his legal brethren found in the young Scot a man possessed of sound legal acquirements which placed him in the first ranks of those lawyers whose ability is handed down as more than ordinary. Especially he recommended himself to their esteem by a high sense of honor, and a courtesy which ruled his conduct at the bar as well as in the business and social relations of life."[5]

It could certainly be said that the year 1806 was the turning point in young Greig's life. Not only had he assumed the job that would propel him to great fortune (and the attendant dominant position), but in that same year he married Clarissa Chapin, the daughter of Captain Israel Chapin and granddaughter of General Israel Chapin, Superintendent of Indian Affairs. If anything, this marriage enhanced Greig's social standing.[6]

By odd coincidence in our "it's a small world" story, 1806 was the same year Augustus Porter left Canandaigua and moved his family to the future Niagara Falls. Who did Porter sell his Canandaigua house to? None other than John Greig, Esq.[7]

From that point, things began to move rapidly in the life of the esteemed Mr. Greig. It was as if the hands of destiny had captured him, guiding him into the current of history, both past and present. After all, within sight of his new home stood the place where Major General John Sullivan set up camp on his march to impede the Seneca from providing military support to their British allies during the Revolutionary War. Only a short walk away, sat the Canandaigua Academy.[8] Greig (along with Howell and three others) would serve on the committee to superintend the academy.[9]

In 1812, Greig would join with fifteen others to announce they intended to apply to charter a bank called the Ontario Farmers' Bank in the Town of Canandaigua. At the same time, he and six others disclosed they would apply to the State Legislature to incorporate the "Village of Canandaigua."[10]

Well, if at first you don't succeed, try, try again.

A year later, Greig would be a part of twenty that would again ask the Legislature to incorporate a bank. This one was called "Ontario Bank."[11] This time, the effort would prove successful. On March 15, 1813, the Legislature would pass an act incorporating Ontario Bank.[12] Greig would serve on the Board of Directors.[13] In 1820, he would be elevated to president.[14]

While the new bank opened its doors in 1813, it would be until 1815 that the Village of Canandaigua would be incorporated.[15]

In the meantime, Greig's American dream moved forward.

In 1816, the commissioners of the Canal and Locks Committee appointed Greig (among a couple dozen others) as a receiver of subscriptions (including land money) for the proposed new canal.[16] In 1819, the Ontario County Agricultural Society was established. Greig was named Secretary.[17]

In 1823, as reported at the time, a treaty "between the Chiefs of the Seneca Indians, and U. States commissioners" made "about 17,000 acres of valuable land on the Genesee river" available.[18] John Greig (along with Henry B. Gibson) purchased this tract and began offering it for sale. Known as the "Gardeau Tract" or "White woman's reservation"[19] (because that's where Mary Jemison lived), it would later become the heart of Letchworth State Park.

A year later, Greig would be named a director of the newly incorporated Western Fire Insurance Company.[20]

Finally, in mid-January 1825, the New York State Senate and Assembly overwhelmingly voted to appoint John Greig a regent of the State University to replace De Witt Clinton who resigned.[21]

There would be greater achievements to come in the life of John Greig, but on the morning of June 7, 1825, you could see the Scotsman had already achieved his American dream.

But the best was about to happen in just a few short hours.

Chapter Thirty-One:
Canandaigua Anxiously Waits Before Jubilation And An Elegant Supper

The young boy was no different from anyone else in the town of Canandaigua. Anxious, fretting, full of anticipation, on the morning of Tuesday, June 7, 1825, they all waited for the word they knew was coming but feared it might not.

Located on the northern tip of the lake that bears its name, Canandaigua housed the first land office in Western New York.

"Most people are not aware of Ontario County. as the 'Queen of Counties' or that Canandaigua was the hub of all Western New York until the opening of the canal just a few years before the visit and that when the War of 1812 threatened our region Rochester was still insignificant!" says Leif Herrgesell, Town Historian for Canandaigua. "Nathaniel Rochester lived in Bloomfield and kept much of his business in what is now West Bloomfield and was there when he laid out the plan for the city that bears his name. For that era, the newspaper of record had been in Canandaigua, all banking, land office, courts and major commerce was carried out in the village and people rode regularly from Geneseo and other points to Canandaigua in order to do business. Monroe County had only been created 4 years before Lafayette's tour! It was a tremendous time in history and Lafayette got to see the corn growing between the stumps as the wilderness faded into pasture."

This former Seneca stronghold sat on the old Genesee Trail, or Central Trail, that cut through the heart of the Iroquois Confederacy. Today we know it as Routes 5 & 20. Back then it had various names, from the Great Genesee Road to the Seneca Turnpike to the Ontario and Genesee Turnpike. Whatever you called it, it was the road everyone heading east or west traveled on.

Lafayette would soon be one of those travelers.

Or would he?

When word first came that Lafayette was visiting the far end of Western New York, the leaders of Canandaigua held a quick assembly. As a result of that meeting, two prominent citizens—Colonel William Blossom, who purchased the Canandaigua Hotel from Amos Read the previous December,[1] and Judge Moses Atwater, a director of Ontario Bank and member of other civic committees, were dispatched to Buffalo. Their mission: do their best to convince Lafayette to stop in their bustling town as he traveled east to Boston.[2]

There was a genuine concern as there were reports Lafayette would bypass the Ontario and Genesee Turnpike in favor of the newly established Erie Canal.[3]

So, the boy, like everyone else, paced with worry. How long would he—and they—have to wait?

It turns out the wait wasn't long at all. Early in the morning, an express messenger rode in from nearby Rochester. "Lafayette is coming!" was the word. The courier promised the General would appear in Canandaigua later that afternoon.[4]

Once the word was received, it spread like wildfire. Those assigned to escort duty quickly gathered. They hopped in their carriages or on their horses. Samuel Greenleaf led a team of four gray horses, pulling "the finest coach that could be obtained." This would be Lafayette's ride. Off they went to Mendon.[5]

The boy had other things on his mind. He was in the Ontario Brass Band. Led by Asa Spaulding, they played an important role in the festivities. About sundown, they marched to the head of Main Street. At roughly half-past eight, the first sighting of the General was announced.[6]

If you thought the people went crazy at the initial early morning announcement, anticipating the approaching General was just too much. The good citizens of Canandaigua simply couldn't contain their excitement. With the firing of the cannon announcing Lafayette's imminent arrival, the best laid plans of an orderly procession went out the door. The crowd went wild, jockeying for the best seats, all searching for the ideal position to get a good glimpse of the Nation's Guest.[7]

Finally, a mature calm settled everyone down. They formed a "lengthy procession of carriages and horsemen, with the multitude on foot" to escort the precious cargo in Greenleaf's carriage down Main Street. The band led the way, alternating with martial music. Cannon salutes were fired from Arsenal hill. The spreading twilight only added to the elegance of the occasion. The darkening skies made the lights from the buildings along Main Street twinkle like diamonds in the sky. The young boy took a look at Blossom's hotel and Kingsley's tavern opposite it. The top-to-bottom illumination dazzled him.[8]

His diary doesn't say whether the awe he was experiencing interfered with his playing.

As he marched down Main Street, the young boy could see women waving their white handkerchiefs. "Welcome," they mouthed as the General passed in his carriage. The boy noted Captain Ira Merrill was there. He was in command of an artillery company, and they proudly displayed their six pounder. He saw Captain James Lyon, too. Captain Lyon led a company of thirty cavalrymen mounted on gray horses.[9]

Countless people, not only from Canandaigua, but from adjacent communities, lined the streets hoping to get an up close and personal view of the General. Some wished Lafayette wasn't in such a hurry.[10] However, that didn't appear to have diminished the honor of his presence.

As the procession came to the hotel, it split to the right and to the left, opening a promenade through which Lafayette's coach could be driven directly to the front door of Blossom's place. As the General stepped down from the carriage, the crowd pressed in.[11]

The committee greeted the General and introduced him to nearly 100 ladies and gentlemen. Once inside the hotel, they had an "elegant" dinner.[12]

Our young friend, who would write his experiences the next day in his diary, was very lucky. As a member of the Ontario Brass Band, he was one of the few allowed into the hotel. Once inside, the doors were shut and guarded.[13]

At about ten o'clock in the evening, the boy and his fellow band members headed out onto the balcony. He peered over the edge. The crowd hadn't moved. It was still there. Anxious. Excited. Anticipating. Suddenly, the General stepped out. Men held candles to each side of his face so the crowd could see him. He took a bow and smiled at the people. He offered a quick speech. It contained the kind words he shared at every stop he made. He added he wished he could have arrived in the daylight. He ended with a polite bow and then returned to the room from which he emerged.[14]

Here's the boy's eyewitness report, as he saw it from the front row at the seat of the action:

> "The General spoke very slow—in broken English—and it was quite difficult to understand him. His son was with him on the balcony. They passed into a large room assigned to them. While on the balcony, I had a fine view of him. In the large room, the ceremony of introduction and a promiscuous hand-shaking took place. The General grasped the hand with much vigor and cordiality. He was quite a stout built man—full florid face, and seemingly very healthy—yet he showed signs of fatigue."[15]

As the evening came to a close, and Lafayette's long day was ending, it was John Greig's time to shine. Of all the people in Canandaigua, and despite the dinner occurring in the hotel, it would be John Greig, who would provide Lafayette with a place to rest for the night.

Greig, who immigrated from Scotland more than twenty-five years earlier, was about to experience the ultimate American dream. He was about to host a hero of the American Revolution. At the conclusion of the hotel event, Lafayette was taken to Greig's mansion where he retired for the evening.

One wishes Greig (or his wife) had a diary in which to record the experience of that evening. For sure Lafayette didn't go immediately to bed. He was too polite not to have some late-night chit chat, away from the crowd, sitting across the kitchen table, in the quiet serenity of the family's home.

Chapter Thirty-Two: How Commonality Saved Captain Williamson And Western New York

He was a proud Tory and Captain in the British army who volunteered to fight for King George III against the rebellious colonists. She was a proud Patriot whose father graciously saw in this prisoner of war a common human element.

Before we get into this backstory, let's review why it's so important.

In December 1786, the states of New York and Massachusetts agreed to resolve a conflict started by the kings of England. Those monarchs made a royal mess of Western New York, at one time or another granting rights to all or portions of it to no less than five colonies.

By the end of the American Revolution, three states had claims to the Greater Western New York region: New York, Massachusetts, and Connecticut (a sliver along the southern tier). With Connecticut quickly quitting its claim, New York and Massachusetts stood nose-to-nose. With the Articles of Confederation dissolving, the two states decided to circumvent that ineffective parchment and meet in neutral territory. Ironically, this meeting took place in the state of Connecticut's capital city.

Those meetings in Hartford proved fruitful. New York and Massachusetts signed the Treaty of Hartford on December 16, 1786. The agreement gave New York political jurisdiction over Western New York but granted the State of Massachusetts preemptive economic rights.

In other words, anyone wishing to develop the land for settlement needed to do two things. They had to purchase the land from the Seneca. Before they could do that, they needed to purchase from Massachusetts the right to negotiate with that member of the Iroquois Confederacy.

Oliver Phelps and Nathaniel Gorham were the first to purchase those preemptive rights. By November 1790, they had sold about a third of the tract between Preemption Line and the Genesee River. When they failed to make payment on the lien Massachusetts held, the rights of the land reverted back to that state. Robert Morris bought the remaining 1,264,000 acres of undeveloped land. He then turned around and sold it to Sir William Pulteney, a British citizen[1].

Only not quite. First, Morris didn't sell to Pulteney. He sold to an "Association" which included Pulteney, John Hornby, and Patrick Colquhoun.[2] Second, because the members of this Association were non-resident aliens, they could not hold deeds to the land. For this, they hired an agent, Captain Charles Williamson. Captain Williamson came to America, became a naturalized citizen, and took the deeds from Morris, putting them in his own name on behalf of the members of The Association.[3] And the rest, as they say, is Western New York history.

How did this boy from Balgray, Scotland, find his way to America?

This wasn't his first time on our continent.

At the outbreak of hostilities in the colonies, Williamson joined the British army. He was officially pronounced an ensign to the 25th Regiment of Foot, commanded by Lord George Henry Lennox. He must have impressed the leaders of the so-called "Edinburgh Regiment" because on June 4th, 1777, he found himself promoted to lieutenant. In 1778, he earned the rank of captain-lieutenant. Finally, on January 17, 1781, the government publication announced he had become a captain.[4]

His unit finally assigned to combat in America, Williamson immediately set sail for the rebellious colonies. He never made it.

Well, he did, but not in the way he intended.

Within sight of the New England shore, his ship ran into a French privateer, which quickly overwhelmed the British crew. The French took them all prisoner, including Captain Williamson. The soldier was brought first to Newburyport before being transferred to Boston. A severely wounded prisoner of war, Williamson was held at the home of Abagail Newell's family. Apparently, it didn't matter that he was an enemy combatant. What mattered was that he was a fellow human being who needed nursing. Abagail was more than obliged to offer such and Charles was more than happy to accept.[5]

There had to be more to what they found in common with each other because, when released on a prisoner exchange in 1781, Abagail went with the captain. The two were very shortly married and spent the next ten years living at his father's estate in Scotland.[6]

A decade later, when thoughts of war had been replaced by thoughts of making money, the British financiers of The Association turned to Williamson to act as their agent. For Charles and Abagail, there was no "us against them." Their actions proved this. They eagerly returned to the United States.

Upon accepting the deeds from Morris, Williamson wrote to Colquhoun. In his letter, he told his backer, "These disinterested accounts, from different people, put the quality of the land in the fairest view. The next object then is to take some liberal and decisive steps to bring them to their value."[7]

After reviewing the land himself, Williamson opened land offices in Bath and Geneva. The former was to be a new settlement, which he laid out in 1792. That same year he forged a crude road to the then unknown territory.[8] To show others it was safe for their families, he built a small log hut there and moved his wife and children into it.[9]

For Geneva, he saw other potential. It already had the crude beginnings of a major east-west road. The Genesee Trail of the Iroquois offered some means of common travel, and settlements had already sprung up on the waterways it crossed. The first few houses of Geneva on Seneca Lake provided one such example.

Williamson took one look at this and immediately decided it wouldn't do. He preferred the much higher bank on the west side of the lake and laid out a street at its summit. To preserve the pristine view, he prohibited the building of any houses between the road and the lake.[10] This was in 1793. There was only one problem. It wasn't clear that he owned the land.

Oh, he bought it. The State issued the land patents and Williamson bought them all. But the State did this before formally accepting the new Preemption Line. The Line, as originally drawn by Colonel Hugh Maxwell in 1788, veered too far to the west. When Joseph Ellicott resurveyed the Line, he determined it should be shifted to the east by a few miles on the shore of Lake Ontario. This triangular slice is known as "The Gore."[11]

Until the State approved the new line, Williamson's deed could not be acted upon. This would inhibit development in the two settlements he aimed to improve: Geneva and Sodus. Fortunately, the State passed legislation favorable to Williamson and Robert Morris released the land to Williamson (a total of 84,000 acres).[12]

With the thumbs up from the State, Williamson wasted no time in developing Geneva. To encourage settlement, he built a spacious hotel there. He set aside two rooms in that hotel for his use. To gauge the success of his efforts in Geneva, one need only look at the population statistics. In 1792, the year before he began to lay out a new version of Geneva, the settlement had no more than three or four families. By 1800, it had at least sixty families, with more coming.[13]

At the same time he was making plans for Geneva, Williamson set his eyes on Sodus. There, he would prove he had more in common with America than with the British army.

While his London employers may have left the war behind, the same could not be said for others. In this case the "other" was John Graves Simcoe, Lieutenant Governor of Upper Canada, who felt Western New York ought to remain in British hands. Other Tories residing in Canada (and their allied sympathizers in America, including the Seneca) plotted to create a new state by having Western New York secede from New York State (but that story could fill a book). Simcoe took a more direct—and military—approach.

You can hardly blame Simcoe's demeanor. Britain was still at war with France. If America would ally itself with the French, that meant Britain would also be at war with America. He had to be prepared.

Upon finding out Williamson sought to establish a settlement on Sodus Bay, Simcoe dispatched his underling Lieutenant Roger Hale Sheaffe with a message for Williamson. Here's how Williamson recounted that exchange:

Lieutenant Sheaffe: *"I am commissioned by Governor Simcoe to deliver the papers, and require an answer."*

Williamson: *"I am a citizen of the United States, and under their authority and protection, I possess these lands. I know no right that his*

Britannic Majesty, or Gov. Simcoe, has to interfere, or molest me. The only allegiance I owe to any power on earth, is to the United States; and so far from being intimidated by threats from people I have no connection with, I shall proceed with my improvements; and nothing but superior force shall make me abandon the place. Is the protest of Gov. Simcoe intended to apply to Sodus, exclusively?"

Lieutenant Sheaffe: *"By no means! It is intended to embrace all the Indian lands purchased since the peace of 1783."*

Williamson: *"And what are Gov. Simcoe's intentions, supposing the protest is disregarded?"*

Lieutenant Sheaffe: *"I am merely the official bearer of the papers; but I have a further message to deliver from Gov. Simcoe; which is that he reprobates your conduct exceedingly for endeavoring to obtain flour from Upper Canada; and that should he permit it, it would be acknowledging the right of the United States to these Indian lands."*[14]

To show his teeth, Simcoe stole a barrel of flour from Williamson. His ire inspired, Williamson set off a nasty dialog between the former British captain and those representing the current British General. The Washington administration stepped in (with President Washington drafted his own snarky letter to the British Embassy) and Williamson was told to "make preparations for defense." At the same time, the Governor of New York State gave him a colonel's commission.[15]

After a brief skirmish not involving Williamson, war was averted, at least for another generation.

Williamson added more to Western New York than simply a colorful story or two. He helped to develop most of the empty space left by Phelps and Gorham. He represented Ontario County in the New York State Legislature from 1796 to 1798.[16] The State appointed him a commission to lay out and open various state roads, including the main road from the Genesee River to Buffalo Creek and to Lewiston.[17]

The Association originally contracted Williamson for a seven-year term, but he served beyond that. When he finally closed the books with them in 1800, the parting was amicable. Sir William Pulteney instructed Williamson's successor to deal with the former agent in a most honorable way. The financier left Williamson with farms, property in both Geneva and Bath, as well as other assets and personal property. Williamson remained in America for several years before returning to Scotland no later than 1804.[18.]

Details of Williamson's death vary. General Peter B. Porter, in an address he prepared to deliver in Geneva, stated that Williamson died in route from England to South America with the idea of participating in the "dawnings of liberty and symptoms of revolution."[19] Another story says the British government appointed him "governor of one of the West India Islands" and he died aboard ship on his way there.[20]

Perhaps it's best to leave with the following summary of Captain Charles Williamson, courtesy of Guy H. McMaster's 1853 biography of him:

> "Captain Williamson having, toward the close of the last century; fairly established himself at Bath, was the greatest man in all the land of the West. His dominion extended from Pennsylvania to Lake Ontario; a province of twelve hundred thousand acres owned him as its lord; Indian warriors hailed him as a great chief; settlements on the Genesee, by the Seneca, and at the bays of Ontario, acknowledged him as their founder; and furthermore, by commission from the Governor of the State of New York, he was styled Colonel in the militia of the Commonwealth, and at the head of his bold foresters, stood in a posture of defiance before the Pro-Consul of Canada, who beheld with indignation a rival arising in the Genesee forests, and taking possession of land which he claimed for his own sovereign, with a legend of New Englanders and Pennsylvanians, mighty men with the axe and rifle, and with colonies of Scotch and Irish boys, who cleaved to the rebellious subjects of the King."[21]

How ever he did it, Captain Williamson found the commonalities in everyone he met. In a life lived constantly with two sides, he saw the unity of one. When confronted with those too arrogant to see how we are all alike in some way, he never backed down from challenging them. That spirit not only forged a new frontier, it saved it in its infancy.

Emphasizing his commonality with them, Charles Williamson successfully bridged the many different cultures he dealt with. In this manner, he displayed the same ability (and bravery) as Lafayette. And while he would not live long enough to meet the Frenchman, Williamson was instrumental in establishing the many places General Lafayette would travel on and to in the Greater Western New York Region.

Chapter Thirty-Three: Pomp and Circumstance Before Lunch In Geneva

General Lafayette rose the morning of Wednesday, June 8, 1825, shortly after sunrise. At 7 o'clock that morning, the French entourage bid John Greig adieu. They climbed aboard their waiting carriage and a military escort led them onto the old Genesee Road (and then the Seneca Turnpike). About ten miles down the road, at Ball's tavern, they'd meet the committee from Geneva and transfer their precious cargo to them.[1]

For the good citizens of Geneva, the largest settlement in the Greater Western New York region, Lafayette was a long time coming. A couple of weeks before, the village appointed a committee of eleven upstanding men to invite the Nation's Guest to visit their fair village. They drafted a letter dated May 28, 1825, for that purpose. Appealing to his sense of nostalgia for the Revolutionary War, they promised, "Our vicinity was the theatre of some very interesting operations, during the Revolutionary war, in which you acted so distinguished a part, with a generosity and disinterestedness which are without a parallel in the annals of the world."[2]

They dispatched the letter immediately to Buffalo. Since they weren't sure where the General was, and if the letter would find him, they sent two men with a second copy of the letter to Rochester. There, they would wait for him. Upon his arrival, they delivered the letter and repeated the citizens of Geneva were most desirous of his honoring them with a visit. Lafayette could not refuse, and word of his acceptance was sent by express to Geneva on June 7th that Lafayette's party would arrive in Geneva the next day.[3]

That Lafayette would accept the invitation shouldn't surprise you for two reasons. First, he rarely said no. Second, the two people sent from Geneva were friends of Lafayette. Major James Rees, a member of the committee, clerked for Robert Morris in Philadelphia during the Revolutionary War. While recovering from his injuries at Brandywine in Philadelphia, Lafayette became good friends with both Morris and Rees. Monsieur Camus accompanied Rees to Rochester. Camus had set up a French language school in Geneva in March of 1825. Among his credentials: a letter of recommendation from Lafayette.[4]

The Geneva Committee had little time to prepare. They immediately informed the neighboring towns. The Yates County Court, being in session, promptly adjourned. Everyone worked to make sure the General would have an unforgettable experience. Captain Sherman, of Yates County, assembled his company of cavalry. William S. De Zeng offered his barouche for the purpose of conveying the General and his companions. Joining De Zeng and Sherman's company was a convoy of private citizens on horseback.[5]

Early on the morning of June 8th, the word came that Lafayette was ready to leave Canandaigua. The reception committee left for Ball's tavern, seven or eight miles to the west of Geneva on the turnpike. There, from his Canandaigua escort, they received the General, along with his son, George Washington Lafayette, his secretary, André-Nicolas Levasseur, and his friends Monsieur Camus and a Mr. Sion.[6]

Meanwhile, just outside the village, several military companies stood at the ready. Captain Lemuel W. Ruggles and Captain Means each commanded a company of cavalry. They were joined by three companies of artillery, commanded by Captain Manning, Captain Bartle, and Lieutenant Lum (for Captain Bayly), two companies of riflemen, commanded by Captain Ottley and Captain Van Auken, and Ensign Brizse led a company of light infantry. With them stood officers of neighboring regiments in full uniform as well as a great many civilians.[7]

The General was spotted at about 10 o'clock.[8] A shot rang out to announce his arrival. The waiting companies all fell into line. Led by Captain Richard M. Bayly, Marshal of the day, with assistance from Captain Dox, Lieutenant Stanley, and Mr. Butler, the long parade marched into the village between two lines of private citizens directing them to the Public Square.[9]

Upon entering the village, Lafayette was greeted "by music from the Banks, the joyous acclamations of the multitude, and the roar of ordnance." The six elegantly adorned white horses leading his open carriage stopped at the Public Square. The General stepped down and, with his suite and the Geneva committee, walked across the square towards a "splendid arch."[10]

Supported by two columns, the arch was "adorned with wreaths and flowers." On one side it proclaimed, "Welcome Lafayette" and on the other side, "Washington and Lafayette." The platform and stage were carpeted. The committee had arranged for a sofa to be placed on the stage for the committee and its guests. From the stage, they had a magnificent view of the lake.[11]

As Lafayette approached the stage, young ladies on either side gently tossed flowers in his direction. They did this while singing an ode composed by the 14-year-old daughter of Doctor Lummis.[12] They sang:

> *"Welcome, Patriot, to the shore*
> > *Where none but Freemen tread!*
> *Welcome to the Land once more*
> > *Where Freedom's warriors bled;*
> > *Columbia's sons shall ne'er forget*
> > *The brave, illustrious La Fayette!*
> *When wrapt in war a terrific gloom,*
> > *Encompass'd round with foes,*
> *You left your country and your home,*
> > *To bleed for foreign woes;*
> *Columbia's sons will ne'er forget*
> > *Their Benefactor, La Fayette!"*[13]

All around, the people of Geneva cheered. From the windows of the houses surrounding the square, women welcomed Lafayette by waiving their handkerchiefs. Closer, but behind the singing ladies, stood a large gathering of men and women, including several Revolutionary War veterans who wore badges to recognize them as such.[14]

After the General and his party were introduced by Major Rees, Colonel Whiting, formally greeting Lafayette to Geneva, gave the following keynote address:

"General La Fayette:"
"The Citizens of Geneva are sensible that to you, who have received the homage of a whole people, their tribute of welcome and congratulations can afford nothing of novelty or interest. We however partake, in common with all our countrymen, in the deep feelings of gratitude and love which your invaluable service in the great cause of American Freedom has inspired; and we were anxious to welcome you to this our free and happy country, to acknowledge that we enjoy this smiling land, with all its blessings of Religion and Laws, under Providence, from the wisdom and valor of our Fathers and their generous Allies; and that among those our benefactors to whom our hearts are drawn by the strongest emotions of gratitude, You, Sir, will ever hold a distinguished rank."

"It is our happiness that we this morning are permitted to realize the truth of history, by having as our Guest, the man of the present age so justly celebrated for his devotedness to the promotion of the great cause of Civil Freedom in both Hemispheres, and for his sufferings under the proscription of Tyrants, the eternal enemies of Liberty."

"We congratulate you that you have in your age witnessed so much of national happiness, resulting from the practical illustration of those liberal principles of government, for the maintenance of which your youthful and disinterested valor was exerted: And our earnest hope is, that your years may by extended until the great maxim of government that 'life, liberty, and the pursuit of happiness' are among the 'unalienable rights' of man, shall have been recognized and adopted by every civilized people on earth."

"In the name of the Magistrates of this Village—in the name of all my Fellow Citizens—I bid you Welcome: And I do not mistake their feeling when I say, that there is not a heart in all this assemblage

which does not pray that your latter days may be as happy as you early life has been honorable to yourself, and useful to our country."[16]

The General responded in kind after which he inspected two brass cannons, both captured during the Revolutionary War, including one from the Battle of Yorktown. After this, he was escorted to the Franklin House where he and 200 others had lunch prepared by Mr. Noyes.[16]

Before the food was served, Lafayette had an opportunity to meet with Revolutionary War veterans. Once again, as in his other visits, familiar stories were shared, he met with those who served under him, and still others who simply knew him. An eyewitness reported, "The age and venerable appearance of these old soldiers excited the most tender sympathies, and all who witnessed the interview were deeply affected by it."[17]

Once he finished his lunch, Lafayette devoted time towards the men, women, and children who went out of their way to see him. Their faces beamed with delight, having had the honor to experience up close the venerable war hero.[18]

At one o'clock in the afternoon, after a non-stop three-hour tour of joyful Geneva, Lafayette and company boarded De Zeng's spacious carriage and Captain Ruggles, with his troop of cavalry, several members of the committee, and many citizens on horseback and in carriages, escorted the Nation's Guest to Waterloo.[19]

Unbeknownst to those smiling happy faces, a terrible tragedy had just occurred at their next destination.

Chapter Thirty-Four:
The Great Central Trail
Becomes The State Road

As General Dwight D. Eisenhower led the Allied effort into the heart of the Nazi regime, he couldn't help but notice the transportation infrastructure that strengthened the defense of his opponent. Hitler began construction of his *Reichautobahn* in the 1930s. Although designed primarily for civilian use, war reports during the Eisenhower's push into Germany in 1944 and 1945 repeatedly referenced the autobahn, "Hitler's Superhighway."[1]

Impressed by these autobahns, Eisenhower proposed an interstate highway system once he became President.[2] It was quickly understood to have military value both in terms of transporting military vehicles and civilian defense.[3,4]

Eisenhower didn't need to wage a world war to learn of the military advantage of roads. Of course, as his headquarters was stationed in England during the war, he would no doubt have traveled on what were once roadways of ancient Rome. Those were primarily military roads. Since Rome relied on its military, its roads were built for the purpose of making it easier for troops to move from one place to another as quickly as possible.[5]

While intended for military use, once that use dissipated, roads proved to offer another advantage. Like natural modes of transport (waterways like streams and rivers), these man-made transportation routes spawned settlements and all that followed.[6]

We often compare the Iroquois Confederacy to the Roman Empire and certainly the two have acclaimed themselves in their military prowess. While lacking the technology of the Romans, the Confederacy also relied on "roads."[7] They weren't exactly autobahns, but they got the job done.

Of all the trails spread across the old Iroquois Confederacy, none was as important as the Great Central Trail. As referenced earlier, in the Greater Western New York Region this trail travels roughly along the Onondaga Escarpment. Barely a foot to a foot-and-a-half wide, centuries of use by man and animal wore it deeply into the ground. Depending on the nature of the soil it cut through, by the time of pioneer emigration, it had become a channel of anywhere from between three and six inches deep. Sometimes the depth could reach twelve inches.[8]

And don't think it only looked that way after the Revolutionary War. When Jesuits saw this trail in the 1600s, they called it "The Beaten Road." Still, it was smooth enough for Indian travelers to cover thirty to forty miles a day on it.[9]

But consider this: imagine walking on it in the midst of a torrential downpour. You'd be literally walking on (and in) water!

When New Englanders came to establish new lives in the Genesee Country, they had little choice but to take this path. Without the benefit of roads, the Central Trail represented the only route to the interior of the Greater Western New York region.[10]

That was about to change.

Dr. Peter Wilson (a.k.a., Wa-o-wa-wâ-na-onk, or *They heard his voice*) succinctly summed what happened as soon as the rush of emigration started. He told the New York Historical Society at its May 1847 meeting, "You have heard a history of the great Indian trails, the geography of the state of New York, before it was known to the Pale Faces. The land of Ga-nun-no, was once laced by these trails from Albany to Buffalo, trails that my people had trod for centuries—worn so deep by the feet of the Iroquois, that they became your own roads of travel, when my people no longer walked in them. Your highways still lie in those paths, the same lines of communication bind one part of the 'Long House' to another. My friend has told you that the Iroquois have no monuments. These are their monuments. The land of Ga-nun-no, the Empire State, is our monument."[11]

Now, how did this "Iroquois monument" evolve from being the Great Central Trail to the State Road to Routes 5&20? As you might expect, what started as a simple exercise quickly became a complicated mess that took more than a century to clean up.

By 1789, Phelps and Gorham finally resolved the issues they had in formally acquiring the land between the Genesee River and Preemption Line whose rights they purchased from Massachusetts. Almost immediately, settlers began to trickle in. They had no choice but to take the Great Central Trail. Settlements began to grow along that path: Auburn, Seneca Falls, Waterloo, Geneva, and Canandaigua. Phelps and Gorham set up their land office in Canandaigua.

Seeing a need for an improved road, the New York State legislature passed an Act on March 22, 1794, to build a road from "Old Fort Schuyler" (now Utica, NY) to the Genesee River. Legally known as the "Great Genesee Road" or the "Main Genesee Road" (until 1800 as we'll soon find out), it was extended to Buffalo by law in 1798.[12]

The law required it to be "laid out 6 rods wide," but allowed the Commissioners to open it four rods wide. They just had to build it "in a line as nearly straight as the situation of the country will admit." Furthermore, as a State Road, towns and counties were forbidden from altering it in any way.[13]

In 1796, the State passed a law "mending the highway commonly called the Great Genesee Road and the bridges thereon."[14] And in 1797, another law was passed appropriating $2,200 "for opening and improving the road commonly called the Great Genesee road, in all its extent from Old Fort Schuyler in the county of Herkimer to Geneva in the county of Ontario."[15]

Despite this, Charles Williamson, who was responsible for overseeing the road from Fort Schuyler to the Genesee River, reported that the road was "little better than an Indian trail." Nonetheless, with the necessary work completed, the road opened on September 30, 1799. To commemorate the event, a stagecoach left Utica. It arrived at the Genesee River terminus three days later.[16]

Things changed on April 1, 1800 (was it a coincidence that this happened on April Fools' Day?). The State passed a law that transformed the Genesee Road into a turnpike. Charles Williamson was named one of the Directors (so was Israel Chapin). For some unknown reason, the law gave the road the formal name "The President and Directors of the Seneca Road Company." Seriously? That's the official name. Apparently, everyone thought it too wordy and just referred to it as the "Seneca Turnpike." [17]

As a turnpike, the specs were more demanding. The law said, "The road was to 'be six rods in width… cleared of all timber excepting trees of ornament, and to be improved in the manner following, to wit, in the middle of the said road there shall be formed a space not less than twenty four feet in breadth, the center of which shall be raised fifteen inches above the sides, rising towards the middle by gradual arch, twenty feet of which shall be covered with gravel or broken stone fifteen inches deep in the center and nine inches deep on the sides so as to form a firm and even surface.' Tollgates were to be established when the road was in proper condition every ten miles; the rates of toll designated in this law will be of interest for comparative purposes:"[18]

One change for the positive occurred on September 4, 1800, when the mile-long Cayuga Bridge opened. It considerably straightened the road, avoiding the awkward bend of sharp turns around Cayuga Lake. Thought to be the longest bridge in America, the Manhattan Company of New York erected it for the cost of $150,000. Built on mud sills, it gave way in 1808.[19]

The members of the Cayuga Bridge Company sure took their time to replace the bridge. If the Company even remained in existence. One of the founders, the omnipresent Charles Williamson, may have never known of the Bridge Collapse. He died at sea the same year returning from Cuba where he was "on some government mission."[20, 21]

Construction on a second bridge began in the winter of 1813. This one was built on piles. The pile driver sat on the ice and punch piles beginning from the east shore about a third of the way across before the ice went out. From there, the crew fashioned a scow which they anchored in. A solitary horse circled the pole to pull up the hammer. Worker received a dollar and a half per day and a dollar and a half for a week's board.[22]

This was the bridge Lafayette would eventually travel on.

But not yet.

Unfortunately, with the opening of the Erie Canal, the Seneca Turnpike's days were numbered. It failed to compete. The railroads only made it worse. On May 7, 1845, the New York State Assembly, by a vote of 95 in favor, 1 against and 32 absent, voted to accept the abandonment of the charter of the Seneca Turnpike Road Company.[23] A week later, on Tuesday, May 13, 1845, the New York State Senate voted unanimously in favor on the same matter.[24] The Great Genesee Road was a public road once again.

It eventually became Routes 5 & 20, a much-traveled route through the heart of Western New York. Motels, shops, and tourist attractions sprung up along its shoulders.

Then Dewey's Folly—the New York State Thruway—appeared, the old Central Trail became an afterthought for long-distance travelers. It hasn't returned to weeds, though, and remains a "Main" street in both a literal and figurative sense.

The Genesee Road had served its purpose, but how much did it really improve things? In 1803, it took Augustus Porter seven days to travel the road from Albany to Canandaigua.[25] Contrast that to the three days it would normally take Iroquois runners to traverse the trail from Albany to Buffalo.[26]

Lafayette, in a rush to get to Boston by June 17, took a day to get from Canandaigua to Syracuse.

And you wouldn't believe the festivities in between.

Chapter Thirty-Five: Wowed Waterloo Overcomes Tragedy to Welcome Hero

The party began early in Waterloo on the morning of Wednesday, June 8, 1825. It was like a festive holiday. A great anticipation thrilled the small village and those visitors who had come to town for the special occasion about to unfold. Revolutionary War hero and valiant icon of freedom, the Marquis de Lafayette was about to visit.

Excitement filled the air. And cannon smoke.

There was no way to contain the enthusiasm. Several villagers expressed this feeling by gathering at Earl's tavern, as the Waterloo Hotel had been known. Ab Falling built the three-story brick structure in 1817. Located in the center of its west side, the main entrance faced the public square. The upper floor had a ballroom and a Masonic Hall.[1]

That same year, Junius Lodge No. 291, F.&A.M. received its charter from the Grand Lodge of New York on June 5. The growing lodge began meeting at the Waterloo Hotel on July 1, 1819. By 1825, only one of the original petitioners—Dr. Jesse Fifield, Treasurer—held a leadership position.[2]

Captain Jehiel P. Parsons was a member of Junius Lodge No. 291.[3] He wasn't among the citizens celebrating at Earl's tavern. Instead, he chose to have breakfast across the street at the Mill. The partiers at the tavern would show their delight for the joyous day by periodically firing the small cannon pointing towards the public square in front of the establishment they were in. To get an increasingly louder report, they'd increase the load each time. As Captain Parsons finished his breakfast, the wannabe cannoneers loaded the muzzle heavy and, using the butt end of an axe, rammed down oakum on top of the load. At that moment, Parsons left the Mill and began walking towards the cannon. One of the men drew a match to it, but it failed to fire. Parsons just happened by and decided to do it himself. In an instant, the cannon blew up. A piece of it angled straight through Parsons above his hips, killing him instantly.⁴

Whatever the shock that must have ensued wore off by shortly before two o'clock in the afternoon. That was the moment Captain Lemuel Ruggles, a Waterloo native and also a member of Junius Lodge No. 291, appeared on horseback with his cavalry troop, all men of Waterloo. They formed the head of the procession leading Lafayette to Waterloo. The cannons roared (at least those didn't blow up), the music played, and the dazzling display of colors and military pronounced the arrival of the Nation's Guest. As the local newspaper reported that day, "With this great character, ideas of all that is dear to Americans in a civil point, is intimately and closely connected. The revolution-the days of our fathers their inflexible patriotism-their unbending firmness, their undaunted courage-their battles and their sufferings in times that tried men's souls, all rush upon the mind at the sight of the General, with sublime and irresistible force."⁵

In a scene familiar to Lafayette, he could hear the music from a distance as he approached the main entrance of the Waterloo Hotel. Above it was a second-floor balcony. On the balcony was a band replete with matching white uniforms. The music played as Lafayette's carriage stopped in front of the door. It continued until Lafayette had entered the building.⁶

There are no official records of the number of people that attended the event. It is only said that the streets were dense with people. At the time, 700 people lived in Waterloo,⁷ with the official 1825 census of Junius (which includes Waterloo and Seneca Falls) listed at 5,113.⁸ The entire county of Seneca had a population of roughly 18,000, or over 23,600 people if you include the towns of Wolcott and Galen, which had recently been taken from Seneca County to form Wayne County.⁹

As with other stops on his tour throughout the United States, Lafayette met with Revolutionary War veterans and members of the Masonic fraternity (often one in the same).¹⁰ Lafayette greeted citizens at the stairs near the entrance of the Hotel. There's a story, written much after the fact, that he recognized one veteran—Rev. John Caton—and called him by name. After spending sufficient time with the people of

Waterloo, Lafayette went up to the lodge room of Junius Lodge No. 291. There, Caleb Fairchild, Master, Oren R. Farnsworth, Senior Warden, and Abraham Lisk, Junior Warden, offered him a Masonic greeting and an opportunity to rest.[11]

After a short visit of about an hour, Lafayette's party boarded their carriage and headed down the main road, crossing the Cayuga bridge before transferring to the Auburn committee in East Cayuga.

Lafayette did not hear of the Parsons tragedy until he arrived in Syracuse.[12] Once aware, he asked Mr. G.A. Gamage of Auburn to look into the matter. Gamage came to Waterloo and interviewed Captain Parsons' mother and surviving sisters. He let Lafayette know the family depended financially on Captain Parsons. Grieved from the unfortunate accident, Lafayette penned the following letter to Captain Parsons' mother:

"Dear Madam:

"The dreadful event, which took place on the morning of my introduction to the citizens of your town, when it became known to me, filled my heart with the most painful and sympathetic emotions. Every subsequent information relative to the melancholy loss of your son, could not but enhance those feelings.

"Permit me to avail myself of our community of regrets, to obtain from you an assent to the offer which may not afford to you, but will to me some consoling relief. Learning the situation of the family, the acceptance of the enclosed bill of One Thousand Dollars, will confer upon me a great obligation. Be pleased, dear madam, to receive my affectionate and condoling respects.

"LaFayette."[13]

Chapter Thirty-Six:
Bigotry Cannot Defeat A
Good And Honorable Man

Why are people so mean? What prompts them to violate the rules of decorum just to get a dig in? How many good men do we lose because of this?

It turns out the Era of Good Feelings was less universal than we think. Or, rather, within those good feelings lay dormant seeds of discord that only needed time, and a good trigger, to flower into tension and, unfortunately, eventually into conflict.

But let's not go there yet. Let's harken back to the source of the unity that the Era of Good Feelings recalled.

While the Revolutionary War can be aptly described as a civil war, its aftermath brought harmony through the commonality of men who served in its victory. Not only did they share the wounds of war, but they also shared within the fellowship of it.

No better manifestation of the fraternity of commonness was the proliferation of Freemasonry both during and after the war. Some postulate that George Washington encouraged his officers to become Masons because "the Lodge was a school of honor." Indeed, one out of seven officers, including 100 generals, belonged to at least one of the 218 Lodges that existed during the Revolutionary War.[1]

But lodges weren't just for officers, they were for everyone. That's apparent by the popularity of Freemasonry among all classes following the end of the Revolutionary War. Even on the frontier, it didn't take long before Masons established lodges in new settlements.

One of those settlements was Aurelius. Captain John L. Hardenburgh first settled in the woods there in 1793. He took the Genesee Road, which was nothing more than a "rude wagon track or trail" hewn by "a party of wood-choppers and emigrants" a couple years earlier.[2]

By 1794, Aurelius had enough people to formally organize as a town.³ By 1800, it had enough people to establish its first Masonic Lodge, Hiram Lodge No. 88.⁴ The Episcopalians began building the first church in 1811 but didn't finish it until several years later.⁵

Located on the primary route of emigration, the Town of Aurelius continued to grow. On April 18th, 1815, the Village of Auburn was legally incorporated by the New York State Legislature. Joseph Colt was named its first president.⁶ On June 10, 1816, a second Masonic Lodge was formed when a charter was issued to St. Paul's Lodge No. 265. Joseph Colt was named its first Master.⁷

On March 12, 1817, the Presbyterians finished their church. "It was a model of taste, and cost nearly seventeen thousand dollars. About sixteen thousand dollars was realized by the first sale of pews."⁸

Enter the Reverend Dirck Cornelius Lansing in November 1816.⁹

Dirck C. Lansing was born in Lansingburg, NY in 1785. That the name of his birthplace rings as his own suggests the status of his family at that time. He graduated from Yale College in 1804. He's been described as "a man after nature's best model. In symmetry of physical frame, in eloquence of speech, in balance of the intellectual and emotional, in generous and noble purpose, in zeal, energy, and perseverance in execution, and in effectiveness as a preacher of the gospel, he had scarcely an equal among his brethren. His own rhetorical powers were eminently fitted to illustrate the importance and value of the department of instruction which he held."¹⁰

A "tall, slender, erect figure" with a "swarthy complexion and coal black hair," he possessed "the keen glance of the dark eye." In Auburn, he stood out as a man in his prime "inspired with an air of lofty courage and self-confidence, that made him dominate every congregation like a king of men."¹¹

How effective a preacher was Rev. Lansing? In his first four years as pastor, he brought in 475 new members. He had a way about him. He had a heart felt personality that saw the good—or the potential of good—in all. He also had something more than faith. He had an intellectual approach that appealed to many and influenced all.¹²

Samuel Miles Hopkins, Professor of Church History at the Auburn Theological Seminary, said of Lansing, "Men shrunk before the glance of that eye as if it were the lightning—before the pointing of his finger as if it were a bare sword."[13]

Now, about that seminary... Lansing was one of its founders as well as one of its professors.[14] As chairman of the Prudential Committee, he had the responsibility to draft the charter as well as pick the location of the buildings which he was tasked to see built. He also had a hand in funding the school and, for five years, he taught Sacred Rhetoric.[15]

As befitted a man of his position, he became a Mason. In that capacity, he was asked to offer the keynote speech during Lafayette's visit in 1825. That would be Dirck C. Lansing's high point in Auburn.

Things began to change in 1826. Always at the vanguard, Rev. Lansing invited Charles G. Finney to help in his ministry in the summer and fall of that year.[16] Finney was a bit of a lightning rod. He referred to Western New York as "a burnt district;" thus, coining the term "burnt-over district."[17]

His revivalist approach during the Second Great Awakening didn't always engender gratitude. He said, "until I arrived at Auburn, I was not fully aware of the amount of opposition I was destined to meet from the ministry."[18]

Ironically, Finney's spartan approach to spiritualism conflicted with Lansing's more eloquent style. Of Lansing's congregation, Finney noted, "The church were (sic) much conformed to the world, and were accused by the unconverted of being leaders in dress, and fashion, and worldliness." It's no wonder then, after Finney presented his fire and brimstone sermon before them, he looked nervously at Lansing to see how the venerable pastor would respond. Much to Finney's delight, Lansing offered a favorable comment.[19]

The moment of relief was short-lived, however. That's when decorum left the building.

A man rose and said to Reverend Lansing in no uncertain terms, "Mr. Lansing, I do not believe that such remarks from you can do any good, while you wear a ruffled shirt and a gold ring, and while your wife and the ladies of your family sit, as they do, before the congregation, dressed as leaders in the fashions of the day.[20]

Crestfallen, Lansing had no response. He fell to his seat and wept visibly. Finney had to close the service.[21]

What happened next tells you everything Reverend Lansing. Here's how Finney told the story:

"I went home with the dear, wounded pastor, and when all the family were returned from church, he took the ring from his finger—it was a slender gold ring that could hardly attract notice—and said his first wife, when upon her dying bed, took it from her finger and placed it upon his with a request that he should wear it for her sake. He had done so, without a thought of its being a stumbling block. Ruffles he said, he had worn them from his childhood, and did not think of them as anything improper. Indeed, he could not remember when he began to wear them, and of course thought nothing about them. 'But,' said he 'if these things are an occasion of offense to any, I will not wear them.' He was a precious Christian man, and an excellent pastor."[22]

What would possess a man to make such a vindictive comment targeting an acknowledged pillar of the community?

It may have its roots in the Abolitionist movement. We know Lansing would later become a member of the American Anti-Slavery Society.[23] We also know there were slaveholders among the early settlers of Auburn, and that, by the spring of 1844, disagreements on the subject at the Seminary would lead to an "alarming falling off in the classes."[24]

It may have been religious bigotry. After all Finney says, "There were several wealthy men in the town who took offence at Dr. Lansing and myself, and the laborers in that revival; and after I left, they got together and formed a new congregation."[25]

Perhaps it was more. Even before the Morgan Affair of September 1826, there was a virulent anti-Masonry strain within at least one community in Auburn. On the other hand, given Dirck Lansing's involvement with the local Masonic Lodge, this might simply reflect a highly competitive environment between different protestant churches.

On February 21st, 1820, the Church of Christ voted "not to fellowship such brethren as do visit the Lodges, or any other of the Masonic meetings." This ban was rescinded later that year on November 4th.[26]

Still, the June 15, 1825, edition of the *Auburn Republican*, while meticulously reporting all other proceedings in great detail, failed to reproduce Lansing's speech to Lafayette.[27] One is left to wonder if this reflects some sort of prejudice against Masonry.

More likely if there was a partiality against Lansing because of Masonry, the Morgan Affair would have exasperated it. This event occurred at the same time as Finney's stay with Lansing.

Within three years, Reverend Lansing would leave Auburn.[28] St. Paul's Lodge No. 265 would close on June 8, 1832, and Hiram Lodge No. 88 would go dark in 1835.[29]

Dirck Cornelius Lansing would die in Cincinnati on March 19, 1857. At a memorial given in his honor by his daughter at Calvary Presbyterian Church in Auburn on September 23, 1883, Professor Hopkins summed up a life well served in this manner:

> "A faithful minister of Christ, an able and zealous preacher of His word, should not be quickly forgotten in the community where he labored. Such a man leaves a legacy of precious memories and precious influences behind him, of which the local church and congregation, at least, should recognize themselves as in some sort the heirs, and claim their share in the bequest."[30]

CHAPTER THIRTY-SEVEN:
THROUGH SENECA FALLS, EAST CAYUGA, THEN A MASONIC WELCOME AND A FINAL ADIEU IN AUBURN

As early as May 12th, 1825, the Village of Auburn expected Lafayette to travel through their growing community. Seventeen men, including two future governors of New York State were appointed to a committee charged with the purpose of preparing for the visit of the French general and American hero. They were "to make suitable arrangements for the occasion; and that they be requested to communicate the doings of this meeting, to the proper military officers, the masonick order, and the surviving revolutionary officers and soldiers, inviting them to co-operate with the citizens of the village, in the proposed expressions of publick attention, to the venerable 'Guest of our Nation,' and its early defender."[1]

A few days later, on May 16th, the officers of the militia met at Strong's tavern. Led by Brigadier General Henry R. Brinkerhoff, they, too, formed a committee to prepare for Lafayette's visit. This committee contained a total of sixteen men, all different from the previous committee and all in charge of specific military units.[2]

Brigadier General Brinkerhoff immediately dispatched a letter to the local newspaper. Addressed "To The Soldiers of the Revolution," he informed them of Lafayette's impending arrival and requested they participate in the reception. He wrote, "Come forward then, and greet your long-departed friend: Come, and welcome him whom our nation delights to honour as her guest." At the same time, he also stated "field and commissioned staff officers will be mounted, and none but such as are in full uniform will be permitted to form in the escort." All others could come in civilian dress and march in the procession.[3]

Word finally came on Tuesday, June 7, 1825, that General Lafayette would soon arrive. To spread the word to everyone in the village and surrounding area, handbills were printed and distributed. In addition, the militia fired a volley of 13 guns to alert those in communities further away.[4]

The *Auburn Press* gleefully reported the news that day. It did, however, regret that this news forced the paper to omit "printing our remarks respecting Gershom Powers' accounts this week, by reason of the press of office business, preparatory to the arrival of Gen. La Fayette; (although we extremely dislike to mention his name in the same paragraph with that of Mr. Powers)."[5]

Located on the right-of-way of the Seneca Turnpike, Auburn was a tavern stop for those emigrating to the west. Some decided to stay. The population had doubled in size between 1815 and 1820. By 1825, the population was 2,982.[6] It was much larger on June 8th.

At 9 o'clock in the morning of Wednesday, June 8, 1825, Captain Benjamin C. Cox of the 13th Regimental Cavalry assembled his company along with several carriages and off-duty officers on horseback. They rode west on the old Genesee Road for 9 miles until they reached the county line at Cayuga bridge. There, they waited. And waited.[7]

At about 4 P.M. they saw the parade from Waterloo approaching. General Lafayette and his party rode in the same barouche provided by W.S. De Zeng, Esq. of Geneva. Pulled by six chestnut horses, the carriage came to a stop upon meeting the Auburn committee.[8]

On behalf of the committee, Enos Thomas Throop, formally welcomed the General. Throop, a former Congressman, was at the time a judge on the Seventh Circuit. Within four years, he would become New York State's tenth Governor. After greeting the French visitor, Throop then introduced Lafayette to the men and women who took the steamboat from the village of Aurora to witness this historic event. When asked, the General "politely consented to appear upon the piazza of Mr. Woolsey's Hotel, and the welkin rang with the three times three of the people." This impromptu reception ended at five o'clock.[9]

Judge Throop joined Lafayette in DeZeng's carriage as the procession departed for Auburn. As they rode, throngs of citizens lined the turnpike, cheering them on.[10]

About 90 minutes later, the parade arrived at the outskirts of the Village of Auburn. There, Captain James Fitch and his Auburn Guards, along with Captain Murphy with his company of Rifle Corps and a Company from Port-Byron under the command of Captain Parks, waited to receive the Nation's Guest.[11]

At this point, where the road rises at the western boundary of the Village, stood an elegant arched bower of shrubbery, built specially for this occasion. In addition to the uniformed troops, nearly 200 Masons and a large number of Revolutionary War veterans stood on either side of the street. As the procession passed, they joined it in an orderly fashion and proceeded under and through the arch.[12]

To give a clear sense of what was happening, take a look at how newspapers of the day reported the event:

> "…an immense concourse of citizens, who had assembled from all parts of the county, to see him, who has excited the admiration and the gratitude of every American heart. The ear was almost deafened with the loud acclamations of our fellow-citizens, who cheered their guest with the greatest enthusiasm, and made the welkin ring with these expressions of their feelings – at the same time, the deep thunder of the ordnance, uniting with the merry peals of the bells, gave to the whole a grandeur that affected every sense."[13]

> "On the procession passing the Arch, surrounded by an immense concourse of the people, who had poured into the village from all quarters, a salute of 24 guns was fired, by a company stationed on an eminence a few rods distant; the bells commenced a merry peal; the citizens with one accord closed their stores, and in the midst of repeated shouts of joy that made the 'welkin ring,' and covered with clouds of dust, under a broiling sun, the veteran Chief rode uncovered through Genesee, North and other streets, to Hudson's Hotel."[14]

Lafayette's carriage passed through a double line of troops who presented arms as the General alighted. The committee escorted him, along with his son and Levasseur, to the awning covered piazza of the second story.[15] Before nearly eight thousand people – four times the population of the Village of Auburn – General Lafayette was introduced to the Honorable John Whitefield Hulbert (a former Congressman from Massachusetts and a recently retired Assemblyman representing Cayuga County) and to the Reverend Dirck C. Lansing, venerable pastor of the Presbyterian Church. Hulbert represented the citizens and Lansing represented the Masons. Each addressed the General as follows:[16]

Hon. John W. Hulbert's Address:

"General,—The people of this village, and of the surrounding country, most respectfully and affectionately welcome you among them. They rejoice in this opportunity afforded them, of testifying to you, personally, their admiration of your character, and their gratitude for the great and inestimable services, which you have rendered to their country.

"Few of us have ever had the happiness, until this day, to behold your face. But where is the American, who would not blush to own his ignorance of the might things you have done for this nation?

"We know that in the dark and perilous day of our revolutionary struggle, when the world looked upon our cause as desperate, when tyrants were rejoicing, and the lovers of freedom were weeping, at our expected downfall—yes, at that hour, when even Hope scarcely dared to linger among us, a light suddenly broke through the gloom—You, general, was [sic] that light! Like the angel of deliverance, you came to our assistance.

"We know that you came not to seek for wealth, ease, or safety. No, you left them all in your native land, and hastened to a foreign country, to [a] land of strangers, where you exhausted your wealth, and poured out your blood, in the cause of an oppressed people struggling for liberty.

"You raised, in this country, numerous troops, fed and clothed them upon your bounty, and led them yourself into the hottest battle.

And, finally, your noble and enthusiastick spirit roused a nation in our defense.

"When the object of your heart was accomplished, when you say our liberty and independence firmly established, you most generously refused all pecuniary compensation. You asked for no reward.—But surely you have received a rich reward in your own consciousness of the good you have done, in beholding the flourishing and happy condition of the country you defended, in the warm and universal gratitude of its people, and in the admiration and applause of all the truly good and virtuous through the world.

"We regret that in your progress through this country you should have had any other than an unmingled emotion of pleasure. But we know that you must have had some reflections, which could not fail to give pain to a heart like yours.—Where, now, are those brave and generous men who were engaged with you in the mighty contest? Where are those who fought by your side in fields of immortal fame? You have found them few in number; yes, you have found them like lonely and shattered trees in the desolate path of the whirlwind.

"You behold a small group of revolutionary soldiers. Providence has sustained them for this glorious day. Their locks are whitened with the frosts of age; the furrows of time are mixed with the scars of battle; yet their eyes are glistening with joy at sight of you.

"But where is your beloved Washington?—Alas, the grave has closed over his body; but never, never, shall it close of his or your renown. You have visited Mount Vernon; you have been near his cold remains—No, cold we will not say, for we will believe, that when La Fayette was kneeling at the tomb of Washington, he immortal spirit was there, and 'even in his ashes lived their wonted fires.'

"We have noticed with priced and with pleasure the course you have pursued since you was last among us. Neither the frowns of kings, the horrors of a dungeon, not threatened death have ever paralyzed your exertions in the great and sacred cause of the rights of man.

"Be assured that we shall never forget the satisfaction, which your presence has this day afforded us. Occasions like this will be rare on earth; — they will be 'like angels' visits, few, and far between.'

"We offer you, General, our best wishes, and our fervent prayers, that after you shall return to the land of your nativity, you may enjoy many years of health and happiness, and that the termination of your bright career on earth may be the commencement of one still brighter, more glorious, and more happy, in the world where virtue like yours will meet, we trust, a blessed and everlasting reward."[17]

Rev. Dirck C. Lansing's Address:

"My Dear General,—Great men are the instruments, by which the Supreme Ruler of the Universe accomplishes the designs of his benevolence. Would he exhibit, as a subject of admiration to the civilized population of our world, the happiness of which his creatures are capable, under the most perfect form of human governments, where the social, civil, political, and religious rights of the people, are the result of voluntary combination, he raises up a nation of freemen, who make their own laws, create and change their own rulers, and retain in their own hands the sovereign power. Such a nation is ours. In those events which gave birth to these free and independent United States, we are furnished with peculiar displays of the resources of divine wisdom, and the energy of divine power.— We discover, most signally, the hand of the great Arbiter of nations, in raising up in one quarter of the globe, a Washington, and in another, a La Fayette, to become the champions of liberty, and the defenders of the rights of man.

"In the departed heroes of our revolution, and in yourself, a most distinguished survivor of them, we recognize, under God, the authors of our free and happy institutions. You adopted our infant country as the object of your patriotick care, and consecrated to it, your talents, your fortune, and your life. After a long absence you have returned to behold the fruits of your early toil, and may I not be permitted to add, to delight yourself in their abundance. The boldest *spirit of prophecy, would scarcely have ventured to predict, what your eyes have seen, and your ears have heard.—'The wilderness has been converted into a fruitful field, and the solitary has become as the garden of the Lord.' The patriot can desire no higher reward, than the pleasure to be derived from contemplating, as the result of his efforts, more than then millions of freemen, the admiration, and the fear of imperial courts the world over. The happiness to be received, from looking at an object, so interesting & commanding, is yours. Your hands have contributed, in no small measure, towards erecting this fair fabric of freedom. The sons and daughters of your coadjutors, in the scenes of the revolution, greet you as their benefactor, and would be delighted to impart to you, any portion of the country you gave them, as a peaceful home for the evening of your days. 'He who was first in war, first in peace, and first in the hearts of his countrymen,' your companion in arms, the immortal Washington, the statesman, the hero, and the Christian, has for years been gathered to the tombs of his fathers. You have knelt in the place, and have wept over the ashes of the illustrious dead. The hearts of his liberated children have dictated his epitaph. 'Tis the proudest and richest that can perpetuate the memory of man—'Here lie the Father of his country.' When La Fayette shall resign his breath to that mighty Being, who raised him up for noble deeds, the children of this father will write upon his tomb-stone, 'Here lies the friend of Washington.'*

"On behalf of the fraternity of free & accepted Masons, as their organ, you will accept, dear sir, the assurance of our high respect, & our grateful recollection of the distinguished blessings which we enjoy, as the fruits of the toils of your patriotism, and the sacrifices of your benevolence. May you at last find a home in the upper Temple of the Eternal, and may the blessedness of our heavenly Father's house be yours, as the purchase of the blood of our glorious Redeemer."[18]

In his entire year-long journey across the United States of America, Dirck Lansing's presentation represents the only time Lafayette was addressed in public by the Masons, according to author Edgar Ewing

Brandon in his book *A Pilgrimage of Liberty*, (The Lawhead Press, Athens, Ohio, 1944). All other times, as in Lockport and Waterloo, Lafayette's meetings with the Masonic fraternity were held in private either in a lodge or at a Masonic Banquet.[19]

General Lafayette offered a brief but polite reply. Once this portion of the ceremony concluded, the General then directed a few words to the crowd. He then met with members of the Masonic order, Revolutionary War veterans, officers of the militia, the local clergy, and many ladies who accompanied them. At 8 o'clock, the assembly gathered to a temporary arbor in a nearby field where Emmanuel Hudson provided an "excellent dinner."[20]

At the dinner, the following toasts have been recorded:

"By Col. J.W. Hulbert. The Nation's Guest."[21]

"By Gen. La Fayette. Cayuga county and Auburn town— May their republican industry and prosperity, more and more give a splendid lie to the enemies of liberty, equality and self-government."[21]

"By Major Smith. The health of G. W. LaFayette."[22]

"By Mr. G.W. La Fayette. A sovereign whose power is felt only when it is wanted—the people."[21]

"The other toasts were given by the gentlemen of the General's suite, copies of which were handed to the chairman, but we regret to say were mislaid."[21]

"By Mr. G.A. Gamage. The eternal continuance of the affections of the American people towards the greatest surviving apostle of freedom on earth – La Fayette."[21]

"By the Hon. G. Powers. The memory of Steuben and Pulaski."[21]

"By Mr. W.H. Seward. Our guest – A safe return to, and happy meeting with his family at La Grange."[21]

"By Mr. J. Pease. Gen. Bolivar, the hero of South America."[21]

After dinner, everyone went to the lavishly decorated Brown's Assembly-Room for a Ball. As reported:

"Here a brilliant circle of the beauty and fashion of the village and vicinity, received the Nation's benefactor, in a manner highly grateful to his feelings. The Hall was very tastefully dressed in shrubbery of various kinds, and in different places appeared the mottos:

"'Washington and La Fayette,'

"'Monmouth and Yorktown,'

"'Nation's Guest,'

"'Kosciusko Pulaski De Kalb Steuben,'

"and over two seperate [sic] arches, a line each, of the following couplet, in letters of evergreen:

"'There's a sweet little cherub that sits up aloft,/To keep watch for the life of the Guest,'

"(in allusion to the recent narrow escape of the General on board the Steam boat *Mechanic*.)"[23]

Following the festivities, Lafayette and his suite once again stepped into a carriage. Mr. J.M. Sherwood graciously volunteered his horses and drivers to convey the guest to their next destination.[24] At 11 P.M. the party, along with the Committee of arrangements, departed Auburn for Syracuse, by way of Skeneateles.[25]

One local paper summarized the day:

"On the whole, such a display was never before witnessed in Auburn; for we have never had an occasion which has so fully elicited the warmest affections of the heart, or aroused the pulsations of patriotism in our bosoms, as that which we have just hastily described. The veterans of the revolution rejoiced to see their old comrade; and all remembered, with gratitude, the disinterestedness, the love of liberty, and the valour of him to whom they were doing honor."[26]

Among the Committee that led the illustrious Lafayette to Syracuse included "a fair-haired youth of twenty-four" by the name of William

Henry Seward.[27] Destined to become New York's twelfth governor, he's perhaps best known for "Seward's Folly," the 1867 purchase of Alaska.

As Lafayette leaves the Greater Western New York Region, it seems appropriate to leave the reader with the General's own thoughts, as recounted by his traveling secretary André-Nicolas Levasseur:

> "This journey confirmed us in the opinion, that no part of America, or, perhaps, of the whole world, contains so many wonders of nature as the state of New York. The lakes of Canandaigua, Seneca and Cayuga, appeared delightful to us from the purity of their waters, the form of their basins, and the richness of their banks. The sight of all these beauties, and still more the kindness and urbanity of the population through which we travelled, often made General Lafayette regret the rapidity with which he travelled. During this journey of upwards of one hundred and thirty miles by land, we travelled night and day, only stopping for a few moments at each village, to enjoy the entertainments, prepared by the inhabitants in honour of their beloved guest, who, said they, by the simplicity, the amenity and uniformity of his manners, towards all classes of citizens, completed the conquest of all hearts, already devoted to him from his adherence to the cause of America in particular, and that of liberty in general."[28]

ACT THREE:

– THE IMPACT –

LAFAYETTE'S LEGACY

Epilogue:
A Favor Returned,
D-Day 50th Anniversary

"France will be free again. I give you my word. Just as Free French troops liberated Corsica, Napoleon's place of birth. I will someday land in France to liberate the birthplace of Lafayette.
— General George S. Patton in the move *Patton*

Patton never landed in France until well after the invasion. He was more valuable as a ruse. Allied leaders leaked to double-agents that Patton had been given the command of the "First United States Army Group." This phantom unit existed to trick the Germans into thinking the actual invasion of France would occur at the Pas de Calais rather than Normandy.

So strong was Patton's stature to Hitler's high command they continued to hold back reinforcements when the actual D-Day landing occurred. They continued to believe Normandy was a diversion and the actual invasion would take place at Pas de Calais under Patton's command.

When the Allies finally liberated France from Nazi occupation, its citizens didn't credit a single individual, but they thanked any soldier who happened to be closest to them.

General Dwight D. Eisenhower was the Supreme Allied Commander that led Operation Overload, the code name for D-Day. Twenty years after the event, he sat down with Madame Simone Renaud, wife of the war-time mayor of Ste. Mere Eglise. This was the first town liberated during D-Day and the pre-invasion drop point of the 82nd and 101st Airborne Divisions. While respectful of Eisenhower, her eyes lit up with excitement when she recalled to him, "I can tell you, this airborne invasion was a wonderful surprise. We dare not believe, we dare not hope such liberation, and it was a wonderful thing that happened to us."[1]

General Eisenhower did not take part in the formal anniversary ceremonies that year. That didn't stop France from celebrating the returning veterans who helped liberate their country. So many towns wanted to thank these old soldiers in person that officials had to stretch out the original single day event over two days.[2]

For some, perhaps twenty years was too soon to revisit the site that turned the tide of WWII. As the years rolled on, however, there grew a need for both sides to recognize the significance of the event.

French native Denise Jones was a young girl during the war. She became a member of the Free French (a.k.a. "Underground") when German troops began their occupation. Each day she lived in a world the average person would fear. She saw friends executed for the slightest indiscretion. Meanwhile, she sabotaged German munition plants, helped allied prisoners escape to England. You know, the usual "Hogan's Heroes" stuff. Except this wasn't funny. It was deadly serious.[3]

Looking back at the liberation of France fifty years later, she couldn't hold back her heart-felt thanks. "You were unselfish," said Jones. "You didn't slink off to some other part of the globe and leave the undesirable job to some other 'Joe.' You are Americans of who we should all be proud."[4]

While Jones had moved to America following the War, those that remained in France thanked the veterans when they returned for the fiftieth anniversary celebration. Michel Thoury, mayor of St. James, proclaimed in his salutatory speech that year, "In 1944, an American soldier spent a few hours with my family. Where is he? I don't know his name, but I remember how strong his arms were when he held me. Today we are free because of the sacrifices of those who rest at your feet. Be the living witnesses to our history. I ask you to come back here in 50 years and cry out, 'Long Live Peace!'"[5]

The sentiments in the France in 1994 echoed those of America in 1825. You could see it in the citizens of those liberated cities. A "majestic, two-color photo of the U.S. military cemetery above Omaha Beach" in *Le Figaro* magazine that carried only the plaintive headline: "Thank You."[6]

The sixtieth anniversary of D-Day had more of the feel of the fiftieth anniversary of American independence that our nation. Like America's reflection in 1824-1825 during Lafayette's farewell tour, a bittersweet mood swept over Normandy in 2004. In both instances, many realized, for them, this would be the last milestone anniversary they would enjoy.

It makes sense, then, that the gratitude expressed by the French had poignant exuberance. French officials, perhaps as a nod to politeness, even spoke in English. [D-Day] "was the longest day, but it was also the dawn of another day for France and for the whole world," said Parliament member Jean-Marc Lefranc. "Thank you, thank you from the bottom of my heart. Thank you for what you did—and did a terrific job. Long live the United States of America!"[7]

As usual, the true measure of thanks came for the townspeople themselves, many of them survivors of the German occupation. "We only think well of them. If they hadn't been here, what would Europe have been like?" said 78-year-old Marie-Therese Leruyer at the Grandcamp-Maisy observance.[8]

It wasn't just their words. It was their actions, too. Like Western New Yorkers in 1825, French citizens decked their homes with American flags and similar bunting. In Omaha, Frank Marino, an 84-year-old veteran from New York, received a memorable non-verbal reaction. "They can't do enough for you," he said. "Oh God, the women come up and kiss me."[9]

Well, if Lafayette kissed the ladies in 1825, then it's only fair play the ladies kissed American veterans in 2004.

In a way, the World Wars of the twentieth century reciprocated what Lafayette (and the French) did for the infant United States of America in the eighteenth century. General Dwight D. Eisenhower summed up in a 1964 interview with Walter Cronkite.

"Walter, D-Day has a special meaning to me," said the former president in 1964. "These men came here, British, and our other Allies, Americans, to storm these beaches for one purpose only. No to gain anything for ourselves. Not to fulfill any ambitions that America had for conquest. But just to preserve freedom, systems of self-government in the world. Many thousands [of] men have died for ideals such as these. And here again in the twentieth century for the second time Americans, along with the rest of the free world, but Americans had to come across the ocean to defend those same values."[10]

Forty years later in 2004, French President Jacques Chirac answered, "France will never forget. She will never forget those men who made the ultimate sacrifice to liberate our soil, our native land, our continent from the yoke of Nazi barbarity and its murderous folly. Nor will it ever forget its debt to America, its everlasting friend."[11]

In a way, Chirac didn't just answer Eisenhower. He also returned the favor of Rev. David Brown. Chosen by the committee to offer Fredonia's welcoming speech on the first day Lafayette stepped foot in Western New York, Brown concluded with:

"As our country's friend and benefactor with heartfelt sincerity and gratitude do I salute you. May that ever gracious Being by whom we are thus favored, strew the path of your pilgrimage with his richest blessings, until at some far distant day He may please to receive you to himself in glory everlasting."[12]

Two nations, two peoples. Bonded by friendship. Eternally indebted to each other.

APPENDIX I:
LAFAYETTE AND FREEMASONRY

contributed by B. Chris Ruli

Like many of his contemporaries, Gilbert Du Motier's curiosity led him to join the Free and Accepted Masons. Colloquially known as the Freemasons, the modern society traces its origins back to the early eighteen century in England and empowers its members, through lessons taught during their initiation, on self-improvement and charitable giving. The fraternity quickly spread throughout western-Europe and the Americas where it became particularly popular amongst the mercantile and upper class. It is no wonder, therefore, why Lafayette became interested in membership.

Curiously, Lafayette's initiation into Freemasonry appears lost to time, with no definitive details as to where or when he joined. Nevertheless, he remained an enthusiastic and steadfast supporter of the world's oldest fraternity throughout his life. According to his own remarks made during a banquet arranged by the Grand Lodge of Tennessee in 1825, Lafayette joined Freemasonry prior to 1777 when he arrived in America to join the Continental Army. This suggests that Lafayette would have been between seventeen or eighteen years old when he joined Freemasonry and may have done so through a lodge attached to a military regiment where he had been stationed back in France. These types of Masonic groups were common in eighteen century France and suffered from a lack of documentation and paperwork that is common in contemporary Masonry.

Lafayette joined George Washington's staff with the rank of major general. We know nothing of Lafayette's thoughts on Freemasonry or activities during this period as there are no surviving letters, meeting ledgers, diaries, or other supporting documentation to provide insight into this part of his life. We do know, however, that there were other

Freemasons on Washington's staff and others serving across the army at the time. Following the war, Lafayette returned to France, attended Masonic meetings, and even served as Master of a French lodge in 1806—*Les Amis de la Vérité* located in Rozay-en-Brie.

Lafayette returned to the United States in 1784-1785 for what became the first of two major publicity tours. Curiously, there are no surviving records to show that Lafayette participated in any Masonic activities during this tour. In his 1904 book, *Washington and Masonic Compeers,* Sidney Hayden claimed Lafayette gifted Washington an apron during his visit to Mount Vernon. This apron was then acquired by the Philadelphia chapter of the Washington Benevolent Society and then transferred over to the Grand Lodge of Pennsylvania's museum after the society dissolved. Hayden goes further to claim that the Madame Lafayette herself had sewn the apron. Unfortunately, Hayden does not provide any references to this claim and a review of newspaper records, diaries, and Masonic records have not been able to affirm Hayden's claim. Lafayette himself never mentions an apron gifted to Washington, and there is no mention of Freemasonry in any surviving letter between both men. While the apron now preserved by the Grand Lodge of Pennsylvania may be associated with George Washington, it has very little, if any, connection to Lafayette.

Almost all of what we know about Lafayette's connection and perspectives on Freemasonry come from his 1824-1825 American tour. Throughout the tour, Lafayette met with Freemasons, visited Masonic Halls, attended meetings and banquets, and spoke publicly about his reverence for the fraternity's principles and values. He attended approximately thirty-nine Masonic meetings: twenty-one craft lodges, ten Grand Lodges, six Royal Arch, and one for both Knight Templar and Scottish Rite. He participated in five Masonic cornerstone ceremonies and dedications, agreed to be initiated into three appendant Masonic bodies (Royal Arch, Knights Templar, and Scottish Rite), and met with Masons outside of a stated meeting dozens of times throughout his tour.

Newspapers covered his visits to Masonic groups in detail and, in many cases, full transcriptions of welcome speeches by grand masters, lodge masters, and Lafayette were reproduced in newspapers for public examination and curiosity. Grand Lodges and their constituent lodges often opened their banquets, lunches, and breakfasts to the public. This not only strengthened their association to Lafayette, but enabled a curious public to catch a glimpse into the fraternity's meeting places, material culture, and traditions.

Lafayette returned to France in the Fall of 1825 and continued to remain active in Freemasonry. In the Spring of 1834, he received word of his election to the 33rd Degree of the Ancient and Accepted Scottish Rite, Cerneau Supreme Council of New York. He transmitted a letter of thanks for this honorary distinction on May 10, 1834, just ten days before his death. In his letter, he summarized his feelings on the fraternity succinctly: "May our ancient institution propagate everywhere the Liberty, the Equality, the Philanthropy, and contribute to the great movement of social civilization which ought to emancipate the two Hemispheres."

B. Chris Ruli is a researcher of early American Freemasonry and its socioeconomic impact on society. He is the author of *Brother Lafayette* and *The White House & The Freemasons* and serves as associate director of The Scottish Rite Research Society and The Philalethes Society.

APPENDIX II:
LAFAYETTE ON THE FOLLY OF TOLERANCE

James Madison served as the fourth President of the United States from 1809 to 1817, immediately preceding James Monroe. History textbooks refer to him as the "Father of the Constitution" as he acted as the driving force in drafting both the Constitution and the Bill of Rights.

A short three years prior to that seminal event, Madison traveled from Baltimore to Fort Stanwix to negotiate with the Iroquois Confederacy. Accompanying him was a young French general and a protégé of George Washington. That would be the Marquis de Lafayette.

This chance meeting formed what would become a lifelong bond between the two men. Very early on, Madison recognized Lafayette's affinity with the American Indians, as well as his key guiding principles. In a 1784 letter to Thomas Jefferson, Madison offers a frank assessment of his French colleague:

> *"In my last I gave you a sketch of what past at Fort Schuyler during my stay there: mentioning in particular that the Marquis had made a Speech to the Indians with the sanction of the Commissioners Wolcot[t] Le[e] Butler. The question will probably occur how a foreigner and a private one could appear on the theatre of a public treaty between United States and the Indian nations and how the Commissioners could lend a sanction to it. Instead of offering an opinion of the measure I will state the manner in which it was brought about. It seems that most of the Indian tribes particularly those of the Iroquois retain a strong predilection for the French and most of the lat[t]er an enthusiastic idea of the Marquis. This idea has resulted from his being a Frenchman, the figure he has made during the war and the*

arrival of several important events which he foretold to them soon after he came to this country. Before he went to Fort S. it had been suggested either in compliment or sincerity that his presence and influence might be of material service to the treaty... The answer of the sachems as well as the circumstances of the audience denoted the highest reverence for the orator. The chief [sic] of the Oneidas said that the word which he had spoken to them early in the war had prevented them from being misled to the wrong side of it. During this scene and even during the whole stay of the M. he was the only conspicuous figure... The time I have lately passed with the M. has given me a pretty thorough insi[gh]t into his character. With great natural frankness of temper he unit[e]s much addres[s] (with very) considerable talents, (a strong thirst of praise and popularity.) In his politics he says his three hob[b]y horses are the alliance between France and the United States, the unio[n] of the lat[t]er and the manumission of the slaves. The two former are the dearer to him as they are connected with his personal glory. The last does him real honor as it is a proof of his humanity. In a word I take him to be as amiable a man as [can be imagined]* and as sincere an American as any Frenchman can be; one whose past services gratitude obliges us to acknowle[d]ge, and whose future friendship prudence requires us to cultivate."[1]

     * originally "his vanity can admit."

 Here you can see Lafayette's ability to not only embrace those of different cultures, but his affinity with the peoples of those cultures. Something about Lafayette drew everyone towards him—whether they be American statesmen or Iroquois chieftains. What stood out about him? What secret to success did he possess?

 The answers to these questions become apparent as we see Lafayette's reception during his farewell tour of America. No matter his birthright, no matter his wealth, no matter his standing, he always greeted everyone he met "on the level." In doing so, he sought and amplified the commonality he had with everyone he met.

Quite simply, he recognized the folly of mere tolerance.

This came up at a meeting between Lafayette's party and James Madison and friends in Virginia from the 15th through the 19th of November, 1824. The following conversation, as witnessed and later published by A. Levasseur, Lafayette's personal secretary during his American tour, expertly brings up the "insult" of "tolerance."

> "After the question of personal slavery in the United States, the equally important question of the spiritual slavery, to which some of the people of Europe are condemned by the *dominant* or *state religions*, was discussed. The friends of Mr. Madison congratulated themselves, that at least this sort of slavery was unknown in their beloved country; they entered into some details which showed me that they were not men to be contented with what we incessantly invoke as a benefit in Europe, that is religious *tolerance*. 'Tolerance,' said one of them, [']is beyond doubt preferable to persecution, but it would always be insupportable in a free country, because it marks an insulting pride. To give one religion the right to tolerate, and subject others to the disgrace of being tolerated, it would be first necessary to prove that the *tolerant* is the only good one, and that all the *tolerated* were bad. This proof is unobtainable, since each believes his own religion to be the best. The word *toleration* is, therefore, an insult, and cannot reasonably be replaced except by the word *liberty*. This liberty we now enjoy in the fullest sense of the term, and we are sure that throughout our twenty-four states, not one is to be found in which it is not better understood than in any part of Europe. However, we have also had our times of *tolerance*, indeed I may say of *intolerance*; before our glorious revolution, for instance, we still groaned under

laws, by which for certain degrees of heresy, a father could be deprived of the privilege of educating his own children. Every individual might lose the rights of citizen, and a part of the protection of the laws, and sometimes even be burnt. At present there is a happy difference; thanks to our new laws, worthy of the immortal sages who framed them, no individual can be forced to observe any religious worship, nor to frequent any place, nor to support any minister, of whatever religion he may be, nor be constrained, retained, disturbed or oppressed in his own person, or his goods; in short he cannot be persecuted in any manner on account of his religious opinions; but all men have liberty *to profess and sustain by reasoning* their religious opinions, and these opinions can neither diminish nor increase any of their civil rights.'"[2]

Note the self-importance implied by tolerance. It suggests your view is the correct view. It's like saying, "I'll allow you to think what you want." This stance subtly tells the other person there's no need to prove the superiority of your view because it is assumed to be the proper view.

From Lafayette's experience, you might imagine how he could interpret "tolerance" as the arrogance of the aristocracy.

Tolerance, therefore, is folly. A conceit of the egotist. A lie to deceive the *hoi polloi*.

Instead, Lafayette championed liberty over tolerance. Liberty is the great leveler. It allows all views to enter freely into the cauldron of ideas. It doesn't suggest they're all good. It leaves it up to real-life to determine the winner.

That doesn't mean proponents of losing ideas should be banished. No. A thriving and growing nation requires a constant inflow of new, different, and competing thoughts. The bond between peoples isn't the similarity in opinion, but in commonality of purpose.

In this case, that purpose is liberty.

Appendix III:
June 17, 1825, Bunker Hill Monument Cornerstone Ceremony

General Lafayette maintained a quick pace through the Greater Western New York Region because he made a commitment he vowed to keep. He promised the City of Boston he would attend the laying of the cornerstone of the Battle of Bunker Hill Monument. The Nation's Guest remained true to that promise.

This wasn't the first cornerstone laying ceremony Lafayette would take part in. Chapter Nine mentions his participation in the cornerstone ceremonies for both the Baron de Kalb and Casimir Pulaski monuments. After the Bunker Hill event, Lafayette would continue his tour into New England. On June 29, 1825, Lafayette laid the cornerstone of what was then known as the University of Vermont's "South College" building in Burlington. Today is it part of the University's "Old Mill" complex.

Two things set apart the Bunker Hill cornerstone ceremony from these other events. First, the laying of the cornerstone of the Battle of Bunker Hill monument drew national attention. This was not simply a local event. Dignitaries from across the region, as well as from the Nation's capital, attended and took part in the ceremonies.

Second, this was a public Masonic ceremony that was documented in detail by the local press. The June 18, 1925 edition of the Boston *Centinel* covered the ceremony and printed nearly everything expect for Daniel Webster's lengthy speech.

Webster's speech is a must read for all those interested in the definition of America. Not only did it accurately reflect the origin story of our new nation, but it exemplified the exuberance of the Era of Good Feelings. As such, it not only captured the tenure of the county on the cusp of its fiftieth birthday, but also the joy of Lafayette's fourteen-month tour across all its states.

The speech can be found online at:

https://www.bostonleadershipbuilders.com/0speeches/1825_webster_bunker_hill.htm.

As for the rest of the ceremony, there is no better way to express it than how it was actually reported at the time. Perhaps it's most meaningful to note the following article appeared not in a Boston newspaper, but in a New York City newspaper. Here in its entirety is the Tuesday, June 21, 1825, page-one story from *The Evening Post*:

"Celebration of the Battle of Bunker Hill"

We give, with much pleasure, an animated and graphic description of the celebration of this national day, as furnished, very appropriately, by one of the Yankee newspapers printed in Boston, in the near vicinity of the battle ground. Its length almost engrosses our columns, and when have they been better occupied?

Of the various contributions of the New-England Muse, on the occasion, we give the preference to the last, by the Revd. Mr. Pierpoint, to the tune of *Scots wha ha*: Its tone and spirit is admirably suited to the occasion—they by Mr. Dawes is harsh and prosaic.

From the *Boston Centinel*, June 18.

Bunker Hill Battle Celebration.—The celebration of the 50th anniversary, of the memorable battle of Bunker Hill and the ceremony of laying the *Foundation Stone* of an Obelisk, to commemorate that great event, have taken place.

As public journalists, it is our duty to record the proceedings of the day; but we feel unable to do any thing like justice to the splendor of the _____ -parsed, or to the excellent spirit and _____ good feelings, which animated, _____ grandeur impulse, an assemblage, we ____ to be no exaggeration to _____ and fifty thousand, collected _____ or the union;

_____ and fair; and all the _____ were executed _____ which could _____ vision of all the _____

_____, having _____, assembled at an early hour in the morning at their Hall, and soon after were visited by their illustrious Brother, Gen. Lafayette, and their respected Brothers George Washington Lafayette, and Le Vasseur, the meeting was most interesting. After the fraternal greeting of Grand Master Abbott, the distinguished Guest expressed the great pleasure he felt in meeting the Brethren in the beloved city of Boston, on the anniversary of the battle of Bunker Hill, and in the Grand Lodge, whose first Grand Master had, in the true spirit of a Mason, shed his blood in defence of the liberties and institutions of his country, on that ever memorable occasion. The assemblage of the fraternity was very numerous. The Grand Lodges of Maine, New Hampshire, Rhode Island, Connecticut, Vermont, and New Jersey, were represented by their Grand Masters, or other distinguished members; and the Grand Royal Arch Chapters of several states by their Grand High Priests, and other officers. The distinguished Visitor was attended from and to his residence, at Mr. Lloyd's, by a deputation composed of Past Grand Masters and Deputies.

The Grand Procession was formed near the State House, with the utmost precision and regularity, under the superintending direction of Brig. Gen. Lyman, assisted by a staff composed of Majors Brimmer and Aspinwall of Boston; Major Edwards, of Brighton; Captains Sprague of Salem; Ford of Milton; Talbot of Dedham; and Young of Charlestown; Lieut. Baxter and Ensign Gardner of Boston.

The military escort was composed of sixteen companies, and a corps of cavalry commanded by Lt. Parker, all volunteers, and in full uniform.—Six of them were of Boston, commanded by Captains Tyler, Howe, Forrie, Prince, Loud, and Gardiner; three of Salem, commanded by Captains Cloutman, Pulsifer and Brown; two of Charlestown, commanded by Capt's Jenkins and Varney; one of Concord, commanded by Capt. Jarvis; one of Roxbury, commanded by Captain Spooner; one of Medford, by Captain Symmes; one from Malden, the Lt. Infantry, Capt. Buck; and one of Cambridge, by Capt. Willard. These formed two regiments, the first under Col. Thos. Hunting, of Boston, and Lieut. Col.

Stratten, of Watertown, and the second under Lt. Col. Stuart, of Boston, Major Baker of Dorchester, and Major Dennis of Boston. The military display was very imposing.

Survivors of the Battle.—These worthies were in eight barouches and carriages, and were about 40 in number—each wearing on his breast a badge, "*Bunker Hill, June 17, 1775,*" and many bearing the implements of wat they used in the fight. Then followed between on or two hundred revolutionary officers and soldiers, each bearing an appropriate badge. Their appearance was truly venerable.

The B.H.M. Association, in full numbers, six deep, all wearing the badge, "B.H.M.A."

The Masonic procession succeeded. This section of the procession was very splendid, and exceeded two thousand of the fraternity, all with their jewels and regalia. The Grand Lodge of this State was fully organized; and bore the implements and vessels used in laying the foundations of ancient edifices. They were followed by the Grand Encampment of the Knight Templars of R. Island, Connecticut, Vermont, Maine, New Hampshire and Massachusetts, in full numbers, with their banners, implements and regalia; by the Grand Lodges of these States; by the Grand Chapters of Royal Arch Masons, and by various subordinate Chapters and Lodges, bearing banners. A full band of music was attached to the masonic procession. Of the regalia of the Grand Lodge, was a gold urn, borne by the Deputy Grand Master, containing a relic of our departed Brother George Washington. We have not room today to enumerate the Great Great, Grand, and eminent Masters who were present.*

Hon. Mr. Webster, president, and other officers of the B.H.M. Association; the Rev. Dr. Kirkland, the Revd. Mr. Thaxter, (a revolutionary chaplain,) and the Rev. Mr. Walker, chaplains of the day; Directors and Committees of the Association; General Lafayette, in a coach and four, accompanied by Lieut. Gen. Lallemand, of Philadelphia; Mr. George Washington Lafayette, and the General's suite, in a carriage; His Excellency the Governor; the Hon. Council, Senate and House of Representatives, accompanied by the

Adjutant General, Secretary, Treasurer, &c.; Governor Fenner, the Secretary of War of the United States, and others; Delegations from various states; Delegation from the Pilgrim Society in Plymouth; Officers of the United States navy and army, and of the militia, in uniform; Citizens.

In this order the whole proceeded from the State-House, about half past 10, and passed on through Park, Common, School, Washington, Union, Hanover, and Prince-streets to Charles-River Bridge, and from thence through Maine, Green, and High-streets, in Charlestown, to the Monumental Square. The front of the procession had nearly reached the bridge, when the rear of it left the Common.

All the streets, the houses to their roofs, and in some instances to chimney tops, and every situation on which a footing could be obtained for a prospect of the procession, were filled with one condensed mass of well-dressed, cheerful looking persons, of all sexes and denominations, many of whom had occupied their station for several hours, and who, at appropriate places, spontaneously rent the air with joyous and orderly acclamation, while the ladies displayed their tokens of smiles, and waving handkerchiefs, as the procession passed, particularly when the Guest was in sight.

Arrived at the Monument spot, the carious sections of the procession, formed in squares around it; when the Grand Master of Massachusetts, accompanied by Gen. Lafayette, President Webster, the Past Grand Masters, the District Deputy Grand Master bearing the Architectural implements, the Grand Wardens bearing the *Corn, Wine,* and *Oil*, in vases, the Grand Chaplain, the Grand Treasurer, and the Principal Architect, repaired around the foundation stone, which having been squared, levelled, and plumbed, by the Grand Master, Brother Lafayette, and Mr. Webster, and declared to be true and proper, a casket was deposited in the cavity of the stone, containing coins, &c. and a silver plate with the following INSCRIPTION.

"On the XVII day of June, M.D.CCCXXV, at the request of the Bunker-Hill Monument Association, the Most Worshipful JOHN ABBOT, Grand Master of Masons in Massachusetts, did, in the presence of Gen. LAFAYETTE, lay this Corner-Stone of the MONUMENT to testify the gratitude of the present Generation to their Fathers, who, on 17th June, 1775, here fought in the cause of their country, and of free institutions, the memorable BATTLE OF BUNKER-HILL, and with their blood vindicated for their posterity the privileges and happiness this land has since enjoyed. Officers of the Bunker-Hill Monument Association. President, DANIEL WEBSTER; Vice Presidents, Thomas H. Perkins, Jospeh Story; Secretary, Edward Everett; Treasurer, Nathaniel P. Russell. [*Here follow a list of 25 Directors.*] Standing Committee for collecting Subscriptions.—Henry A. S. Dearborn, John C. Warren, Edward Everett, George Blake and Samuel D. Harris. Committee on the form of the Monument.—Daniel Webster, L. Baldwin, G. Stuart, Washington Alston, and G. Ticknor.

President of the United States.—John Quincy Adams. Governor of Massachusetts.—Levi Lincoln. Gov. of New Hampshire.—David L. Morrell. Gov. of Connecticut.—Oliver Wolcott.—Gov. of Vermont.—C.P. Van Ness. Gov. of Rhode Island.—James Fenner. Gov. of Maine.—Albion K. Paris. Alexander Parris, Architect."

The Grand Chaplain, the R.W. Br. Allen, of Chelmsford, then pronounced a benediction; the Grand Master strewed the *Corn*, *Wine*, and *Oil*, and delivered the implements of Architecture to the Master Builder, with orders to erect the Monument on the true principles of Masonry, to which the Architect made the following reply:

Most Worshipful Grand Master.—I receive form your hands these implements of science and labor, belonging to my *craft* and *professions*, with feelings of great personal diffidence, but still in the strongest confidence and faith that such is the triumphant spirit of the age, and such the numbers, ability, and power of those who have ordered the *craftsmen* to commence building, that the work with *go bravely on*, and the fathers who have this day come up, resting each upon his staff to see you lay the Corner-Stone, will live long enough to witness the dedication at the completion of the structure.

The benediction being repeated, the G.M. pronounced the ceremonies ended.

The procession, which was inside the lines, then cheered, and salutes were fired on Bunker Hill by the Charlestown Artillery, Capt. Sanders, and on Copps Hill in Boston, by the Sea Fencibles commanded by Lieut. Lewis.

The procession then moved to an ampitheatrical area, where accommodations had been made, on a most ample scale, for the accommodation of the auditors of the Address of the President of the Association. They included a large portion of the north-eastern declivity of the battle hill. In the centre of the base, a rural arch and bower, surmounted by the American Eagle, was formed for the government of the Association, and some of the Guests, in front of which, after the venerable Mr. Thaxtor had addressed the Throne of Grace, the Orator, *sub caelo*, pronounced an Address, which none but its author is capable of doing justice to in a summary, and which will be printed and read with a pleasure equalled only by that which electrified the vast assemblage who listened to it for nearly one hour and a quarter. It is enough for us to say, that it was in every particular worthy of the celebrity of the orator, and that his address to the silver-headed worthies of the Revolution, and to the distinguished Guest of the Nation, filled every heart with transport. On each side of the bower, seats, with awnings, had been prepared, and were filled by over on thousand Ladies, from all parts of the Union, presenting a spectacle of animated beauty and intelligence, and offering a fine contrast to the other parts of the auditory. The exercises commenced and closed with the following Hymns, sung by a powerful choir, to the two good old tunes. An Ode, written for the occasion, was omitted for want of time.

FIRST HYMN.

By the Rev. J. Pierpont.—*Tune*, "Old Hundred."

    O, is not this a holy spot!
        'Tis the high place of Freedom's birth:—
God of our Fathers! is it no
        The holiest spot of all the earth?
Quenched is thy flame on Horeb's side:
        The robber roams o'er Sinai now;
And those old men, they seers, abide
        No more on Zion's mournful brow.

But on *this* Hill thou, Lord, has dwelt,
    Since round his head the war-cloud curled,
And wrapped our fathers, where they knelt
    In prayer and battle for a world.
Here sleeps their dust: 'tis holy ground:
    And we, the children of the brave.
From the four winds are gathered round,
    To lay our offering on their grave.
Free as the winds around us blow,
    Free as yon waves below us spread,
We rear a pile, that long shall throw
    Its shadow on their sacred be.
But on their deeds no shade shall fall,
    While o'er their couch thy sun shall flame:
Thine ear was bowed to hear their call,
And thy right hand shall guard their fame.

SECOND HYMN
By the Rev. James Flint—*Tune, "St. Martin's."*
    O Glorious day! that saw the array
        Of freemen in their might,
When here they stood, unused to blood,
    Yet dared th' unequal fight.
The sons are met to own the debt
    Due to their fathers' fame;
And here they place the column's base
    To bear their deathless name.
'Tis not that here the victor's cheer
    Rung o'er the falling foe,—
That earth here drank, of many a rank,
    The life-blood's gushing flow:
The pledge here given to earth and heaven,
    Freemen to live or die—
This gives their fame its sacred claim
    To immortality.
To God, who willed a state to build,
    Based on the rights of man—
Glory we give, who this day live
    To hail th' accomplished plan.

The Dinner, — The guests and subscribers to the dinner were then escorted to Bunker Hill, where an edifice, covering 38,400 square feet of ground, had been erected; and in which, at twelve tables, running its entire length, 400 feet, 4000 plates were laid, which were all occupied. A spacious gallery contained an excellent band of music; and the following toasts, interspersed with songs and martial airs, were announced by Mr. F.C. Whiston, amidst the most deafening bursts of applause. The scene defies description: and as much order prevailed, as was compatible with the festivity of the occasion, and the magnitude of the company.

TOASTS.

1st. *The 17th of June*, 1775—The marble may moulder; but while a heart beats in an American's bosom, there will be a *tablet* from which the record of that day's glory shall never be effaced.

ODE.

By Rufus Dawes, Esq.

Let Freedom's banner swell with patriot pride!
While Glory's iron heralds proclaim along the shore.
The Day! when Albion crimsoned Charle's tide,
And Bunker shook beneath the battle's roar:
How majestic the Spirit, that rode upon her thunder,
Whose bolts, indignant, broke Oppression's chains asunder;
When first our yeoman band,
The bulwark of the land,
Like monarch oaks, withstood
The dark, contending flood,
And bought with blood a freeman's rights, our heritage to be.
Huzza! Huzza! Huzza! Huzza! Huzza!
Our Genius gave the mandate, declaring we were free,
Huzza! Huzza! Huzza! Huzza! Huzza!
And Independence sealed the high decree.
Arise! Arise! ye patriot spirits, rise!
And hail the glorious morn, when your star of freedom rose;
When Bunker hurled her lightning, like the skies,

And poured a flaming torrent on her foes;
When our sires, our gallant sires, their dearest birthright shielded,
And wrote our Magna Charta in the sacred blood they yielded!
    Whose monument shall stand
    In Alpine glory grand;
    Where our mountain bird shall soar,
    When around the tempests roar,
Their lifted pile's gigantic strength exultingly to see.
    Huzza! Huzza! &c. &c. &c.
    Should hostile legions darken round the land,
Your rock-encompassed shore presuming to invade;
    The towering temple, Liberty! would stand,
To blast thy fell oppressors with its shade:
In grandeur unrivaled, they pillared dome ascending,
Shall strengthen on, from age to age our father's fame extending:
    While round thee fanes decay,
    Exempt from ruin's sway,
    Thy stately front sublime,
    Shall stand the proof of time,
And, midst its beating storm, secure, unshaken ever be.
    Huzza! Huzza! &c. &c. &c.
    Arise! Arise! ye patriot spirits rise!
Our jubilee of Glory demands a nations song;
    Triumphant music wake, with glad surprise,
Till Echo every rapturous strain prolong;
Let the clarion of Fame, from shore to shore be sounded;
And lo Paeans ring, through Heaven's high arch unbounded!
    Let the trumpet proudly swell;
    Wake, wake the inspiring shell!
    While the rosy cup goes round,
    With ruby nectar crowned,
And we drink to them, who nursed with blood our drooping freedom tree!
    Huzza! Huzza! &c. &c. &c.

    2d. *The Militia.* — What more than to name the spot whereon we stand, to proclaim its character to the world.

Tune—"*Yankee Doodle.*"

3d. *The Committee of Safety.* — The early guardians of our nation's rights; fearless, as faithful in the execution of their trust.

Tune—"*Rise Columbia*"

4th. *The Martyrs of Bunker Hill Battle.* —We inhale the air they breathed; we tread the ground they trod; we surround the altar where their lives were offered; we swear devotion to their cause! (drank standing.)

ODE.

By Thomas Wells, Esq.

Ye Shades of martyred heroes,
    Who rallied here in fight;
Whose hearts of oak the onset braved
    That shook old Bunker's height;
Who, with your Warren, proved yourselves
    The Spartans of the field, —
Here ye stood—here your blood
    Freedom's sacred charter sealed;
Here to Liberty you pledge ye gave,
    And the sacred charter sealed.
Where Britain launched her lightning,
    On Havoc's wing that swept;
There, reckless of the fray, ye still
    The van of danger kept: —
Unawed by tyrant power, yet then
    Your lusty sinews steeled
In the might—of your right,
    When ye Freedom's charter sealed;
When submission proudly ye forswore,
    And the sacred charter sealed.
Ye brave, in death triumphant!
    In Glory's rest that sleep;
Your country shall your ashes guard,
    Her watch around you keep; —
Your Spirits here that walk abroad,
    Have not unheard appealed
From the sod where ye trod,

    And the sacred charter sealed;
Where ye gathered with your hardy few
    And the sacred charter sealed.
Here fond Remembrance lingers,
    On your renown to dwell;
And Gratitude decrees the pile
    Where ye devoted fell; —
Where, prodigal of life, ye met
    Your heritage to shield;
Be the spot ne'er forgot
    Where ye Freedom's charter sealed,
Where the earnest *to be free* ye gave,
    And the sacred charter sealed.
Behold!—our Nation's Champion,
    Who shared with us the fight;
Behold!—he comes your shrine to bless,
    To mingle with the rite: —
In peril's hour, the righteous sword,
    Who dared for us to wield,
When we broke Thraldom's yoke,
    And our independence sealed;
When to arms each hill and valley rung,
    And the noble cause was sealed.
Your fame, ye patriot fathers,
    Enrolled on Glory's page,
Shall live beyond the Pyramid,
    And brighten on with age;
The deeds your valor wrought shall be
    From sire to son revealed,
Where ye stood—where your blood
    Freedom's sacred charter sealed;
Where to Liberty your pledge was given,
    And the glorious cause was sealed.

5th. *Bunker Hill Monument.* — Its proud summit shall brighten with the morning's *first* beam, and the evening's last ray; it shall glow with a still richer and purer light in speaking *their* deeds who repose beneath it.

ODE.
                    By Dr. Percival
When our Patriot Fathers met
    In the dark and trying hour,
While the hand of Britain yet
    Pressed us with its weight of power,
Still they dared to tell the foe,
    They were never made for slaves, —
Still they bade the nations know,
    They were free as ocean's waves.
Yonder is the glorious hill,
    Where their blood was nobly shed—
Never with a firmer will
    Hearts of freemen beat and bled:
Shall the son forget his sire?
    No—the admiring world shall see
High a pillared tomb aspire,
    Like a tower of Liberty.
Now the arch of empire swells
    Proud and daring, fixed and strong,
While the hand of ruin fells
    Nations that have flourished long;
Loftier the temple springs—
    Telling on its front sublime,
How it scorns the rage of kings
    And the wasting tooth of time.
From its high and lifted brow,
    See! it sends a wakening light,
Where a world is slumbering now
    In the shades of eastern night:
They shall feel the quickening fire —
    Rise and run to meet the day,
And their hearts shall never tire,
    Till their chains are rent away.
None shall ever rashly dare
    Lift his hand against this shrine,
While its pediment shall bear
    Names, so honored and divine:
High above the sacred band,

There its light unfading set,
Like twin stars of glory, stand
Washington and Lafayette.

6th. *The Survivors of Bunker Hill Battle.* — The *gloom* of *that* day may dwell on their recollection: but in the *brightness* of *this*, they feel, that they fought under the auspices of Heaven.

Tune—*Adams and Liberty*

The Orator of the Day. —A statesman and patriot, who knows no party but his country, who feels no impulse but her welfare.

7th. *Lexington and Concord.* — There the earnest was given, that a people, *resolved to be free*, can never be enslaved! Tune—"*Old Soldier.*"

8th. The President of the United States.
"*Washington's March.*"

9th. The Governor of the Commonwealth."
"Gve. Bacts, March."

10th. The Continental Army—Whom victory could not elate, whom defeat could not depress—their cause their country, their trust their God!

ODE.

By Rev. John Pierpont/
Tune—"*Sesti whobut,*" lze.

"Spread your brother to _____!
Let the red cross dance on _____
Charge! their unfledged bird will fly
    When our trumpets blow.
When they hear our Lion roar,
From the ships and from the shore,
Then, my lads, you'll see no more,
    Of your rebel foe!"
"Stand! The ground's your own, my braves!
Will ye give it up to slaves?
Will ye look for greener graves?
    Hope ye mercy still?
What's the mercy despots feel?

Hear it in that battle peal!
Read it on yon bristling steel!
    Ask it—ye who will.
Fear ye foes who kill for hire?
Will ye to your *homes* retire?
Look behind you! they're on fire!
    And, before you, see
Who have done it! — From the vale
On they come! — and will ye quail? —
Leaden rain and iron hail,
    Let their welcome be.
In the God of battles trust!
Die we may—and die we must: —
But, O, where can dust to dust
    Be consigned so well,
As where heaven its dues shall shed
On the martyr'd patriot's bed,
And the rocks shall raise their head,
    Of his deeds to tell."

11th. *The Memory of Washington.*   Dirge.

12th. *The Continental Congress.* — *The embodied wisdom of the nation*; which wrought the freedom of one hemisphere, and promulgated the principles which will emancipate the other.

13th. *The Memory of Warren.* — Associated with this occasion; his name comes to us "as the gentle rain from Heaven, refreshing the place beneath."

After the regular toasts the President of the Association said,

He rose to propose a toast, in behalf of the Directors of the Association. Probably, he was already anticipated, in the name which he should mention. It was well known, that the distinguished personage near him, from the time when he first became acquainted with the object of the Association, had taken much interest in it, and had expressed an intention to be present at the ceremony of laying the Corner Stone. This primus he had kindly remembers, through the long course of his visits to the several states. It was not at all necessary to say—indeed it could not be said—how much his presence had added to the interest and pleasure of the occasion. He should proceed at once to the grateful duty which the Directors had enjoined on him, and propose to the company

"Health and long life to Gen. LAFAYETTE."

On which Gen. Lafayette rose, and expressed himself:

Gentlemen,—I will not longer trespass on your time than to thank you in the name of my Revolutionary companions in arms and myself for the testimonies of esteem and affection, I may say, of filial affection, which have been bestowed upon us on the memorable celebration of this Anniversary day, and to offer our fervent prayers for the preservation of that Republican freedom, equality, and self-government, that blessed union between the States of the confederacy for which we have fought and bled, and on which rests the hopes of mankind. Permit me to propose the following sentiment: —

Bunker Hill, and the holy resistance to oppression which has already enfranchised the American hemisphere, — the next half Century Jubilee's toast shall be, — *to Enfranchised Europe.*

The business of the United States, and that of the State of New York, prevented the attendance of the President and Gov. Clinton, on the memorable celebration.

One of the old soldiers, who took a part in the Bunker Hill Battle, was present at the celebration with the same coat which he wore in the battle, and which has in it no less than *nine bullet holes*!

* Note.—The following address of the M.E. John H. Sheppard, Grand King of the Grand Royal Arch Chapter of Maine, (which formed a splendid part of the cortege) was delivered to the Grand Master of Massachusetts, immediately after laying the Corner Stone, by direction of the Chapter, and will afford the reader better information on the subject on the Masonic part of the ceremony than any we are able to give :—

"*M.W. Grand Master of the Grand Lodge of Massachusetts.*

"I have the honor in behalf of Grand Royal Arch Chapter of Maine, to present to you our felicitations on the interesting ceremonies of this memorable day. Your invitation has assembled, we have reason to believe, a larger number of organized fraternities on the first Battle Ground of American Independence, than have ever met together since the completion and dedication of the Temple of Solomon, where the Masons of all countries were spectators of the scene. Under your direction this great body have laid the Corner Stone of a Monument to be erected as a lasting memorial to the first battle which changed the moral and political destiny of a new continent, the celebration of this event in the splendid manner we have this day witnessed, will be ever dear to our recollection, not only as brethren of the great Masonic Family, but as citizen, of an immense Republic, whose greatest glory is the happiness of all its individual members. We have also had the satisfaction of witnessing your interview with the illustrious Lafayette, whose name is so justly endeared to every good man, and of assuring him in your presence of our perfect concordance with the sentiments you expressed. Allow me also, M.W.G. Master to communicate to you, the high sense entertained by the M.E.G. High Priest, and by the Grand Royal Arch Chapter of the State of Maine, of the attention we have received on this occasion."

To which the M.W. Grand Master made an appropriate and affectionate reply.

BIBLIOGRAPHY

Auburn Theological Seminary 1820-1870, Dennis Bro's & Thorne, Auburn, 1870

Badger, Joseph, *A Memoir of Rev Joseph Badger*, ed. by Henry Noble Day, Sawyer, Ingersoll and Company, Hudson, Ohio, 1851

Barber, John W., and Howe, Henry, *Historical collections of the state of New York*, S. Tuttle, New York 1842

Barbour, Lucius Barnes, *Families of Early Hartford, Connecticut*, Genealogical Publishing Co., Inc., Baltimore, 1977

Becker, John E., *A History of the Village of Waterloo*, Waterloo Library and Historical Society, Waterloo, New York, 1949

Beers, F.W., *Gazetteer and Biographical Record of Genesee County*, J.W. Vose & Co., Publishers, Syracuse, NY, June 1890

Belloc, Hilaire, *The Road*, for The British Reinforced Concrete Engineering Co. Ltd., Charles W. Hobson, Manchester, 1923

Brackenridge, H.M., *History of the Late War Between the United States and Great Britain*, Cuming & Jewitt, Baltimore, 1818

Brandon, Edgar Ewing, *A Pilgrimage of Liberty*, The Lawhead Press, Athens, Ohio, 1944

Broadhead, John Romeyn, *Documents Relative to the Colonial History of the State of New York, Vol VI*, E.B. O'Callaghan, ed, Weed, Parsons & Co, 1855

Broadhead, John Romeyn, *Documents Relative to the Colonial History of the State of New York, Vol X*, E.B. O'Callaghan, ed, Weed, Parsons & Co, 1858

Brown, William Mosely, *George Washington Freemason*, Garrett & Massie, Inc., Richmond, 1952

Census Of the State Of New York, For 1865, New York State Library

Chadwick, G. H., "Large fault in western New York," *Geological Society of America, Bulletin, Vol. 31*, New York, 1920

Chappell, Josephine Gregg, "Early History of the Genesee Country—Events and Men," *Rochester Historical Society Publication Fund Series Vol. 2*, 1923

Chautauqua History Company, *The Centennial History of Chautauqua County Vol. I*, Jamestown, 1904

Chautauqua History Company, *The Centennial History of Chautauqua County Vol. II*, Jamestown, 1904

Child, Hamilton, *Gazetteer and Business Directory of Chautauqua County, NY for 1873-4*, Journal Office, Syracuse, 1873

Child, Hamilton, *Gazetteer and Business Directory of Monroe County*, NY for 1869-70, Journal Office, Syracuse, 1869

Child, Hamilton, *Gazetteer and Business Directory of Niagara County, NY for 1869*, Journal Office, Syracuse, 1869

Clark, James, A., *The chronological history of the petroleum and natural gas industries*, Clark Book Co., Houston, 1963

Cruikshank, Lt-Col. E., *The Documentary History of the Campaigns Upon The Niagara Frontier in 1812-4, Vol IX, December 1813 to May, 1814*, The Lundy's Lan Historical Society, Tribune Office, Welland, 1908

Downs, John P. & Fenwick Y. Hedley, *History of Chautauqua County New York and Its People-Vol. 1*, American Historical Society, 1921

Dwight, Timothy, *Travels in New England and New York Vol. IV*, Willams Baynes and Son, London, 1823

Edson, Obed (Historian), History of Chautauqua County New York, Georgia Drew Merrill, Editor, W.A Fergusson & Co, Boston, Mass, 1894

Emerson, ed. Edgar C., ed., *Our County and Its People A Descriptive Work on Jefferson County*, The Boston History Company, 1898

Evans, Paul Demund, *The Holland Land Company*, Buffalo Historical Society, Buffalo, NY 1924

Everts, Ensign & Everts, *History of Ontario County, New York With Illustrations*, Philadelphia, 1878

Everts, Ensign & Everts, *History of Seneca County*, J.B. Lippincott & Co., Philadelphia, 1876Fay, H.A., *Collection of the Official Accounts in Detail of All the Battles Fought by Sea and Lan, Between the Navy and Army of the United States, and the Navy and Army of Great Britian, During the Years 1812, 13, 14, & 15.*, E. Conrad, New York, 1817

Finney, Charles G., *Memoirs of Rev. Charles G. Finney*, Fleming H. Revell Company, New York, 1876

Ford, Worthington Chauncey, *The Writings of George Washington, Vol. XIV. 1798-1799*, The Knickerbocker Press, G.P. Putnam's Sons, New York, 1983

"George Washington Papers, Series 2, Letterbooks 1754-1799," Library of Congress

Gibson, Campbell, "Population of the 100 Largest Cities and Other Urban Places In The United States: 1790 to 1990," U.S. Census Bureau, June 1998

Gottschalk, Louis, *Lafayette Comes to America*, University of Chicago, 1975

Granger, J. Albert, "The History of Canandaigua," *Ontario Repository and Messenger*, 1876

Hall, Henry, *The History of Auburn*, Dennis Bro's & Co., Auburn, NY, 1869

Hastings, Hugh, ed., *Military Minutes of the Council of Appointment of the State of New York 1783-1821, Vol III*, James B. Lyon, State Printer, Albany 1901

Hill, Henry Wayland, *Municipality of Buffalo New York A History 1720-1923, Volume I*, Lewis Historical Publishing Company, New York, 1923

Hotchkin, James H., *A History of the Purchase and Settlement of Western New York: and of the rise, progress and present state of the Presbyterian Church in that section*, M.W.Dodd, Birck Church Chapel, New York, 1848

Hough, Franklin B., *A History of St. Lawrence and Franklin Co*, Little & Co, Albany 1853

Hough, Franklin B., *Census of the State of New York for 1865*, Charles Van Benthuysen & Sons, Albany, 1867

Hulbert, Archer Butler, *Pioneer Roads and Experiences of Travelers (Volume II)*, by, The Arthur H. Clark Company, Cleveland, Ohio

In Memoriam Dirck C. Lansing, D.D., Knapp, Peck, & Thomson, Auburn, 1883

Johnson, Crisfield, *History of Erie County*, Printing House of Matthews & Warren, Buffalo, NY, 1876

Kelsey, John, *The Lives and Reminiscences of the Pioneers of Rochester*, J. Kelsey, Rochester, 1854

Ketchum, William, *History of Buffalo Vol II*, Rockwell, Baker & Hill, Buffalo, NY, 1864

Kramer, Lloyd S., *Lafayette in Two Worlds: Public Cultures and Personal Identities in an Age of Revolutions*, The University of North Carolina Press, 1999

Krieger, Amo, *Sesquicentennial Souvenir Program And History of the Town of Mendon*, O'Brien Bros. Printing, Honeoye Falls, NY, 1963

Lane, Jason, *General and Madame de Lafayette: Partners in Liberty's Cause in the American and French Revolutions*, Taylor Trade Publishing, 2003

Leepson, Marc, *Lafayette: Lessons in Leadership from the Idealist General*, St. Martin's Press, 2011

Levasseur, André-Nicolas, *Lafayette in America in 1824 and 1825, Vol. I*, John D. Godman translation, Philadelphia, Carey and Lea, 1829

Levasseur, André-Nicolas, *Lafayette in America in 1824 and 1825, Vol. II*, John D. Godman translation, Philadelphia, Carey and Lea, 1829

Lewis Historical Publishing Company, *Genealogical and Family History of Northern New York Vol. II*, 1910

Lossing, Benson J., *The Pictorial Field-Book of the War of 1812*, Harper & Brothers, New York, 1868

Main, William, *Charles Williamson*, Cowan & Co., Ltd., Perth, 1899

Mathews, Lois Kimball, The Expansion of New England, (Boston: Houghton Mifflin Company), 1909

McIntosh, W.H., *History of Ontario County, New York*, Everts, Ensign & Everts, Philadelphia, 1876

McMaster, Guy H., *History of the Settlement of Steuben County*, R.S. Underhill & Co, Bath, NY, 1853

Miner, Julius, *Buffalo Medical and Surgical Journal, Vol. VIII*, Warren, Johnson & Co., 1869

Morgan, Lewis H., *League of the Ho-de-no sau-nee or Iroquois*, Herbert Lloyd, ed., Dodd, Mead and Company, 1904 [reprint, 1851]

Morrison, William, *History of Monroe County*, Everts, Ensign & Everts, Philadelphia, 1877

New York (State), *Documents of the Senate of the State of New York, Volume 5*, 1886

O'Reilly, Henry, *Settlement in the West. Sketch of Rochester with Incidental Notices of Western New York*, William Alling, Publisher, Rochester, 1838

Parker, Arthur C., *Red Jacket, last of the Seneca*, McGraw-Hill, New York, 1952

Proceedings of the New-York Historical Society, January-May, 1847, William Van Norden, New York, 1847

Robinson, Charles Mulford, "The Life of Judge Augustus Porter," *Publications of the Buffalo Historical Society Vol VII*, Buffalo Historical Society, Buffalo, 1904

Rochester Historical Society, *Rochester Historical Society Publication Fund Series Vol. 14*, Rochester, 1936

Rubin, Zoe, "The Tories of 1812," *The Yale Historical Review*, Volume V Issue II, Spring 2016

Sanford, Laura G., *The History of Erie County, Pennsylvania*, (Philadelphia: J.B. Lippincott & Co.), 1862

Sandford & Co., *History of Niagara County, NY*, New York

Severance, Frank H., ed.. *The Picture Book of Earlier Buffalo*, [*Buffalo Historical Society Publications, Volume Sixteen*], Buffalo Historical Society, Buffalo, NY, 1912

Seward, Olive Risley, "The Marquis De Lafayette. His Great Service to our Country and His Visit to Chautauqua County," *The Centennial History of Chautauqua County Vol I*, Chautauqua History Company, Jamestown, 1904

Spafford, Horatio Gates, *Pocket Guide for the Tourist and Traveller Along the Canals*, T. and J. Swords, New York, 1824

Stone, William Leete, *The Life and Times of Sir William Johnson*, Bart, Volume II, Munsell, Albany, 1865

Storke, Elliot G., *History of Cayuga County*, D. Mason & Co., Syracuse, NY, 1879

Taylor, Horace Clefton, *Historical Sketches of the Town of Portland*, W. McKinstry & Son, Printers, Fredonia, NY, 1873

The Times, *A History of the City of Buffalo and Niagara Falls*, Buffalo, NY, 1896

Turner, Orsamus, *Pioneer History of the Holland Purchase of Western New York*, Jewett, Thomas & Co., 1849

Turner, Orsamus, *Pioneer History of the Phelps and Gorham's Purchase and Morris Reserve (supplement of Monroe County)*, William Alling, Rochester, 1851

Turner, Orsamus, *History of the Pioneer Settlement of Phelps & Gorham's Purchase, and Morris' Reserve*, William Alling, Publisher, Rochester, 1852

Upton, Harriet Taylor, *History of the Western Reserve*, Lewis Publishing Company, Chicago, 1910

Walker. John, *Elements of Geography and of Natural and Civil History, 3rd ed.*, Darton & Harvey, London, 1800

Warren, Emory F., *Historical Sketches of Chautauque County*, J. Warren Fletcher, Jamestown, NY, 1846

Young, Andrew W., *History of Chautauqua County*, Printing House of Matthews & Warren, Buffalo, NY, 1875

ENDNOTES

Chapter 1: What Took Congress So Long?
[1] *Richmond Enquirer*, Thursday, March 4, 1824, p.4
[2] *Richmond Enquirer*, Friday, April 2, 1824, p.3
[3] Ibid.
[4] *Richmond Enquirer*, Saturday, January 17, 1824, p.2
[5] Ibid.
[6] Ibid.
[7] *The Evening Post*, Saturday, January 24, 1824, p.2
[8] *The Charleston Mercury*, Friday, February 6, 1824, p.2
[9] *The Evening Post*, Monday, February 2, 1824, p.2
[10] *Knoxville Register*, Friday, March 5, 1824, p.2
[11] *Alexandria Gazette*, Thursday, February 12, 1824, p.3

Chapter 2: The Duty That Held Him Back
[1] Gottschalk, Louis, *Lafayette Comes to America*, University of Chicago, 1975, p.26
[2] Ibid., p.2
[3] Source: Paritius (1709) link Comparison of Coinslink © Matthias Böhne / Olaf Simons, 2004. Retrieved January 20, 2024
[4] Source: https://www.in2013dollars.com/uk/inflation/1770. Retrieved January 20, 2024
[5] Source: https://www.xe.com/currencyconverter/convert/. Retrieved January 20, 2024
[6] Leepson, Marc, *Lafayette: Lessons in Leadership from the Idealist General*, St. Martin's Press, 2011, p.10
[7] Lane, Jason, *General and Madame de Lafayette: Partners in Liberty's Cause in the American and French Revolutions*, Taylor Trade Publishing, 2003, p.10
[8] "From Geo. Washington to Benj. Harrison, August 19, 1777." National Archives. Retrieved January 20, 2024
[9] Leepson, p.36-37
[10] Leepson, p.37
[11] Ibid.
[12] *Burlington Sentinel*, Friday, April 2, 1824, p.3

Chapter 3: A Message From An Old Friend
[1] Kramer, Lloyd S., *Lafayette in Two Worlds: Public Cultures and Personal Identities in an Age of Revolutions*, The University of North Carolina Press, 1999, p.71
[2] Ibid., p.73
[3] "From The Foreign Journals," *Aberdeen Journal, and General Advertiser for the North of Scotland*, Wednesday, February 4, 1824, p.4

⁴ Levasseur, André-Nicolas, *Lafayette in America in 1824 and 1825*, John D. Godman translation, Philadelphia, Carey and Lea, 1829, p.10
⁵ Ibid., p.10
⁶ *Gettysburg Compiler*, Wednesday, May 5, 1824, p.3
⁷ *The National Gazette*, Monday, April 26, 1824, p 2
⁸ Levasseur, p.10
⁹ *The Portland Gazette*, Tuesday, June 1, 1824, p.3

Chapter 4: America In 1824
¹ Rubin, Zoe, "The Tories of 1812," *The Yale Historical Review*, Volume V Issue II, Spring 2016, p.120

Chapter 5: And The Lucky Winner Is…
¹ *The National Gazette*, Thursday, March 4, 1824, p.2
² *Richmond Enquirer*, Friday, April 2, 1824, p.3
³ Ibid.
⁴ *Vermont Gazette*, Tuesday, April 13, 1824, p.2
⁵ *The National Gazette*, Monday, April 26, 1824, p.2
⁶ *Vermont Republican and American Yeoman*, Monday, May 3, 1824, p.2
⁷ *Woodstock Observer* [Vermont], Tuesday, May 4, 1824, p.2
⁸ *Gettysburg Compiler*, Wednesday, May 5, 1824, p.3
⁹ *Gettysburg Compiler*, Wednesday, June 9, 1824, p.3
¹⁰ *The Pittsfield Sun*, Thursday, June 24, 1824, p.3
¹¹ *Georgia Journal and Messenger*, Wednesday, June 30, 1824, p.3
¹² Levasseur, A., *Lafayette in America in 1824 and 1825*, John D. Godman translation, Philadelphia, Carey and Lea, 1829, p.11
¹³ *The National Gazette*, Saturday, March 6, 1824, p.2
¹⁴ *The Pittsfield Sun*, Thursday, June 17, 1824, p.2
¹⁵ *Richmond Enquirer*, Tuesday, June 29, 1824, p.2
¹⁶ Levasseur, p.13
¹⁷ *Poughkeepsie Journal*, Wednesday, August 25, 1824, p.3

Chapter 6: America Welcomes The Nation's Guest
¹ Levasseur, A., *Lafayette in America in 1824 and 1825. Vol. 1*, John D. Godman translation, (Philadelphia: Carey and Lea, 1829), p.13
² *Georgia Journal and Messenger*, Wednesday, August 4, 1824, p.3
³ Ibid.
⁴ Ibid.
⁵ http://www.fortwiki.com/Fort_Lafayette_(2) [Retrieved February 10, 2024]
⁶ http://www.fortwiki.com/Fort_Lafayette_(1) [Retrieved February 10, 2024]
⁷ Levasseur, p.14
⁸ *Poughkeepsie Journal*, Wednesday, August 25, 1824, p.2

⁹ Levasseur, p.14
¹⁰ *Poughkeepsie Journal*, Wednesday, August 25, 1824, p.2
¹¹ Ibid., p.15
¹² Ibid.
¹³ Ibid.
¹⁴ *Poughkeepsie Journal*, Wednesday, August 25, 1824, p.2
¹⁵ Ibid.
¹⁶ Levasseur, p.16
¹⁷ *Poughkeepsie Journal*, Wednesday, August 25, 1824, p.3

Chapter 7: Why Lafayette?
¹ *The Bath Chronicle* [Bath, Avon, England], Thursday, August 27, 1778, p.3
² *The Leeds Intelligencer and Yorkshire General Advertiser* [Leeds, West Yorkshire, England], Tuesday, August 28, 1781, p.3
³ *The Freeman's Journal or The North American Intelligencer* [Philadelphia, Pennsylvania], Wednesday, July 11, 1781, p.3
⁴ "Lafayette and the Virginia Campaign 1781," National Park Service, https://www.nps.gov/york/learn/historyculture/lafayette-and-the-virginia-campaign-1781.htm, retrieved February 18, 2024
⁵ *Cambridge Chronicle and Journal* [Cambridge, Cambridgeshire, England], Saturday, October 28, 1780, p.1
⁶ *The Writings of George Washington, Vol. XIV. 1798-1799*, Worthington Chauncey Ford, The Knickerbocker Press, G.P. Putnam's Sons, New York, 1983, p.452-453
⁷ Ibid., p.128
⁸ "Republicanism in France," *Vermont Republican and American Yeoman*, Monday, June 1, 1818, p.3
⁹ "Will Be Exhibited," 1805.08.23 *Lancaster Intelligencer and Journal* [Lancaster, Pennsylvania], Friday, August 23, 1805, p.3
¹⁰ "Gen. La Fayette, and Col. Willet," *North Star* [Danville, Vermont], Thursday, November 7, 1822, p.1
¹¹ Ibid.

Chapter 8: Overview Of 1824-1825 American Visit (Part I)
¹ Levasseur, A., *Lafayette in America in 1824 and 1825. Vol. I*, John D. Godman translation, (Philadelphia: Carey and Lea, 1829), p.iii
² This isn't a complete list of stops. For that, go to https://lafayette200.org/, [Retrieved February 24, 2024]
³ *Poughkeepsie Journal*, Wednesday, August 25, 1824, p.3
⁴ Levasseur, A., *Lafayette in America in 1824 and 1825. Vol. II*, John D. Godman translation, (Philadelphia: Carey and Lea, 1829), p.9
⁵ Ibid., p.10

⁶ Ibid., p.30
⁷ Ibid., p.30

Chapter 9: Overview Of 1824-1825 American Visit (Part II)

¹ Levasseur, A., *Lafayette in America in 1824 and 1825. Vol. II*, John D. Godman translation, (Philadelphia: Carey and Lea, 1829), p.31
² Ibid., p.42
³ https://www.scgrandlodgeafm.org/grand-masters-news/message-from-the-grand-master3224245, [Retrieved February 24, 2024]
⁴ Levasseur, *Vol. II*, p.63
⁵ Ibid., p.87-88
⁶ Ibid., p.89
⁷ Ibid., p.130
⁸ Ibid., p.149
⁹ "La Fayette," *The Evening Post* [New York, New York], Friday, May 27, 1825, p.2
¹⁰ Levasseur, *Vol. II*, p.159
¹¹ "LaFayette's Papers," *Buffalo Emporium and General Advertiser*, Saturday, July 9, 1825, p.3
¹² Levasseur, *Vol. II*, p.182-183

Chapter 10 – Lafayette Prepares To Enter The Greater Western New York Region

¹ https://www.calculatorsoup.com/calculators/time/sunrise_sunset.php, [Retrieved March 9, 2024] If this seems odd, remember there was no Daylight Savings Time and, indeed, we wouldn't have Standard Time until 1883.
² "LaFayette in Fredonia," *Fredonia Censor*, August 21, 1872, p.1-2
³ Documents of the Senate of the State of New York, Volume 5, by New York (State). 1886, p.438
⁴ Ibid.
⁵ Sanford, Laura G., *The History of Erie County, Pennsylvania*, (Philadelphia: J.B. Lippincott & Co.), 1862, p.59-60
⁶ Ibid. p.97
⁷ Mathews, Lois Kimball, The Expansion of New England, (Boston: Houghton Mifflin Company), 1909, p.151
⁸ "Arrival of Gen. La Fayette at Erie," *Erie Gazette*, Wednesday, June 9, 1825, p.3
⁹ Ibid.
¹⁰ Ibid.
¹¹ Ibid.
¹² Ibid.
¹³ Levasseur, A., *Lafayette in America in 1824 and 1825. Vol. II*, John D. Godman translation, (Philadelphia: Carey and Lea, 1829), p.185
¹⁴ Ibid, *Erie Gazette*

Chapter 11 – The State Of Greater Western New York In 1825

[1] Turner, Orsamus, *History of the Pioneer Settlement of Phelps & Gorham's Purchase, and Morris' Reserve*, William Alling, Publisher, Rochester, 1852, p.106

[2] O'Reilly, Henry, *Settlement in the West. Sketch of Rochester with Incidental Notices of Western New York*, William Alling, Publisher, Rochester, 1838, p.128

[3] Turner, p.107

[4] O'Reilly, p.127

[5] McIntosh, W.H., *History of Ontario County, New York*, Everts, Ensign & Everts, Philadelphia, 1876, p.37

[6] Hough, Franklin B., *Census of the State of New York for 1865*, Charles Van Benthuysen & Sons, Albany, 1867

[7] Turner, p.109

[8] Turner, p.110

[9] *History of Niagara County, NY*, Sandford & Co., New York, p.41

[10] Ibid, p.88

[11] Hotchkin, James H. A history of the purchase and settlement of western New York: and of the rise, progress and present state of the Presbyterian Church in that section. New York: M.W. Dodd, 1848. Pdf. Retrieved from the Library of Congress April 24, 2024, <www.loc.gov/item/a40001696/>, p.4

[12] Johnson, Crisfield, *History of Erie County*, Printing House of Matthews & Warren, Buffalo, NY, 1876, p.207

[13] Beers, F.W., *Gazetteer and Biographical Record of Genesee County*, J.W. Vose & Co., Publishers, Syracuse, NY, June 1890, p.396

[14] Warren, Emory F., Historical Sketches of Chautauque County, J. Warren Fletcher, Jamestown, NY, 1846 p.60

[15] Turner, p.456

[16] Census Of the State Of New York, For 1865, New York State Library, retrieved November 12, 2023, https://nysl.ptfs.com/#!/s?a=c&q=*&type=16&criteria=field11%3D4750890&b=0

[17] O'Reilly, p.24

[18] Gibson, Campbell, "Population of the 100 Largest Cities and Other Urban Places In The United States: 1790 to 1990," U.S. Census Bureau, June 1998, retrieved April 17, 2024, https://www.census.gov/library/working-papers/1998/demo/POP-twps0027.html

Chapter 12: The Buffalo And Erie Road

[1] William Bell letter, *Westfield Republican*, Wednesday, April 5, 1871

[2] Upton, Harriet Taylor, *History of the Western Reserve*, Lewis Publishing Company, Chicago, 1910, p.40

³ Stone, William Leete, *The Life and Times of Sir William Johnson*, Bart, Volume II, Munsell, Albany, 1865, p.469
⁴ Broadhead, John Romeyn, *Documents Relative to the Colonial History of the State of New York, Vol X*, E.B. O'Callaghan, ed, Weed, Parsons & Co, 1858, p.255
⁵ Broadhead, John Romeyn, *Documents Relative to the Colonial History of the State of New York, Vol VI*, E.B. O'Callaghan, ed, Weed, Parsons & Co, 1855, p.837
⁶ Broadhead, *Vol VI*, p.834
⁷ Taylor, Horace Clefton, *Historical Sketches of the Town of Portland*, W. McKinstry & Son, Printers, Fredonia, NY, 1873, p.403
⁸ "George Washington Papers, Series 2, Letterbooks 1754-1799," Library of Congress, https://tile.loc.gov/storage-services/service/mss/mgw/mgw2/015/015.pdf [retrieved April 24, 2024]
⁹ Taylor, p.81
¹⁰ Upton, p.17, 21
¹¹ Taylor, p.81
¹² Ibid., p.82
¹³ Badger, Joseph, *A Memoir of Rev Joseph Badger*, ed. by Henry Noble Day, Sawyer, Ingersoll and Company, Hudson, Ohio, 1851, p.32
¹⁴ Ibid., p.39
¹⁵ Warren, Emory F., *Historical Sketches of Chautauque County*, J. Warren Fletcher, Jamestown, NY, 1846, p.36
¹⁶ Young, Andrew W., *History of Chautauqua County*, Printing House of Matthews & Warren, Buffalo, NY, 1875, p.74
¹⁷ Ibid.
¹⁸ "New York: Consolidated Chronology of State and County Boundaries." *New York Atlas of Historical County Boundaries*, Copyright The Newberry Library 2008, [retrieved November 23, 2023]
¹⁹ Evans, Paul Demund, *The Holland Land Company*, Buffalo Historical Society, Buffalo, NY 1924, p.280
²⁰ Edson, Obed (Historian), *History of Chautauqua County New York*, Georgia Drew Merrill, Editor, W.A Fergusson & Co, Boston, Mass, 1894, p.175
²¹ Evans, p.96
²² Taylor, p.82
²³ Edson, p.611
²⁴ *Tables Giving Detailed Information and Present State of all State and County Highways – 1915*, J.B. Lyon Company, Printers, Albany, 1916, p. 278
²⁵ *Dunkirk Evening Observer*, Friday, May 20, 1927, p.11
²⁶ *Dunkirk Evening Observer*, Saturday, March 5, 1932, p.7
²⁷ Taylor, p.93-93
²⁸ Warren, p.96

Chapter 13 – Special Delivery To Westfield, A Fitting First

[1] *Buffalo Emporium and General Advertiser*, Saturday, June 25, 1825, p. 3
[2] *Fredonia Censor*, Wednesday, May 25, 1825, p.3
[3] "La Fayette," *Fredonia Censor*, Wednesday, June 1, 1825, p. 3
[4] Seward, Olive Risley, "The Marquis De Lafayette. His Great Service to our Country and His Visit to Chautauqua County," *The Centennial History of Chautauqua County Vol I*, Chautauqua History Company, Jamestown, 1904, p.457
[5] "LaFayette in Fredonia," *Fredonia Censor*, August 21, 1872, p.1-2 (reprint of the June 8, 1825 edition)
[6] "Arrival of Gen. La Fayette at Erie, *Erie Gazette*, Wednesday, June 9, 1825, p.3
[7] "LaFayette in Fredonia"
[8] Ibid.
[9] Ibid.
[10] Ibid.
[11] Ibid.
[12] Ibid.
[13] Ibid.
[14] Ibid.
[15] Ibid.
[16] Ibid.

Chapter 14: Gaslighting The General

[1] "1925: Temperature reaches 100 degrees in Washington DC," This Date in Weather History website, https://shows.acast.com/this-date-in-weather-history/episodes/1925-temperature-reaches-100-degrees-in-washington-dc, [retrieved May 6, 2024]
[2] Jamestown Weather in 1925, Extreme Weather Watch website, https://www.extremeweatherwatch.com/cities/jamestown-ny/year-1925#june, [retrieved May 6, 2024]
[3] "Dedication of Memorial To Gas Discovery," *The Fredonia Censor*, Wednesday, June 10, 1925, p.1
[4] "Commemorate Visit Of General Lafayette," *The Westfield Republican*, Wednesday, June 17, 1925, p.2
[5] "Dedication of Memorial Will Occur Thursday," *The Fredonia Censor*, Wednesday, June 3, 1925, p.1
[6] *The Fredonia Censor*, June 10, 1925, p.1
[7] "Dedication Address By Mrs. Charles White Nash," *The Fredonia Censor*, Wednesday, June 17, 1925, p.13
[8] *The Fredonia Censor*, June 10, 1925, p.1
[9] *The Fredonia Censor*, Wednesday, August 31, 1825, p.2
[10] "True Story Of Natural Gas Is Here Recorded," *The Fredonia Censor*, Wednesday, January 7, 1925 p.1, p.4

[11] "Gas and Oil Notes – New York," *Engineering and Mining Journal v.41*, 1886 Jan-Jun, p.156

[12] Childs, Hamilton, *Gazetteer and Business Directory of Chautauqua County, NY for 1873-4*, Journal Office, Syracuse, 1873. p.143

[13] Edson, Obed, Historian, *History of Chautauqua County New York*, Georgia Drew Merrill, Editor, W.A Fergusson & Co, Boston, Mass, 1894 p.42

[14] Chautauqua History Company, *The Centennial History of Chautauqua County Vol. I*, Jamestown, 1904, p.274

[15] Downs, John P. & Fenwick Y. Hedley, *History of Chautauqua County New York and Its People-Vol. 1*, American Historical Society, 1921, p.71

[16] Clark, James, A., *The chronological history of the petroleum and natural gas industries*, Clark Book Co., Houston, 1963, p.15

[17] Ibid., p.16

[18] "Fredonia's Part In History Of Gas Business Is Reviewed By Distributing Company's Writer," *Dunkirk Evening Observer*, Thursday, October 4, 1945, p.10

[19] "Fortune Hunters Still Drilling For Natural Gas In NY Areas," *Star-Gazette* (Elmira), Friday, February 19, 1965, p.3

[20] Shepard, Douglas H., "One Park Place," 2005 https://chqgov.com/sites/default/files/document-files/2019-09/One%20Park%20Place%20%28PDF%29.pdf, [retrieved May 6, 2024]

[21] *Fredonia Censor*, Wednesday, August 31, 1825, p.2

[22] *Fredonia Censor*, Wednesday, November 30, 1825, p.3

[23] *Fredonia Censor*, Wednesday, November 26, 1826, p.3

[24] Levasseur, André-Nicolas, *Lafayette in America in 1824 and 1825, Volume I*, John D. Godman translation, Philadelphia, Carey and Lea, 1829, p.166

[25] Samford, Patricia, "Gas Lighting in Baltimore, 19th-Century Style," *Maryland History by the Object*, September 13, 2018 by Patricia https://jeffersonpatterson.wordpress.com/2018/09/13/gas-lighting-in-baltimore-19th-century-style/ [retrieved June 1, 2024]

Chapter 15: Fast Fredonia Frenzy

[1] Levasseur, André-Nicolas, *Lafayette in America in 1824 and 1825, Volume II*, John D. Godman translation, Philadelphia, Carey and Lea, 1829, p.185

[2] Evans, Paul Edmund, *The Holland Land Company*, Buffalo Historical Society, Buffalo, NY 1924, p.273

[3] Seward, Olive Risley, "The Marquis De Lafayette. His Great Service to our Country and His Visit to Chautauqua County," *The Centennial History of Chautauqua County Vol I*, Chautauqua History Company, Jamestown, 1904, p.458-459

[4] "A Glimpse of the Past," *Fredonia Censor*, March 10, 1886, p.1

[5] Seward, p.459

⁶ Edson, Obed, Historian, *History of Chautauqua County New York*, Georgia Drew Merrill, Editor, W.A Fergusson & Co, Boston, Mass, 1894, p.481
⁷ Levasseur, p.185
⁸ "LaFayette in Fredonia," *Fredonia Censor*, August 21, 1872, p.1
⁹ Levasseur, p.185
¹⁰ "LaFayette in Fredonia," p.1
¹¹ Ibid.
¹² Ibid.
¹³ Edson, p.461
¹⁴ Ibid., p.288
¹⁵ Levasseur, p.186

Chapter 16: Dunkirk, The Last Frontier
¹ Edson, Obed, Historian, *History of Chautauqua County New York*, Georgia Drew Merrill, Editor, W.A Fergusson & Co, Boston, Mass, 1894, p.512
² Ibid., p.513
³ Chautauqua History Company, *The Centennial History of Chautauqua County Vol I*, Jamestown, 1904, p.80
⁴ Morgan, Lewis H., League of the Ho-de-no sau-nee or Iroquois, Herbert Lloyd, ed., Dodd, Mead and Company, 1904 [reprint, 1851], p.128
⁵ Taylor, Horace Clefton, *Historical Sketches of the Town of Portland*, W. McKinstry & Son, Printers, Fredonia, NY, 1873, p.336
⁶ Edson, p.523
⁷ Chautauqua History Company, *The Centennial History of Chautauqua County Vol II*, Jamestown, 1904, p.422
⁸ Ibid., p.422
⁹ Ibid., p.430
¹⁰ Taylor, p.515
¹¹ Downs, John P. & Fenwick Y. Hedley, *History of Chautauqua County New York and Its People-Vol. 1*, American Historical Society, 1921, p.42
¹² *The Centennial History of Chautauqua County Vol II*, p.432
¹³ *The Centennial History of Chautauqua County Vol I*, p.461

Chapter 17: To The Dunkirk Dinghy By The Dawn's Early Light
¹ Chautauqua History Company, *The Centennial History of Chautauqua County - Vol I*, Jamestown, 1904, p.401
² "LaFayette in Fredonia," *Fredonia Censor*, August 21, 1872, p.1-2
³ Downs, John P. & Fenwick Y. Hedley, *History of Chautauqua County New York and Its People-Vol. 1*, American Historical Society, 1921, p.146
⁴ "In Memoriam—Walter Smith," *Fredonia Censor*, September 30, 1874, p.3
⁵ Chautauqua History Company, *The Centennial History of Chautauqua County Vol II*, Jamestown, 1904, p.494-496

⁶ Ibid., p.432
⁷ Ibid., p.435
⁸ Edson, Obed, Historian, *History of Chautauqua County New York*, Georgia Drew Merrill, Editor, W.A Fergusson & Co, Boston, Mass, 1894, p.522
⁹ Ibid., p.524
¹⁰ *The Centennial History of Chautauqua County Vol II*, p.432
¹¹ "LaFayette in Fredonia"
¹² "The Progress of La Fayette," *Albany Argus*, Tuesday, June 14, 1825, p.2
¹³ "Arrival of Gen. La Fayette," *Fredonia Censor*, Wednesday, June 15, 1825, p.2&3
¹⁴ "LaFayette in Fredonia"
¹⁵ Levasseur, André-Nicolas, *Lafayette in America in 1824 and 1825, Volume II*, John D. Godman translation, Philadelphia, Carey and Lea, 1829, Levasseur, p.186

Chapter 18: Rebuilt Buffalo

¹ "Resolution," *Buffalo Emporium and General Advertiser*, Saturday, July 22, 1826, p.3
² Ketchum, William, *History of Buffalo Vol II*, Rockwell, Baker & Hill, Buffalo, NY, 1864, p.166
³ Turner, Orsamus, *Pioneer History of the Holland Purchase of Western New York*, Jewett, Thomas & Co., 1849, p.452-453
⁴ Ketchum, p.144
⁵ Ibid., p.154
⁶ *Extra Number Issued as a Souvenir of the International Industrial Fair Paper Sept. 4-14, 1888*, Buffalo Express, p.8
⁷ Dwight, Timothy, *Travels in New England and New York Vol. IV*, Willams Baynes and Son, London, 1823, p.56-58
⁸ Ketchum, p.157
⁹ Sheldon, James, *The life and public services of Oliver Forward*, read before the Buffalo historical society, January 25, 1875
¹⁰ *Extra Number*, p.6
¹¹ Sheldon, p.3
¹² Cruikshank, Lt-Col. E., *The Documentary History of the Campaigns Upon The Niagara Frontier in 1812-4, Vol IX, December 1813 to May, 1814*, The Lundy's Lan Historical Society, Tribune Office, Welland, 1908, p.46
¹³ *Buffalo Gazette*, Wednesday, February 5, 1812, p.3
¹⁴ Cruikshank, p.123
¹⁵ Ibid., p.26
¹⁶ Fay, H.A., *Collection of the Official Accounts in Detail of All the Battles Fought by Sea and Lan, Between the Navy and Army of the United States, and the Navy and Army of Great Britian, During the Years 1812, 13, 14, & 15.*, E. Conrad, New York, 1817, p.114

[17] Chapin's letter to Gen. Dearborn appeared (at least) in the Friday, August 6, 1813 editions of *The Raliegh Minerva*, p. 2 col. 2, the *War Journal*, p.4, and the *Martinsburg Gazette*, (WV), p.3
[18] Miner, Julius, *Buffalo Medical and Surgical Journal, Vol. VIII*, Warren, Johnson & Co., 1869, p.121
[19] Cruikshank, p.122
[20] Ibid., p.120
[21] Brackenridge, H.M., *History of the Late War Between the United States and Great Britain*, Cuming & Jewitt, Baltimore, 1818, p.265
[22] Cruikshank, p.67
[23] *Kingston Gazette*, Wednesday, January 5, 1814
[24] Hill, Henry Wayland, *Municipality of Buffalo New York A History 1720-1923, Volume I*, Lewis Historical Publishing Company, New York, 1923, p.162
[25] Sheldon, p.3
[26] Dwight, p.57
[27] Ibid., p.56

Chapter 19: Regal Reception In Buffalo's Blossoming Queen City

[1] Lossing, Benson J., *The Pictorial Field-Book of the War of 1812*, Harper & Brothers, New York, 1868, p.379
[2] Turner, Orsamus, *Pioneer History of the Holland Purchase of Western New York*, Jewett, Thomas & Co., 1849, p.641
[3] Evans, Paul Demund, *The Holland Land Company*, Buffalo Historical Society, Buffalo, NY 1924, p.292
[4] Turner, p.641
[5] Evans, p.292
[6] Sheldon, James, *The life and public services of Oliver Forward*, read before the Buffalo historical society, January 25, 1875, p.6
[7] Levasseur, André-Nicolas, *Lafayette in America in 1824 and 1825, Volume II*, John D. Godman translation, Philadelphia, Carey and Lea, 1829, p.186-187
[8] "Arrival of Gen. La Fayette," *Fredonia Censor*, Wednesday, June 15, 1825, p.2&3
[9] "The Progress of La Fayette," *Albany Argus*, Tuesday, June 14, 1825, p.2
[10] *Fredonia Censor*
[11] "The Nation's Guest," *Buffalo Emporium and General Advertiser*, Saturday, June 11, 1825, p.2
[12] Ibid.
[13] *Fredonia Censor*
[14] Parker, Arthur C., *Red Jacket, last of the Seneca*, McGraw-Hill, New York, 1952, p.86
[15] "LaFayette in Fredonia"
[16] Levasseur, André-Nicolas, *Lafayette in America in 1824 and 1825, Volume II*, John D. Godman translation, Philadelphia, Carey and Lea, 1829, Levasseur, p.186

Chapter 20: Peter B. Porter's Home Sweet Home
[1] Turner, Orsamus, *Pioneer History of the Holland Purchase of Western New York*, Jewett, Thomas & Co., 1849, p.612
[2] Robinson, Charles Mulford, "The Life of Judge Augustus Porter," *Publications of the Buffalo Historical Society Vol VII*, Buffalo Historical Society, Buffalo, 1904, p.242
[3] Turner, p.612
[4] Ibid.
[5] Robinson, p.242
[6] Cozzens, Frederic S., *Colonel Peter A Porter - A Memorial*, D. Van Norstrand, New York, delivered before The Century December 1864, p.9
[7] Ibid., p.10
[8] https://billofrightsinstitute.org/essays/the-battle-of-saratoga-and-the-french-alliance retrieved May 25 [retrieved May 25, 2024]
[9] https://www.napoleon-series.org/military-info/Warof1812/2009/Issue12/c_Artillery.html [retrieved May 26, 2024]
[10] Cozzens, p.13-14
[11] Ibid., p.14
[12] Lossing, Benson J., *The Pictorial Field-Book of the War of 1812*, Harper & Brothers, New York, 1868, p.426
[13] Ibid., p. 627
[14] *The Long Island Star*, Wednesday, January 26, 1814, p.3
[15] Ibid.
[16] Severance, Frank H., ed.. *The Picture Book of Earlier Buffalo*, [*Buffalo Historical Society Publications, Volume Sixteen*], Buffalo Historical Society, Buffalo, NY, 1912, p.259
[17] "Communicated for the Star," *The Long Island Star*, Wednesday, August 10, 1831, p.3

Chapter 21: Breakfast At Black Rock Then On To Tonawanda
[1] "Termination of the Grand Canal," *Black Rock Gazette*, Tuesday, June 7, 1825, p.3
[2] Ibid.
[3] Ibid.
[4] Ibid.
[5] "The Nation's Guest," *Buffalo Emporium and General Advertiser*, Saturday, June 11, 1825, p.2
[6] "General La Fayette," *Black Rock Gazette*, Tuesday, June 7, 1825, p.3
[7] Levasseur, André-Nicolas, *Lafayette in America in 1824 and 1825, Volume II*, John D. Godman translation, Philadelphia, Carey and Lea, 1829, p.188
[8] "General La Fayette," *Black Rock Gazette*, Tuesday, June 7, 1825, p.3
[9] Ibid.
[10] Ibid.

[11] Ibid.
[12] Levasseur, p.188

Chapter 22: Augustus Porter Could Have Danced All Night

[1] https://www.findagrave.com/memorial/115608447/anna_foster [retrieved June 1, 2024]
[2] Turner, Orsamus, *Pioneer History of the Holland Purchase of Western New York*, Jewett, Thomas & Co., 1849, p.470-471
[3] Ibid.
[4] Turner, Orsamus, *Pioneer History of the Phelps and Gorham's Purchase and Morris Reserve (supplement of Monroe County)*, William Alling, Rochester, 1851, p.384
[5] Turner, 1849, p.471
[6] https://harrisfamilynews.com/direct_harris_nathan.htm [retrieved June 2, 2024]
[7] Turner, 1851, p.384
[8] Ibid.
[9] Robinson, Charles Mulford, "The Life of Judge Augustus Porter," *Publications of the Buffalo Historical Society Vol VII*, Buffalo Historical Society, Buffalo, 1904, p.229
[10] Turner, 1849, p.358
[11] Robinson, p.236
[12] Turner, 1849, p.406
[13] Robinson, p.236
[14] Ibid., p.238-239
[15] Ibid., p.241
[16] Ibid., p.245
[17] Ibid., p.239
[18] Ibid., p.243
[19] Ibid., p.246
[20] Child, Hamilton, *Gazetteer and business directory of Niagara County, NY for 1869*, Journal Office, Syracuse, 1869, p.92-93
[21] Robinson, p.257
[22] Ibid., p.259

Chapter 23: The Natural Wonder Of Niagara Falls, Goat Island, And Lewiston

[1] The Times, *A History of the City of Buffalo and Niagara Falls*, Buffalo, NY, 1896, p.322
[2] Ibid. p. 347
[3] "History Pages in a Hotel Register; Recollections of the Cataract House," *Buffalo Evening News*, Saturday, October 20, 1945, p.13
[4] Levasseur, André-Nicolas, *Lafayette in America in 1824 and 1825, Volume II*, John D. Godman translation, Philadelphia, Carey and Lea, 1829, p.188

⁵ "More Recollections of 1825," *The Buffalo Commercial*, Thursday, June 17, 1897, p.12
⁶ "General Alarm Sounded For Cataract Fire," *Buffalo Courier Express*, Monday, October 15, 1945, p.7
⁷ Famous Hotel Destroyed at Niagara Falls," *Oswego NY Daily Times*, Thursday, January 3, 1918, p.1
⁸ "General Alarm Sounded For Cataract Fire," *Buffalo Courier Express*, Monday, October 15, 1945, p.7
⁹ Levasseur, p.188
¹⁰ Ibid., p.190
¹¹ "The Progress of La Fayette," *Albany Argus*, Tuesday, June 14, 1825, p.2
¹² Taussig, Ellen, "Lewiston's Kelsey-Hall House Once Welcomed Gen. Lafayette," *Buffalo Evening News*, Saturday, August 10, 1963, p.7
¹³ Ibid.

Chapter 24: Riding The Ridge (Road)
¹ Chadwick, G. H., "Large fault in western New York," *Geological Society of America, Bulletin, Vol. 31*, New York, 1920, p.117-120
² *History of Niagara County*, Sanford & Co, New York, 1878, p.229
³ Turner, Orsamus, *Pioneer History of the Holland Purchase of Western New York*, Jewett, Thomas & Co., 1849, p.497
⁴ *History of Niagara County*, p.229
⁵ "Tour through Niagara County in 1810," *Niagara Falls Gazette*, Wednesday, January 5, 1859, p.1
⁶ Ibid.
⁷ Turner, p.23
⁸ "Tour through Niagara County in 1810"

Chapter 25: Fort Niagara And The Man-Made Wonder Of Lockport
¹ Klements, Elizabeth, "Alexander Ramsey Thompson (1793–1837)," *Veterans Legacy Program*, The University of Central Florida & the National Cemetery Administration https://vlp.cah.ucf.edu/biographies/sanc/BPYR-0-ATHOMPSON-F.html [retrieved June 10, 2024]
² "The Progress of La Fayette," *Albany Argus*, Tuesday, June 14, 1825, p.2
³ Levasseur, André-Nicolas, *Lafayette in America in 1824 and 1825, Volume II*, John D. Godman translation, Philadelphia, Carey and Lea, 1829, p.190-191
⁴ "The Progress of La Fayette"
⁵ *A History of the City of Buffalo and Niagara Falls*, The Times, Buffalo, NY, 1896, p.346
⁶ "Lafayette in Lockport," *The New York Times*, Tuesday, May 8, 1883, p.5
⁷ O'Reilly, Henry, *Settlement in the West. Sketch of Rochester with Incidental Notices of Western New York*, William Ailing, Rochester, 1838, p.382-383

⁸ Ibid., p.184
⁹ Levasseur, p.191
¹⁰ Lewis, Clarence O., "Howell Tavern One of Oldest," *Niagara Falls, Gazette*, Wednesday, April 2, 1969, p.37
¹¹ *History of Niagara County*, Sanford & Co, New York, 1878, p.229
¹² Ibid., p.231
¹³ Levasseur, p.191
¹⁴ Ibid., p.192
¹⁵ "Lafayette in Lockport," *The New York Times*, Tuesday, May 8, 1883, p.5
¹⁶ Levasseur, p.192

Chapter 26: Remembering Silvius Hoard

¹ "Visit of Lafayette," *Rochester Telegraph*, Wednesday, June 15, 1825, p.2
² Hough, Franklin B., *A History of St. Lawrence and Franklin Co*, Little & Co, Albany 1853, p.422-423
³ https://www.findagrave.com/memorial/27408796/silvius_hoard [Retrieved June 5, 2024]
⁴ Lewis Historical Publishing Company, *Genealogical and Family History of Northern New York Vol. II*, 1910, p.628
⁵ "Hoard, Charles Brooks," Biographical Directory of the United States Congress, https://bioguide.congress.gov/search/bio/H000658 [Retrieved June 14, 2024]
⁶ Emerson, ed. Edgar C., ed., *Our County and Its People A Descriptive Work on Jefferson County*, The Boston History Company, 1898, p.452
⁷ *Genealogical and Family History of Northern New York Vol. II*, p.628
⁸ Ibid.
⁹ Hough, Franklin B., p.422-423
¹⁰ *Our County and Its People A Descriptive Work on Jefferson County*, p.333
¹¹ Ibid., p.463
¹² Ibid., p.246-247
¹³ Hough, p.94
¹⁴ *Our County and Its People A Descriptive Work on Jefferson County*, p.474
¹⁵ Hastings, Hugh, ed., *Military Minutes of the Council of Appointment of the State of New York 1783-1821, Vol III*, James B. Lyon, State Printer, Albany 1901, p.1980
¹⁶ Ibid., p. 2140
¹⁷ https://www.findagrave.com/memorial/27408795/nancy_mary_hoard [Retrieved June 5, 2024]
¹⁸ "Lafayette and Retinue Paid Visit to Rochester One Hundred Years Ago," Democrat and Chronicle, Sunday, June 14, 1925, p.1
¹⁹ Ibid.

[20] 1820 Census Antwerp, Jefferson Co., NY: Heads of Households, https://jefferson.nygenweb.net/census/1820antwerpcensus.htm [Retrieved June 17, 2024]

[21] "Big Ship Canal Monument To Silvius Hoard," *The Odgensburg Republican-Journal*, Monday, December 16, 1929, p.3

[22] "Visit of Lafayette," *Rochester Telegraph*, Wednesday, June 15, 1825, p.2

[23] "List of Letters," *Monroe Republican*, Wednesday, March 16, 1926, p.3

[24] *Genealogical and Family History of Northern New York Vol. II*, p.628

Chapter 27: Competing Memories Turn Lafayette's Rochester Visit From History To Mystery

[1] "Visit of Lafayette," *Rochester Telegraph*, Wednesday, June 15, 1825, p.2

[2] "Lafayette in Lockport," *The New York Times*, Tuesday, May 8, 1883, p.5

[3] "Visit of Lafayette"

[4] "General La Fayette," *Rochester Telegraph*, Tuesday, June 7, 1825, p.3

[5] Spafford, Horatio Gates, *Pocket Guide for the Tourist and Traveller Along the Canals*, T. and J. Swords, New York, 1824, p.42

[6] Levasseur, André-Nicolas, *Lafayette in America in 1824 and 1825, Volume II*, John D. Godman translation, Philadelphia, Carey and Lea, 1829, p.192-193

[7] 1855 *Greece Daily Union*, reprinted in "From The Arm Chair," *The Greece Press*, Friday, December 21, 1934, p.3

[8] "Rochester's Celebration on Opening of Erie Canal and Arrival of Lafayette," *Rochester Democrat and Chronicle*, Sunday, April 21, 1929, p.49

[9] *The Greece Press*, Friday, December 21, 1934

[10] "Visit of Lafayette"

[11] Ibid.

[12] Ibid.

[13] Ibid.

[14] 1855 *Greece Daily Union*, reprinted in "From The Arm Chair," *The Greece Press*, Friday, December 28, 1934, p.2

[15] Ibid.

[16] "Visit of Lafayette"

[17] Levasseur, p.193

[18] *The Greece Press*, Friday, December 28, 1934

[19] "Lafayette and Retinue Paid Visit to Rochester One Hundred Years Ago," *Democrat and Chronicle*, Sunday, June 14, 1925, p.1-2

[20] Ibid.

[21] 1855 *Greece Daily Union*, reprinted in "From The Arm Chair," *The Greece Press*, Friday, January 11, 1935, p.2

[22] McKelvey, Blake, From Stagecoach Taverns to Airline Motels, *Rochester History Vol. 31 No.4*, October 1969, p.6-7

[23] "Visit of Lafayette"

²⁴ Kramer, David, "Sarah, We Were There Too! 'Lafayette in the Somewhat United States' and Rochester," *Talker of the Town*, posted November 24, 2015, https://talkerofthetown.com/2015/11/24/sarah-we-were-there-too-lafayette-in-the-somewhat-united-states-and-rochester/ [retrieved June 15, 2024]
²⁵ "Lafayette and Retinue Paid Visit to Rochester One Hundred Years Ago"
²⁶ McKelvey, Blake, p.3-4
²⁷ *The Greece Press*, Friday, January 11, 1935

Chapter 28: Timothy Barnard, A Soldier's Story
¹ "Another Revolutionary Patriot Gone," *Geneva Courier*, Tuesday, April 13, 1847, p. 2
² https://www.findagrave.com/memorial/16676793/ebenezer_barnard [Retrieved June 22, 2024]
³ Barbour, Lucius Barnes, *Families of Early Hartford, Connecticut*, Genealogical Publishing Co., Inc., Baltimore, 1977, p. 31-32
⁴ Yates, Anah B., "The Pioneers of Mendon," *The Honeoye Falls Times*, Thursday, November 4, 1920, p.1
⁵ "Biographies of Monroe County People," GenWeb Monroe County, NY website, p. 42, https://mcnygenealogy.com/bios/biographies042.htm [Retrieved June 23, 2024]
⁶ Yates, p. 1
⁷ *Daughters of the American Revolution Magazine*, July - December 1915, p.263-264
⁸ Yates, p. 1, 6
⁹ *Daughters of the American Revolution Magazine*
¹⁰ Turner, Orsamus, *Pioneer History of the Phelps and Gorham's Purchase and Morris Reserve (supplement of Monroe County)*, William Alling, Rochester, 1851, p. 530
¹¹ Morrison, William, *History of Monroe County*, Everts, Ensign & Everts, Philadelphia, 1877, p. 264
¹² "Ontario Agricultural Society," *Ontario Repository*, Tuesday, February 23, 1819, p. 3
¹³ *History of Ontario County, New York With Illustrations*, Everts, Ensign & Everts, Philadelphia, 1878, p.49
¹⁴ *Ibid.*, p.37
¹⁵ 1855 *Greece Daily Union*, reprinted in "From The Arm Chair," *The Greece Press*, Friday, December 28, 1934, p.2
¹⁶ Ibid.
¹⁷ Ibid.

Chapter 29: Dispelling Mendon Myths
¹ https://www.findagrave.com/memorial/69604859/samuel-hildreth [retrieved June 24, 2024]

² Turner, Orsamus, *Pioneer History of the Phelps and Gorham's Purchase and Morris Reserve (Monroe)*, William Alling, Rochester, 1851, p.527

³ Morrison, William, *History of Monroe County*, Everts, Ensign & Everts, Philadelphia, 1877, p.236

⁴ Child, Hamilton, *Gazetteer and Business Directory of Monroe County*, NY for 1869-70, Journal Office, Syracuse, 1869, p.83

⁵ Everts, Ensign & Everts, *History of Ontario County, New York With Illustrations*, Philadelphia, 1878, p.55

⁶ "La Fayette," *Ontario Repository*, Wednesday, June 8, 1825, p.2

⁷ Rochester Historical Society, *Rochester Historical Society Publication Fund Series Vol. 14*, Rochester, 1936, p.235

⁸ Turner, Orsamus, p.530

⁹ Ibid.

¹⁰ Fisher, J. Sheldon, and Douglas A. Fisher, "Revolutionary War hero came calling," *Democrat and Chronicle*, Wednesday, June 7, 2000, p.13A

¹¹ 1855 *Greece Daily Union*, reprinted in "From The Arm Chair," *The Greece Press*, Friday, December 28, 1934, p.2

¹² Morrell, Alan, "Stone-Tolan House oldest in county," *Democrat and Chronicle*, Friday, June 17, 2016, p,10A

¹³ "Pittsford has historical points of interest," *Democrat and Chronicle*, Friday, August 24, 2001, p.13F

¹⁴ Krieger, Amo, *Sesquicentennial Souvenir Program And History of the Town of Mendon*, O'Brien Bros. Printing, Honeoye Falls, NY, 1963, p.27

¹⁵ "The Progress of La Fayette," *Albany Argus*, Tuesday, June 14, 1825, p.2

¹⁶ 1855 *Greece Daily Union*

Chapter 30: John Greig Lives The American Dream

¹ https://www.findagrave.com/memorial/7574413/john-greig [Retrieved June 26, 2024]

² https://bioguide.congress.gov/search/bio/G000449 [Retrieved June 26, 2024]

³ Chappell, Josephine Gregg, "Early History of the Genesee Country—Events and Men," *Rochester Historical Society Publication Fund Series Vol. 2*, 1923, p.280,283

⁴ Kelsey, John, *The Lives and Reminiscences of the Pioneers of Rochester*, J. Kelsey, Rochester, 1854, p.106

⁵ Chappell, p.283

⁶ Granger, J. Albert, "The History of Canandaigua," *Ontario Repository and Messenger*, 1876, p.13

⁷ Turner, Orsamus, *Pioneer History of the Holland Purchase of Western New York*, Jewett, Thomas & Co., 1849, p.374

⁸ Everts, Ensign & Everts, *History of Ontario County, New York With Illustrations*, Philadelphia, 1878, p.16

⁹ "Canandaigua Academy," *Ontario Repository*, Wednesday, December 25, 1810, p.1

[10] *Ontario Repository*, Tuesday, January 28, 1812, p.4
[11] *Ontario Repository*, Tuesday, January 19, 1813, p.3
[12] "Ontario Bank" *Ontario Repository*, Tuesday, April 6, 1813, p.1
[13] *The Geneva Gazette*, Wednesday, June 25, 1817, p.3
[14] https://bioguide.congress.gov/search/bio/G000449 [Retrieved June 26, 2024]
[15] Granger, p.10
[16] *The Geneva Gazette*, Wednesday, August 7, 1816, p.2
[17] "Ontario County Agricultural Society, *The Republican Agriculturist*, Thursday, March 18, 1819, p.1
[18] *New-York Evening Post*, Monday, September 22, 1823, p.2
[19] *Geneva Palladium*, Wednesday, September 24, 1823, p.3
[20] "Law of New-York," *Ontario Repository*, Wednesday, April 14, 1824, p.2
[21] *The Troy Sentinel*, Friday, January 14, 1825, p.3

Chapter 31: Canandaigua Anxiously Waits Before Jubilation And An Elegant Supper

[1] *Ontario Repository*, Tuesday, March 9, 1825, p. 1
[2] "Lafayette in Canandaigua," *Ontario County Times*, Wednesday, June 7, 1911, p.6
[3] *Albany Argus*, June 10, 1825
[4] "Early History Continued," *Ontario County Times*, January 30, 1873, p. 3
[5] "Lafayette in Canandaigua"
[6] Ibid.
[7] Ibid.
[8] Ibid.
[9] Ibid.
[10] "La Fayette," *Ontario Repository*, Wednesday, June 8, 1825, p. 2
[11] "Lafayette in Canandaigua"
[12] "La Fayette"
[13] "Lafayette in Canandaigua"
[14] Ibid.
[15] Ibid.

Chapter 32: How Commonality Saved Captain Williamson And Western New York

[1] O'Reilly, Henry, *Settlement in the West, Sketches of Rochester*, William Ailing, Rochester, 1838, p.150
[2] Turner, Orsamus, *Pioneer History of the Phelps and Gorham's Purchase and Morris Reserve (Monroe)*, William Alling, Rochester, 1851, p.244
[3] Ibid., p.252
[4] Main, William, *Charles Williamson*, Cowan & Co., Ltd., Perth, 1899, p.5
[5] Ibid.
[6] Ibid., p.6

[7] Turner, 1851, p.252
[8] O'Reilly, p.151
[9] Ibid., p.152
[10] Walker. John, *Elements of Geography and of Natural and Civil History, 3rd ed.*, Darton & Harvey, London, 1800, Supplement by Charles Williamson, p.1229
[11] Turner, 1851, p.261
[12] O'Reilly, p.163
[13] Ibid. p.153-154
[14] Turner, Orsamus, *Pioneer History of the Phelps and Gorham" Purchase and Morris Reserve, (Ontario, Yates)*, William Alling, Rochester, 1852, p.317
[15] McMaster, Guy H., *History of the Settlement of Steuben County*, R.S. Underhill & Co, Bath, NY, 1853, p.104-106
[16] Turner, 1851, p.273
[17] Turner, Orsamus, *Pioneer History of the Holland Purchase of Western New York*, Jewett, Thomas & Co., 1849, p.417
[18] Turner, 1851, p.277-78
[19] Turner, 1849, p.665
[20] Ibid., p.330
[21] McMaster, p.99

Chapter 33: Pomp And Circumstance Before Lunch In Geneva

[1] "La Fayette," *Ontario Repository*, Wednesday, June 15, 1825, p.2
[2] "General La Fayette," *Geneva Palladium*, Wednesday, June 15, 1825, p.2
[3] Ibid.
[4] Sutton, Ernest and Janet Sutton, "Lafayette Trivia: AFL Fall Gazette Geneva," *The Gazette of the American Friends of Lafayette, No. 87*, October 2017, p.74
[5] *Geneva Palladium*, Wednesday, June 15, 1825, p.2
[6] Ibid.
[7] Ibid.
[8] "General La Fayette," *Geneva Palladium*, Wednesday, June 8, 1825, p.2
[9] *Geneva Palladium*, Wednesday, June 15, 1825, p.2
[10] *Geneva Palladium*, Wednesday, June 8, 1825, p.2
[11] *Geneva Palladium*, Wednesday, June 15, 1825, p.2
[12] Ibid.
[13] Ibid.
[14] Ibid.
[15] Ibid.
[16] Ibid.
[17] Ibid.
[18] Ibid.
[19] Ibid.

Chapter 34: The Great Central Trail Becomes The State Road

[1] "Six Towns Captured in Drive to the Roer; Elas Rules Salonika," *Buffalo Evening News*, Tuesday, December 12, 1944, p.1

[2] Moley, Raymond, "Fallacies in Highway Plan," *The Times Record*, Monday, March 28, 1955, p.12

[3] "New Interstate Highway New to Aid CD Evacuation," *Brooklyn Daily*, Friday, June 14, 1957, p.4

[4] Powell, Roland, "Repair Problems on Interstate," *The Buffalo News*, Sunday, October 25, 1981, p.67

[5] Belloc, Hilaire, *The Road*, for The British Reinforced Concrete Engineering Co. Ltd., Charles W. Hobson, Manchester, 1923, p.101

[6] Ibid., p.133

[7] Morgan, Lewis H., *League of the Ho-de-no sau-nee or Iroquois*, Herbert Lloyd, ed., Dodd, Mead and Company, 1904 [reprint, 1851], p.206

[8] Ibid, p.94

[9] Ibid., p.205

[10] Ibid., p.,103-104

[11] *Proceedings of the New-York Historical Society*, January-May, 1847, William Van Norden, New York, 1847, p.65

[12] Hulbert, Archer Butler, *Pioneer Roads and Experiences of Travelers (Volume II)*, by, The Arthur H. Clark Company, Cleveland, Ohio, 1904, p.96-100

[13] Ibid., p.101

[14] Ibid., p.106

[15] Ibid., p.107

[16] Hotchkin, Rev. James H., *A History of the Purchase and Settlement of Western New York*, M.W.Dodd, Birck Church Chapel, New York, 1848, p.19

[17] Hulbert, p.109-110

[18] Ibid., p.110-111

[19] Barber, John W., and Howe, Henry, *Historical collections of the state of New York*, S. Tuttle, New York 1842, p.79-80

[20] Everts, Ensign & Everts, *History of Seneca County*, J.B. Lippincott & Co., Philadelphia, 1876, p.12

[21] Parker, Arthur C., *Charles Williamson, Builder of Genesee Country*, Rochester Historical Society, Volume VI, Rochester, New York, 1926, p.34

[22] *History of Seneca County*, p.43

[23] *Journal of the Assembly of the State of New York*, Carroll and Cook, Albany, p.1118

[24] *Journal of the Senate of the State of New York*, E, Mack, Albany, p.760

[25] Turner, Orsamus, *Pioneer History of the Holland Purchase of Western New York*, Jewett, Thomas & Co., 1849, p.494

[26] Morgan, p.105

Chapter 35: Wowed Waterloo Overcomes Tragedy To Welcome Hero

[1] "Waterloo Factory Burned 45 Years Ago," *Rochester Democrat and Chronicle*, Wednesday, May 17, 1922, p.13
[2] Becker, John E., *A History of the Village of Waterloo*, Waterloo Library and Historical Society, Waterloo, New York, 1949, p.74-75
[3] Ibid., p.390
[4] *Auburn Free Press*, Wednesday, June 15, 1825, p.2
[5] *Seneca Farmer*, Wednesday, June 8, 1825 [via *Waterloo Observer*, Friday, March 13, 1903, p.1]
[6] "Would Name Waterloo Park After Lafayette," *Geneva Daily Times*, Friday, June 10, 1921, p.5
[7] Becker, p.98
[8] 1865 NYS Census data on 1825 Census
[9] Becker, p.99
[10] Wilcox, William, "General Lafayette," *Waterloo Observer*, Thursday, June 8, 1922, p.7
[11] Becker, p.99
[12] *Auburn Free Press*
[13] Becker, p.100

Chapter 36: Bigotry Cannot Defeat A Good And Honorable Man

[1] Brown, William Mosely, *George Washington Freemason*, Garrett & Massie, Inc., Richmond, 1952, p.169-170
[2] Hall, Henry, *The History of Auburn*, Dennis Bro's & Co., Auburn, NY, 1869, p.42
[3] Ibid., p.58
[4] Auburn Masonic Lodge #124 History, https://sites.google.com/site/auburnmasoniclodge124/history [retrieved July 20, 2024]
[5] Hall, p.100
[6] Ibid., p.126
[7] Auburn Masonic Lodge #124 History, https://sites.google.com/site/auburnmasoniclodge124/history [retrieved July 20, 2024]
[8] Hall, p.143
[9] Ibid., p.144
[10] *Auburn Theological Seminary 1820-1870*, Dennis Bro's & Thorne, Auburn, 1870, p.13-15
[11] *In Memoriam Dirck C. Lansing, D.D.*, Knapp, Peck, & Thomson, Auburn, 1883, p.7
[12] Storke, Elliot G., *History of Cayuga County*, D. Mason & Co., Syracuse, NY, 1879, p.198
[13] *In Memoriam Dirck C. Lansing*, p.7

¹⁴ *Auburn Theological Seminary 1820-1870*, p.13
¹⁵ Ibid., p.14
¹⁶ Finney, Charles G., *Memoirs of Rev. Charles G. Finney*, Fleming H. Revell Company, New York, 1876, p.192
¹⁷ Ibid., p.78
¹⁸ Ibid., p.192
¹⁹ Ibid., p.199
²⁰ Ibid., p.200
²¹ Ibid., p.200
²² Ibid., p.200
²³ American Anti-Slavery Society (AASS), http://www.americanabolitionists.com/american-anti-slavery-society.html [retrieved July 21, 2024]
²⁴ Hall, p.391
²⁵ Ibid., p.199
²⁶ Storke, p.306
²⁷ Brandon, Edgar Ewing, *A Pilgrimage of Liberty*, The Lawhead Press, Athens, Ohio, 1944, p.413
²⁸ Hall, p.144
²⁹ Auburn Masonic Lodge #124 History, https://sites.google.com/site/auburnmasoniclodge124/history [retrieved July 20, 2024]
³⁰ *In Memoriam Dirck C. Lansing*, p.6

Chapter 37: Through Seneca Falls, East Cayuga, Then A Masonic Welcome And A Final Adieu In Auburn

¹ "La Fayette," *Auburn Free Press*, Wednesday, May 18, 1825, p.2
² Ibid.
³ "To The Soldiers of the Revolution," *Auburn Free Press*, Wednesday, May 25, 1825, p.2
⁴ *Auburn Republican*, Wednesday, June 15, 1825 [via Brandon, Edgar Ewing, *A Pilgrimage of Liberty*, The Lawhead Press, Athens, Ohio, 1944, p.410]
⁵ *Auburn Free Press*, Wednesday, June 8, 1825, p.2
⁶ Hall, Henry, *The History of Auburn*, Dennis Bro's & Co., Auburn, NY, 1869, p. 172
⁷ *Auburn Republican*
⁸ Ibid.
⁹ *Cayuga Patriot*, Wednesday, June 15, 1825 [via Brandon, Edgar Ewing, *A Pilgrimage of Liberty*, The Lawhead Press, Athens, Ohio, 1944, p.410]
¹⁰ *Auburn Republican*
¹¹ *Auburn Free Press*, Wednesday, June 15, 1825, p.2
¹² *Auburn Republican*

[13] *Auburn Free Press*, Wednesday, June 15, 1825, p.2
[14] *Auburn Republican*, Wednesday, June 15, 1825 [via Brandon, Edgar Ewing, *A Pilgrimage of Liberty*, The Lawhead Press, Athens, Ohio, 1944, p.411]
[15] Ibid.
[16] *Auburn Free Press*, Wednesday, June 15, 1825, p.2
[17] Ibid.
[18] Ibid.
[19] Brandon, Edgar Ewing, *A Pilgrimage of Liberty*, The Lawhead Press, Athens, Ohio, 1944, p.479
[20] *Auburn Republican*, Wednesday, June 15, 1825 [via Brandon, Edgar Ewing, *A Pilgrimage of Liberty*, The Lawhead Press, Athens, Ohio, 1944, p.413]
[21] *Auburn Free Press*, Wednesday, June 15, 1825, p.2
[22] *Cayuga Patriot*
[23] *Auburn Republican*, Wednesday, June 15, 1825 [via Brandon, Edgar Ewing, *A Pilgrimage of Liberty*, The Lawhead Press, Athens, Ohio, 1944, p.414]
[24] *Auburn Free Press*, Wednesday, June 15, 1825, p.2
[25] *Auburn Republican*
[26] *Auburn Free Press*, Wednesday, June 15, 1825, p.2
[27] Seward, Olive Risley, "The Marquis De Lafayette. His Great Service to our Country and His Visit to Chautauqua County," *The Centennial History of Chautauqua County Vol I*, Chautauqua History Company, Jamestown, 1904, p.454
[28] Levasseur, André-Nicolas, *Lafayette in America in 1824 and 1825, Volume II*, John D. Godman translation, Philadelphia, Carey and Lea, 1829, p.193-194

Epilogue: A Favor Returned, D-Day 50th Anniversary

[1] "CBS Reports: D-Day Plus 20 Years - Eisenhower Returns To Normandy," Aired Sunday, June 5, 1964
[2] "D-Day Veterans Assemble For Anniversary Tributes," *Wellsville Daily Reporter*, Friday, June 5, 1964, p.1
[3] Jones, Denise, F., "From This French Heart, Thanks," *The Wichita Eagle*, Sunday, June 5, 1994, p.18
[4] Ibid.
[5] "Cemetery Rites Honor Paratroopers—French Ceremonies Celebrate Liberation," *The Idaho Statesman*, Tuesday, May 31, 1994, p.4
[6] Crary, David, "Thanks For The Liberation, But…," *Daily Citizen*, Friday, May 20, 1994, p.5
[7] Leicester, John, "French Town Thanks, U.S.," *Fort Worth-Telegram*, Sunday, June 6, 2004, p.11
[8] Ibid.
[9] "Return Bittersweet For Men Of D-Day," *The Times Leader*, Friday, June 4, 2004, p.6

[10] "CBS Reports: D-Day Plus 20 Years - Eisenhower Returns To Normandy"
[11] "D-Day: Surviving, Fallen Vets Lauded," *The Atlanta Constitution*, Monday, June 7, 2004, p.A7
[12] "LaFayette in Fredonia," *Fredonia Censor*, August 21, 1872, p.1-2

Appendix II: Lafayette On The Folly Of Tolerance

[1] James Madison to Thomas Jefferson, October 17, 1784, James Madison Papers, Library of Congress, Washington, DC, National Archives Database, https://founders.archives.gov/documents/Madison/01-08-02-0064 [retrieved April 7, 2024]

[2] Levasseur, André-Nicolas, *Lafayette in America in 1824 and 1825, Volume I*, John D. Godman translation, Philadelphia, Carey and Lea, 1829, p.222-223

INDEX:

"the year without a summer", 52
1812 Overture, 18
Abell Tavern, 69, 72
Abell, Col. Thomas G., 69, 83
Abell, Mosley W., 69, 76
Abolitionist movement, 167
Adams, John, 33, 34
Adams-Onis Treaty, 2
Alleghany River, 54
American Anti-Slavery Society, 167
American Dictionary of the English Language., 19
Ames Royal Arch Chapter No. 88, 114, 116, 123
Annin, 103
anti-Masonry, 167
Antwerp, 120, 121
Aquirre Mission, 2
Articles of Confederation, 144
Association, The, 145, 146, 148
Astor, John Jacob, 104
Atwater, Judge Moses, 141
Auburn, 158
Auburn Theological Seminary, 166
Aurelius, 164, 165
Aurora, 170
Averill, L., 60
Babcock, Joshua R., 60
Badger, Joseph, 56
Ball Tract, 134
Ball's tavern, 151, 152
Barcelona, 54, 78
Barker, Zenas W., 85
Barnard, 130
Barnard, Daniel G., 128
Barnard, Ebenezer, 128, 129, 134
Barnard, Fran H., 129
Barnard, Samuel, 129

Barnard, Timothy, 128-135
Barnstable, Massachusetts Colony, 128
Barritt, Alfred, 113, 117
Bartle, Capt., 152
Barton, Benjamin, 103
Batavia, 52, 96, 110
Bath, 146, 149
Battle of Lake Erie, 44
Bayly, Capt. Richard M., 152
Beach's Tavern, 135
Beaten Road, The, 157
Benjamin Prescott Chapter Daughters of the American Revolution, 66, 67
Birch, Thomas, 20
Black Rock, 88, 94, 98, 99
Bloomfield, 128, 130, 140
Blossom House, 142
Blossom, Col. William, 141, 142
Bonaparte, Napoleon, 13, 15, 181
Bouck, William C., 93, 97, 99, 113
Bourbon Restoration, 15
Brandywine, Battle of, 12, 29, 41, 152
Breckinridge, John, 96
Brent, William Leigh, 8
Brewster wagon, 126
Brigham Road, 79, 80
Brigham, John, 79
Brighton, 194
Brinkerhoff, Brig. Gen. Henry R., 169
Brizse, Ens., 152
Brown, 184
Brown, Capt. (of Fredonia), 72
Brown, David, 72, 184
Brown, James, 9, 16
Brown, Royal Arch Ames Chapter Member, 117
Budd, Captain, 44

Buffalo, 52, 53, 84, 88
Buffalo and Erie Road, 57, 59, 71, 79
Buffalo Bills, 70
Buffalo Creek, 54, 84, 87, 89, 148
Buffalo, burning of, 96
Buffalo, first school built, 85
Bunker Hill Monument, x, 35, 42, 59, 192, 203
Burdge, Dr. Howard G., 67
Burgoyne, surrender of, 20, 95
burnt district, 166
Busti, Paul, 89
Butler, 152
Butler, Colonel John, 51
Butler, Pennsylvania, 41
Butler, Wolcott, 188
Byron, 52
Cadmus, 22, 24, 25, 26
Calvary Presbyterian Church (Auburn), 168
Cambria, 110, 113
Camden, Battle of, 38
Campbell, Thomas B., 60, 61
Camus, 152
Canada, i, 19, 50, 51, 95, 109, 110, 111, 121, 147, 148, 149
Canadaway Creek, 68, 69
Canandaigua, viii, x, 51, 94, 95, 96, 101, 102, 103, 104, 127, 133-143, 152, 158, 160, 178
Canandaigua Academy, 138
Canandaigua Hotel, 141
Canandaigua, Village of, 138, 139
Canfield Road, 128
Carroll Street, 127
Cass, Jonathan, 60
Cataract Hotel, 106
Cato, Clarence, 67
Caton, Rev. John, 162
Cayuga Bridge, 159
Central Avenue, 79, 80, 82
cessation, 42

Chadwick, 110
Chadwick, George H., 110
Chamber of Deputies, 14, 15
Chancellor Livingston, 26, 27
Chapin, Captain Israel, 138, 158
Chapin, Clarissa, 138
Chapin, Dr. Cyrenius, 84-89,
Chapin, General Israel, 138
Chautauqua County, 54-60, 65, 68, 78, 81
Chautauqua Lake, 54
Christopher, John G., 127
Christopher's Mansion House, 127
Church of Christ (Auburn), 168
Civil War, 2
Clarendon-Linden Fault System, 110
Clark, William, 39
Clay, Henry, 104
Cleveland, Palmer, 124
Clinton Hotel. *See* Clinton House
Clinton House, 125, 126, 127
Clinton, De Witt, 104, 110, 111, 112, 139, 207
Coffen, Stephen, 54, 55
Coit, George, 89
Colquhoun, Patrick, 137, 145, 146
Colt, Joseph, 165
Colt, Judah, 44
commonality, 150, 164, 190, 191
Condict, Lewis, 8
Connecticut Fire Lands. *See* Connecticut Reserve
Connecticut Reserve, 55, 56, 103
continental army, 28
Cook, Harriet Howell, 110
Cooper, James Fenimore, 19
Corn Planter, 104
Cornwallis, 12, 13, 20, 29, 30, 131
Cox, Benjamin C., 170
Crosby, Dr., 76
Cross Roads, 56, 57
cuesta, 110

Cusick, Chief Nicholas, 108
Daughters of the American Revolution, 129
de Kalb, Baron, 38, 192
De Lancey, James, 55
De Zeng, William S., 152, 155, 170
December 16, 1786, 50
Declaration of Independence, vi, 3, 20
Demming, Fenn, 60
Democratic-Republican Party, 2
DeVillers, Lewis, 120, 121
DeVillers, Nancy Mary, 120
DeWitt, Simeon, 111
Dexter, John, 60
Dobbins, Daniel, 44
Dox, Capt. M.M., 93, 152
Drake, Mary Ann, 79
Drummond, Lieutenant-General Sir Gordon, 86, 87
Duck Soup, 70
Dunkirk, vii, ix, 59, 77-82
Dunkirk Bay, 78, 79, 82, 83
Duquesne, Marquis, 54
Dwight, Timothy, 85, 87
Dye, Claude R., 66
Eagle Hotel, 105, 106, 107
Earl's tavern, 161
earthquake, 110
East Avenue, 134, 135
East Bloomfield, 102, 133
East Cayuga, 163
Eddy, Thomas, 111
Edinburgh Regiment, 145
Edson, John M., 76
Edson, Obed, 72
Eisenhower, Dwight D., 156, 181, 182, 183, 184
Eleven Thousand Acre Tract, 130, 134
Ellery, Town of, 61
Ellicott Road. *See* Buffalo and Erie Road
Ellicott, Andrew, 43

Ellicott, David, 57
Ellicott, Joseph, 51, 57, 71, 84, 88, 89, 102, 146
Ely, Heman, 79
Era of Good Feelings, 2, 7, 18, 49, 164, 192
Erie Canal, 50, 53, 79, 80, 89, 90, 97, 98, 116, 118, 123, 141, 160, 230
Erie County, ii, 43, 87, 89, 104
Erie County Fair, 87
Erie Road. *See* Buffalo and Erie Road
Erie Triangle, 42, 43
Erie, Pennsylvania, 41, 42, 54, 59, 79
Escarpment, 109, 110, 112, 116, 157
Eustis, William, 21
Fairchild, Caleb, 163
Farmer's Brother, 104
Farnsworth, Joseph, 60
Farnsworth, Oren R., 163
Federalist Party, 2, 19
Fifield, Dr. Jesse, 161
Finger Lakes, 109
Finney, Charles G., 166, 167, 168
First Restoration, 27
Fishers, 135
Fitzhugh basin, 124
Fitzhugh Street, 123
five flights, 117
Forrest Gump, 128
Fort Erie, 85
Fort Lafayette, 24, 25, 26
Fort Niagara, v, x, 85, 86, 103, 113, 114, 228
Fort Stanwix, 92, 188
Forward, Oliver, 85, 88, 89, 90
Foster, Anna Spencer, 102, 104
Franklin, 155, 211, 219, 229
Franklin, Ben, 33
Franklin, Pennsylvania, 41
Fredonia, vii, viii, ix, 59, 65-92, 184
Fredonia Normal School, 67
Freemasonry, x, 38, 164, 185-187

Freemasons. *See* Freemasonry, *See* Freemasonry, *See* Freemasonry
French and Indian War, 54, 55
French Revolution, 3, 13, 15, 33
Gamage, G.A., 163, 176
Gardeau Tract, 139
Gardiner, Edith, 67
Gardiner, Mrs. A.J., 67
Genesee Country, 44, 49, 94, 130, 137, 157
Genesee County, 57
Genesee River, 101, 110, 123, 126, 144, 148, 158
Genesee Road, 140, 151, 158, 160, 164, 170
Genesee Trail. *See* Great Central Trail
Geneva, 51, 146-158
Gibson, Henry B., 139
Gilbert's Basin, 124, 126
glacier, 109, 110
Goat Island, ix, 103-105, 107
Goat Island Bridge, 107
Gorham, Nathaniel, 144
Gould, Jacob, 124, 127
Gould, John, 113, 115
Grand Island, 105
Grand Lodge of South Carolina, 38
Grayson, Letitia, 96
Great Britain, i, 2, 31, 92
Great Central Trail, x, 109, 140, 156-160
Greece, 124
Greenleaf, Samuel, 136, 141, 142
Greig, John, x, 103, 137-143, 151
Grétry, André, 26
Groucho Marx, 70
Hardenburgh, Capt. John L., 164
Harris, Nathan, 101, 103
Hart, Eli, 85
Hart, William A., 68, 69
Hart, William L., 67
Harvard, 33, 34

Hendricks Reef, 26
Henricks, Walter A., 66
Herkimer, 51, 158
Hildreth, Samuel, 133
Hiram Lodge No. 88, 165, 168
Hoard, Charles Alexander, 120
Hoard, Charles Brooks, 119, 120
Hoard, Daniel, 120
Hoard, Silvius, x, 118, 119, 120, 121
Hoard's Tavern, 121, 127, 131, 135
Holland Land Company, 57, 89, 102
Holland Land Purchase, 57, 84
Hopkins, Samuel Miles, 166, 168
Hornby and Colquhoun, Estate of, 137
Hornby, John, 137, 145
Howell, Judge Nathaniel W., 137, 138
Howell, William, 110, 111, 112, 113
Howell's Tavern, 111, 112, 115
Hulbert, John Whitefield, 172, 176
husking frolic, 101
Indian trails, 55, 109, 158
Indonesia, 52
interstate highway system, 156
Irondequoit, v, 101
Iroquois, 51, 157, 160, 188, 189
Iroquois Confederacy, 50, 109, 140, 144, 156, 157, 188
Iroquois Trail, 110
Irving, Washington, 19
Jackson, Andrew, 40
Jay, John, 33
Jefferson County, 120, 121
Jefferson County Agricultural Society, 120
Jefferson County Bank, 120
Jefferson, Thomas, 35, 188, 239
Jemison, Mary, 139
Jesuits, 157
John Trumbull, 20
Johnstone, John, 137
Junius, 162

Junius Lodge No. 291, F&AM, 161-163
Keating, Kenneth Barnard, 134, 135
Kelsey, Martha, 108
Kelsey, Thomas, 108, 113
Kelsey's Tavern, 108, 114
Kennedy, Robert F., 134
King George III, 144
King's Basin, 117, 123, 124
Kingsley's Tavern, 142
Lafayette Guards, 27
Lafayette, George Washington, 33, 92, 93, 117, 152, 194, 195
Lake Erie, 20, 43, 44, 54, 55, 56, 83, 88, 93, 95, 98, 109
Lake Iroquois, 110
Lake Ontario, 109, 110, 112, 114, 146, 149
Lansing, Rev. Dirck C., 165-168, 172, 174, 175
Le Couteulx, Louis Stephen, 84, 85, 90, 93
Leatherstocking Tales, 19
Lee, Oliver, 60
LeFebvre, Louis Charles Aime. *See* DeVillers, Lewis
lemonade, 115
LeRoy, 110
Lessees, 50, 51
Letchworth State Park, 139
Levasseur, André-Nicolas, 17, 26, 33, 34, 37, 40, 45, 70, 71, 72, 83, 89, 99, 106, 107, 115, 116, 123, 124, 125, 152, 172, 178, 194
Lewis and Clark, 39
Lewiston, ix, 52, 103, 105, 107, 108, 110, 111, 113, 148, 227, 228
liberty, 7, 12, 13, 14, 27, 28, 38, 40, 62, 63, 73, 74, 91, 116, 149, 154, 172-178, 190, 191
Lisk, Abraham, 163
Livingston, James K., 124

Lockport, x, 113-117, 123, 124, 176
Louis XV, 12
Louis XVI, 15
Louis XVIII, 15
Lower Mountain Road, 115
Lum, Lt., 152
Lummis, Doctor, 153
Lyon, Capt. James, 142
Mack, Daniel, 127
Madison, James, 35, 190
Main Road. *See* Buffalo and Erie Road
Maine, 19
Manchester, 105
Manning, Capt., 152
Marshall, J.L., 98
Matteson, David J., 76
Maxwell, Colonel Hugh, 146
Maytum, Arthur R., 66, 67
Mayville, 54, 89
McClure, General George, 84, 85, 86
McHenry, Edward, 56
McKelvey, Blake, 126
McMahan, James, 56, 57
Meadville, Pennsylvania, 41
Mechanic, sinking of, 40
Mendon, iii, iv, x, xv, 128, 130, 133-136, 141
Mendon (Hamlet), 135
Mendon Hotel, 135
Mercer, Pennsylvania, 41
Merrill, Capt. Ira, 142
Miller, Aaron, 52
Missouri Compromise, 2, 19
Mitchell, George E., 8
Monmouth, Battle of, 27, 29, 177
Monroe County, 20, 123, 128, 129, 130, 140
Monroe Doctrine, 3
Monroe, James, i, 13, 16, 17, 19, 20, 21, 104, 188
Morgan Affair, 167, 168
Morgan, Lewis, 79

Morris, Governor, 111
Morris, Robert, 145, 146, 147, 152
Mount Tambora, 52
Mount Vernon, 33, 34, 173, 186
Musketeers, 11, 12
Napoleonic Wars, 2, 18
Nash, Mrs. Charles White, 66, 67
natural gas, 68, 69, 70, 72
New Connecticut. *See* Connecticut Reserve
New England, 42, 56, 102, 145, 192
New France, 54, 114
New Orleans, 8, 39, 40
New York City, 13, 23, 24, 28, 34, 129, 137, 193
New York Genesee Land Company, 50
New York Harbor, 24, 25, 26
New York Historical Society, 28, 111, 129, 157
New York State Society of Cincinnati, 28
Newark, 52, 85, 86
Newberry, Roger, 129
Newburyport, 145
Newell, Abagail, 145
Niagara County, vii, 57, 85, 89, 100, 113, 115,
Niagara County Agricultural Society, 87
Niagara Escarpment, 109, 110
Niagara Genesee Land Company, 50, 51
Niagara River, 85, 88, 95, 96, 103, 104, 105, 106, 107, 111, 114
Niagara Street. *See* Schimmelpenninck Avenue
Niagara-on-the-Lake. *See* Newark
Norfolk, Virginia, 22, 36, 37
North, William, 111
Norton, Zebulon, 134
Norton's Mills, 134

Ogdensburg Turnpike Company, 121
Ohio River, 40, 54
Old Fort Schuyler, 158
Old French Road. *See* Portage Road
Olmutz, 75, 93
Onondaga Escarpment, 109, 110
Ontario and Genesee Turnpike, 140, 141
Ontario Bank, 139, 141, 233
Ontario Brass Band, 136, 141, 142
Ontario County, 51, 57, 95, 101, 102, 128, 130, 131, 133, 140, 148
Ontario County Agricultural Society, 130, 139, 233
Ontario Farmers' Bank, 138
Osborne, T.A., 60
Ottley, Capt., 152
Paine, Edward, 56
Paine's Road, 56, 57
Painted Post, 110
Palmyra, 101
Panic of 1819, 19
Pardee, Silas, 135
Parish, David, 120
Parishville, 120
Parsons, Capt. Jehiel P., 161, 162, 163
Peacock, William, 60, 61, 89
Pearl Street, 85
Perry, Commodore Oliver Hazard, 20, 44, 45, 91
pewter chandelier, 106
Phelps, 133
Phelps and Gorham, 50, 101, 102, 148, 158
Phelps, Oliver, 144
Phoenix Hotel, 135
Pittsburgh, 40, 41, 55
Pittsford, 133, 135, 232
Portage Escarpment, 56, 109
Portage Road, 54, 55, 56, 79
Porter, Augustus, ix, 95, 101, 102, 103, 104, 107, 134, 138, 160

Porter, Peter B., ix, 88, 94, 95, 98, 99, 102, 103, 111, 134, 149
Portland, 55, 58, 60, 61, 71, 79
Potter, Col. H.B., 90, 92
Powers, Gershom, 170, 176
Preemption Line, 50, 51, 102, 144, 146, 158
Presqu' Isle, 43
Presque' Isle, 79
Prevost, Sir George, 86
Pulaski, Casimir, 38, 39, 176, 177, 192
Pulteney, Sir William, 137, 145, 148
Putnam, Rufus, 17
Queenston Heights, Battle of, 95, 105
Rathbun, Capt. (of Buffalo), 90
Read, Amos, 141
Red Jacket, 92, 104
Red Tavern, 115
Red Tavern, 113
Rees, Major James, 151, 152, 154
Rensselaer, Stephen Van, 111, 113, 116
Revolutionary War, viii, i, 2, 3, 7, 8, 12, 13, 20, 26-29, 31-33, 36, 38, 40, 42, 44, 49, 50, 51, 55, 65, 66, 78, 85, 95, 113, 121, 126, 129, 130, 131, 138, 151-153, 155, 157, 161, 162, 164, 171, 176
Rich, Charles, 8
Ridge Road, 110, 111, 123
Rip Van Winkle, 19
Ripley, vi, 60, 61
Risley, Hanson A., 71
Risley, Hiram, 81
Risley, Jr., Major General Elijah, 81, 82, 83, 93
Robert Fulton, 26
Rochester, 118, 123, 124
Rochester, Judge William Beatty, 123, 126

Rochester, Nathaniel, 118, 123, 124, 126, 140
Rochesterville, 123
Roman Empire, 156
Ross, Harriet, 67
Route 104, 111
Route 18, 57
Route 425, 115
Route 5, 57
Routes 5&20, 109, 157
Royal Arch Masons, 114, 117, 186, 194, 195, 207, 208
Ruggles, Capt. Lemuel W., 152, 155, 162
Rush-Bagot Treaty, i
Russell, Benjamin, 2
Sampson, Judge Ashley, vii, 123, 124, 125, 126, 127, 131, 135
Saxton, Col. Asher B. Saxton, 113, 115, 116
Schimmelpenninck Avenue, 84
Second Great Awakening, 166
Second Restoration, 27
Seminole Wars, 2
Seneca Chief, 99
Seneca Falls, 158, 162
Seneca Nation, 50, 51, 56, 79, 104, 138, 139, 140, 144, 147, 149
Seneca Road Company, 159
Seneca Turnpike, 140, 151, 159, 160, 170
Seneca Turnpike Road Company, 160
Seward, Olive Risley, vii, 59, 71, 72, 76, 81
Seward, William Henry, 176, 178
Seward's Folly, 178
Shattuck, Samuel, 55, 65
Sheaffe, Lt. Robert Hale, 147, 148
Sherman, Capt., 152
Sherwood, J. M., 177
Simcoe, John Graves, 147, 148
Sinclairville, 76

Sion, 152
Sir William Johnson, 54, 214, 220
Six Nations, 50
Sixty Years' War, 18
slavery, 2, 19, 190, 237
Smith, Walter, 59, 81, 82, 83, 176
Sodus, 147, 148
Sodus Bay, 147
Spencer, Silas, 60
St. Lawrence County, 120
St. Paul's Lodge No. 265, 165, 168
Stanley, Lt., 152
State Line (in the Town of Ripley), 60
State Road, 157, 158
State Street. *See* Carroll Street
Staten Island, 24, 26
Steam Boat Hotel, 98
Stone, Moody, 101
Stone-Tolan House, 135
Storrs, Col. (of Buffalo), 90
Sullivan, Major General John, 138
Superior, 78, 82, 83, 89
Swan Street, 85
Tariff Act of 1816, 19
Tchaikovsky, 18
Temple Street, 80
Thatcher, Dr. James, 8, 21
Thayer's Hotel, 99
The Last of the Mohicans, 19
The Legend of Sleepy Hollow, 19
The Pioneers, 19
The Star-Spangled Banner, 18
Thompson, Maj. Alexander Ramsay, 113
Throop, Enos Thomas, 170
Thruway, 110, 123, 128, 160
Tinker, E.L., 60
Tolerance, x, 188, 190, 191
Tompkins, Daniel, 24, 25
Tonawanda. *See* Tonnewanta, *See* Tonnewanta
Tonnewanta, 87, 98, 100, 105

Touzard, General, 85
Townsend, Charles, 89, 92
Treaty of 1818, i, 18
Treaty of Hartford, 50, 144
Turner, Orsamus, 52
Tuscarora, 108
U.S. Route 20, 57, 59
Upham, E.P., 60
Utica, 94, 103, 158
Valentine Hill, 129
Valley Forge, 13, 129, 130
Van Auken, Capt., 152
Verrazano-Narrows Bridge, 26
Victor, 135
von Steuben, Baron Friedrich Wilhelm, 30
Wadsworth, Jeremiah, 130, 134
Walden, Ebenezer, 85, 92
Wallace, General B., 44
Wangum Mills, 135
War of 1812, i, 2, 18, 19, 20, 26, 43, 44, 51, 53, 95, 120, 140
Ward, Dr. Levi, 124
Warren, Judge E.F., 52
Washington D.C., 34, 35, 40, 87
Washington, George, vi, xiv, 2, 12, 13, 16, 17, 19, 20, 30, 31, 33, 40, 43, 55, 78, 130, 135, 164, 185, 186, 188, 195
Waterford, 42, 44
Waterford, Pennsylvania, 41
Waterloo, x, 15, 155, 158, 161-163, 170, 176, 209, 236
Waterloo Hotel, 161, 162
Webster, Daniel, 19, 192, 197
Welland Canal, 121
West Bloomfield, 140
West Bloomfield Road, 128
West Mendon, 134
Western Fire Insurance Company, 139
Western Reserve. *See* Connecticut Reserve

Westfield, v, ix, 55, 56, 57, 59, 60, 61, 65, 70, 71, 79, 82
Wheaton, Joseph, 7, 21
White woman's reservation, 139
Whiting, Col., 154
Whitney, Parkhurst, 105, 106, 114
Whitney, Solon, 106
Whitney, Warham, 114
Wilkeson, Samuel, 89
Willet, Colonel Marinus, 27, 32
Williams, Lewis, 8
Williamson, 148
Williamson, Charles, 137, 145-150, 158, 159
Williamson, Sarah, 128
Wilson, Dr. Peter, 157
Woolsey's Hotel, 170
X, go to www.ChrisCarosa.com/secret, iv
Yale, 34, 85, 94, 102, 165
Yates County, 152
Yates, Anah Babcock, 129
Yorktown, 13, 30, 35, 55, 77, 130, 131, 155, 177

ABOUT THE AUTHOR

Christopher Carosa, Deputy Historian for the Town of Mendon, NY, is a popular and entertaining speaker who has appeared from coast to coast. As an award-winning financial writer, his thoughts and opinions have been sought out by such major media outlets as *The Wall Street Journal, The New York Times, USA Today, Barron's*, CNBC, CNN, and Fox Business News. But his work isn't limited to money talk. A long-time newspaper columnist writing on everything from white cream donuts to international geopolitics, he's been recognized by the New York Press Association for his editorial writing, features writing, columnist writing, and online news video production. A Past President of the National Society of Newspaper Columnists, he currently serves on its Board as well as the Board of the NY Press Association.

In addition to serving as senior contributor to *Forbes.com*. Chris is the publisher of the *Mendon-Honeoye Falls-Lima Sentinel*, chief contributing editor for *FiduciaryNews.com*, and a columnist and free-lance writer for various print and digital publications.

In 2018, Chris published one of his most popular books, *Hamburger Dreams*, which is the subject of many of his interviews. Inspired by his previous work and research for *50 Hidden Gems of Greater Western New York*, the book uses classic crime solving techniques and other investigative tools to crack the mystery behind who sold the world's first hamburger. The book has led many to dub him "The Hamburger Historian" as he has spoken around the country sharing his findings with the culinary world and enthusiasts alike. Other works include *A Pizza The Action: Everything I Ever Learned About Business I Learned Working in a Pizza Stand at the Erie County Fair* and finance books including *From Cradle to Retirement: The Child IRA, Hey! What's My Number, 401(k) Fiduciary Solutions* and *The Parents' Guide To Turning Your Teenager Into A Millionaire Before High School Graduation*.

Carosa earned his undergraduate degree In Physics and Astronomy from Yale University and MBA from the Simon Business School. He has been designated a Certified Trust and Fiduciary Adviser by the Institute of Certified Bankers. He has three children, Cesidia, Catarina, and Peter and currently lives in Mendon with his wife, Betsy, and their beagle, Wally.

If you'd like to read more by Mr. Carosa, feel free to browse his author's site, ChrisCarosa.com; LifetimeDreamGuide.com, a site to another book he's working on; his site devoted to his first love, AstronomyTop100.com; and, TheMacaroniKid.com, a musical/comedy stage play he wrote that has played to sold-out community theater crowds. Not bad for a Physics and Astronomy major.

Did You Enjoy *History Unleashed?*

[Click here to buy a print copy](#) and give it to a friend, family member, or budding entrepreneur because that's the best way to say "thank you" to the author!

Readers who enjoyed *History Unleashed* also enjoyed *50 Hidden Gems of Greater Western New York!* Would you like to?

[Click here to enjoy *50 Hidden Gems of Greater Western New York!*](#)

Readers who enjoyed 50 Hidden Gems also enjoyed A PIZZA THE ACTION. Would You like to?

[Click here to buy a print copy](#) and give it to a friend, family member, or budding entrepreneur because that's the best way to say "thank you" to the author!

Hungry For More? How About Some Hamburger Dreams?

Click here to buy it to discover what they never told you about the true and uncensored history of the hamburger!

www.ingramcontent.com/pod-product-compliance
Lightning Source LLC
Chambersburg PA
CBHW050549160426
43199CB00015B/2592